For Vicky and Will,
my own slices of heaven.

And for Sam Sadin,
a modern day wise man
and true mensch.

P·I·Z·Z·A

A Slice of Heaven

THE ULTIMATE GUIDE AND COMPANION

WITHDRAWN

~ ED LEVINE ~

Universe Publishing

First published in the United States of America in 2005
by UNIVERSE PUBLISHING
A Division of Rizzoli International Publications, Inc.
300 Park Avenue South
New York, NY 10010
www.rizzoliusa.com

Original Essays: page 18: copyright © Sam Sifton; page 166: copyright © Ruth Reichl;
page 173: copyright © Nicholas Dawidoff; page 185: copyright © Alan Richman; page 198: copyright
© Laura Lippman; page 209: copyright © Robb Walsh; page 220: copyright © Don McLeese;
page 245: copyright © Heartburn Enterprises; page 255: copyright © Brian Koppelman;
page 288: copyright © Mario Batali; page 292: copyright © Corby Kummer; pages 304, 311: copyright
© www.danielyoung.fr; page 309: copyright © Eric Karpeles; page 313: copyright © David Downie.

Photo Permissions: pages 5, 57, 110: courtesy Carusone family;
title page, page 338: copyright © 2004 Jeff Topping; page 6: copyright © 1985 G. B. Trudeau. DOONESBURY
distributed by UNIVERSAL PRESS SYNDICATE. All rights reserved; pages 31, 86, 93: courtesy Lombardi's;
pages 39, 50: courtesy Roberto Caporuscio; pages 45, 125, 144, 153, 194, 205, 249, 254, 280,
299, 310: © TongRo Image Stock/Inmagine; pages 88, 354: courtesy Totonno's Pizzeria Napolitano;
pages 144, 167, 170, 175, 228, 303, 368: courtesy Peter Cunningham; page 156: courtesy DeLorenzo's;
page 246: courtesy Greg Lindgren; page 289: copyright © Scott Morgan;
page 349: courtesy John Angelis; page 351: courtesy Sally's Apizza.

2005 2006 2007 2008 2009 / 10 9 8 7 6 5 4 3 2 1

Printed in the United States of America

ISBN: 0-7893-1205-0

Library of Congress Catalog Control Number: 2004112325

Thanks to Mystic Pizza®, Mystic, CT, for the use of its slogan "a slice of heaven."

Please note that while, to the best of our knowledge, the information contained in this book was accurate
at the time of printing, it is always best to call ahead to confirm that the information is still up to date.

WITH CONTRIBUTIONS BY

ERIC ASIMOV

MARIO BATALI

ROY BLOUNT JR.

JOHN T. EDGE

NORA EPHRON

CORBY KUMMER

ED NORTON

RUTH REICHL

PETER REINHART

ALAN RICHMAN

JEFFREY STEINGARTEN

CALVIN TRILLIN

among others

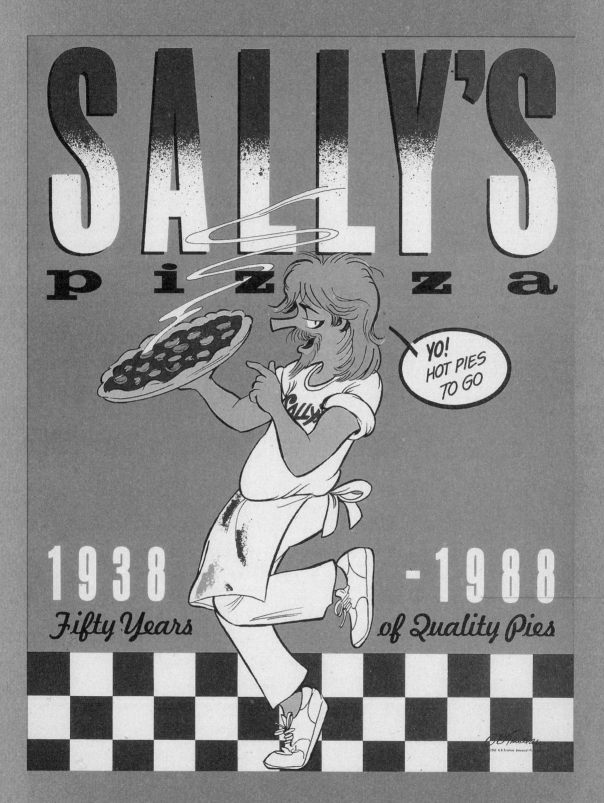

C·O·N·T·E·N·T·S

INTRODUCTION

WHEN I WAS DOING "PRIMARY RESEARCH" FOR THIS BOOK, that is, eating pizza in San Francisco, I called my sixteen-year-old son, Will, from my hotel room after a typical six-pizza day in the Bay Area. We exchanged greetings before Will asked, "So how's the work—quote unquote—going, Dad?" I admit it's easy to be skeptical about the motivation (and sanity) of a grown man who would consider eating nothing but pizza for twelve months. But I love pizza. If my editor had asked me to visit and review all 63,873 pizza purveyors in America, plus another couple of thousand in Italy, I would have happily accepted the challenge. (We decided, in the end, to list only those places that I—and other food critics whose opinion I respect—have found to serve truly *great* pizza.)

As I said, I love pizza. And why not? In its simplest, most elemental form, pizza is melted cheese . . . on good bread . . . with tomato—one of the all-time great food combinations. Pizza is a perfect food. It is always some combination of sweet, creamy, salty, hot, crisp, chewy, tangy and crunchy. You can eat it standing up or sitting down or even walking. You can eat it with your hands. It's priced just right (even an expensive pizza is an affordable indulgence). It's filling, relatively nutritious and, if you're going the low-carb route, you can eat just the toppings. Anyone—vegetarians, carnivores, even vegans—can find sustenance and satisfaction in pizza, and even in the *same* pizza if you go half and half. Could pizza be the catalyst for world harmony? A candidate for the Nobel Peace Prize? The appeal of pizza crosses all ethnic, racial and class lines. Everybody, from working class families to college kids to multibillionaires, loves pizza.

Then there are the poetic, artistic elements of pizza. If you have ever made pizza from scratch, or simply added your own toppings to commercial dough, you know that pizza can bring out the artist in just about anyone, even the most kitchen-phobic. So imagine the poetry that can happen when someone chooses to make pizza for a living. The pizza world is filled with idiosyncratic characters obsessed with making the perfect pie. Many of them, such as Arizona's Chris Bianco and New Jersey's Anthony Mangieri, put their heart and soul into every pie. They serve not slices but works of art. You will meet Anthony and Chris, and many others like them, in *A Slice of Heaven*.

And what about pizza history? When and how did pizza get its start in America? Where did the concept of Chicago pizza come from—and is it pizza or just a casserole? What role has organized crime played in the development of pizza? Which world war brought pizza to Main Street? Why does there seem to be a photo of Frank Sinatra in every pizzeria in New York, New Jersey and Connecticut? How much pizza did Ol' Blue Eyes eat, anyway? *A Slice of Heaven* will unravel all these mysteries.

A Slice of Heaven will help you find a fine slice wherever you go. I'll tell you where to eat pizza in what I call the Pizza Belt, which runs from Washington, D.C., up through Providence. That corridor, which includes Philadelphia, New Jersey, New York, New Haven, Boston and Providence, is the epicenter of high-quality Neapolitan-American pizza in this country. I'll also guide you to the tastiest pizza in California, and will introduce you to the finest pizza in America (and the world, for that matter), in the unlikely town of Phoenix, Arizona. Where should you order your pie in Seattle or New Orleans or Atlanta? I asked leading food critics across the country for their suggestions, so you'll never be left stranded when you crave a slice. I've no doubt missed some fine local pizzerias here and there (I look forward to hearing about them from readers), but I've tried my best to be comprehensive.

In compiling *A Slice of Heaven*, I wanted to entice some of my favorite writers to contribute their take on pizza—to wax poetic on this minimalist masterpiece. Turns out I didn't need to entice them at all. I felt a bit like Tom Sawyer, when nearly a score of writers came through to help paint the fence. Calvin Trillin gave permission to reprint his brilliant profile of the late Fats Goldberg, who brought Chicago-style pizza to New York. Other people I know and respect had already weighed in on pizza in their own books. I loved what they had written, so I asked them for permission to run those stories. Jeff Steingarten offered his hilarious, quasi-scientific assessment of Neapolitan-American pizza. Roy Blount Jr. wanted to share his poetic essay, "Pretty Decent Pizza," and Eric Asimov at the *New York Times* agreed to share his "genealogy" of New York's pizza families. Emboldened by these friends' enthusiasm for the project, I approached other writers whose work I admired. Screenwriter and director Nora Ephron responded to my query with a pithy piece about the intricacies of eating pizza on a first date in Los Angeles in the 1950s. She was only one of many who came through for the cause. Nobody, it seems, doesn't like pizza.

So, to answer your question, Will, I've been "working" hard, very hard. All of it a labor of love, and all of it to further the enjoyment of pizza lovers everywhere. Over this last twelve months I have consumed at least a thousand slices of pizza (roughly three per day) in twenty states as well as Canada and Italy. And that's not counting the *ten thousand* slices I consumed in my first fifty years of life on Planet Pizza, starting at Cairo's Restaurant in Inwood, New York. (My family's Sunday eating ritual was to grill steak and order a pizza from Cairo's.) I tasted and took notes, burned fingers and tongue countless times, and ruined more pairs of pants than you can imagine—all in the cause of guiding you to the best pizza . . . the perfect pie . . . the slices of heaven that I've found through my passion for pizza. I'm sure I ate the truly fantastic slices too quickly, and I ate more bad pizza in the name of "primary research" than you'd want to think about. Yes, Will, my work is never done, but in this case, that's a good thing. Ten thousand slices later, I can honestly say I'm looking forward to my next great pizza, wherever I might find it.

LAST LICKS: Serious pizzerias are springing up like mad even as we go to press. Craig Stoll, chef/owner of the great San Francisco restaurant Delfina, is planning to open a pizzeria. Ditto for Waldy Malouf, chef/owner of Beacon in New York. Michael Ayoub has just opened Fornino, complete with wood-burning oven, in trendy Williamsburg, Brooklyn. Bake on, my pizza-loving friends. May your mozzarella always be snow-white, creamy and fresh, and your crust chewy, tender and crisp. I promise I'll find you, and the others I might have missed this time around, for the next *Slice of Heaven*.

CHAPTER
1

The Perfect Pizza

THE PERFECT INGREDIENTS FOR THE PERFECT FOOD

WHAT GOES INTO A PERFECT PIZZA? THE TANGIBLE ELEMENTS are as follows:

THE FUEL SOURCE

In my opinion, coal-fired and wood-fired ovens produce the best pizza. The high heat given off by both charcoal and wood can char a pizza crust to perfection, and when coal or wood is piled directly into the oven it imparts a smoky flavor to the pizza. Christophe Hille, chef at San Francisco's A16, told me he believes that the flames, and not the wood itself, flavor the pie. Gas-fired ovens can also create a great pizza. Nick Angelis of Nick's gets a fantastic char on his crusts from his Woodstone gas-fired ovens. As he points out, pizza crust gets its char from high heat consistently applied to the dough, and his gas ovens can easily maintain 800°F heat. Conventional gas ovens, such as those made by Bakers Pride and Bari, can maintain temperatures of only around 600°F.

THE OVEN

How do you get an oven to reach eight hundred degrees and stay there? There's no way around it: You line the floor and top with bricks and/or stones to help maintain heat. I am sickened by all of the awful pizza places that tout their "brick" ovens, just because they have a couple of bricks somewhere in the vicinity of the restaurant. So next time you see brick-oven pizza advertised, investigate. Become a "Pizza P.I." Are those real bricks you see—or a faux-brick façade? Is the oven encased in brick, or are the bricks positioned only at the corners? It's the brick and stone acting in concert with the fuel source that imparts flavor. If you have an oven that doesn't maintain high heat, the pizza is going to be inferior, no matter how you slice it.

THE CRUST

I like my crust puffy, chewy and pliant. A great pizza crust should be like a great football defense. It should bend but never break. The superior pizza crust is neither cracker-thin nor thick as bread. It should have a veneer of crispness and be softer and more tender on the inside. A great pizza crust should have browned and blackened charred spots. They lend a needed bit of smoky flavor. I love a pizza crust with a few of those raised blisters. They lighten the overall effect of eating pizza. The interior of the crust should have the hole structure of well-made and well-baked bread.

Pizza is as simple a great food as there is. But a pizza crust becomes great not just because of the quality of the ingredients, but also because of the skill of the "pizzaiolo," the person who makes it (in New York and New Haven the pizzaiolo is more commonly known as the pie man). It's all in the hands.

THE MOZZARELLA

I love the clean, milky taste of fresh cow's-milk mozzarella (*fior di latte*, in Italian) on my pizza. It's easy to tell if a pizzeria uses fresh mozzarella: It's white. Aged mozzarella, used by the great majority of pizza makers in this country, is that color I call pizza yellow. Because it's aged, it has a certain tanginess. A few pizzerias across the country, including Salvatore's in Port Washington, New York, and Pizzeria Bianco in Phoenix, Arizona, make their own whole-milk mozzarella fresh every day. Most good by-the-slice pizzerias use a commercial aged mozzarella made by Grande, a large cheese purveyor in Wisconsin. Mozzarella made from the milk of water buffaloes is called *mozzarella di bufala*. True *mozzarella di bufala* is produced mostly in Italy, although there is one farm in Vermont that makes it domestically. It's tangy, very creamy (it's actually wet and quite oily when it melts), slightly tart and unbelievably delicious. It's also quite expensive (even in Italy). In Naples you can get a pizza made with *mozzarella di bufala* called a DOC (see glossary) for a slight premium. In the States, only a few pizzerias with the Vera Pizzeria Napoletana (or VPN, see chapter 16) designation offer it as an option, and only Anthony Mangieri of Una Pizza Napoletana uses it exclusively on his pizza.

The only slice I've ever seen made with *mozzarella di bufala* is baked in Midwood, Brooklyn, at Di Fara Pizza. Unbelievably, Domenico DeMarco uses a blend of fresh *mozzarella di bufala* and fresh cow's-milk mozzarella on slices that are an absolute steal at $2.50.

OTHER CHEESES

Chris Bianco of Pizzeria Bianco goes to the trouble of smoking his own mozzarella in his wood-burning pizza oven using pecan wood. The result is the best smoked mozzarella I have ever tasted, which he uses on his Wiseguy pie along with roasted onions and sweet fennel-laced sausage. Many first-rate pizzerias use a judicious sprinkling of freshly grated Romano and/or Parmigiano-Reggiano to flavor their pizzas. DeMarco and Lawrence Ciminieri of Totonno's both use freshly grated Romano to lend a little saltiness and tang to their pies. La Pizza Fresca uses a dusting of Parmigiano-Reggiano on its pizza, which lends it a slightly nutty flavor. As Dan Young notes on page 304, pizzerias in the south of France use Cantal (a mild Cheddar) and Gruyère on their pizza instead of mozzarella. Chefs like Todd English, Mario Batali and Alice Waters use goat cheese and Gorgonzola on particular pizzas.

THE SAUCE

The best pizza sauces are made with uncooked canned tomatoes, from either California or Italy, that have been strained and seasoned with salt and maybe some oregano. Pizza sauce should not be slow-cooked. It should not taste like pasta sauce or marinara sauce. Some people think you have to use San Marzano tomatoes, grown in that town in Italy, that have been designated DOP (Denominazione di Origine Protetta; see glossary). They are very expensive, and I have found wonderful pizza sauces made with other Italian tomatoes or even high-quality California tomatoes. Some people doctor their sauce with sugar, giving it an excessive sweetness that I don't care for. If the tomatoes used are good enough, they will be plenty sweet on their own. Fresh tomatoes are generally not used to make the sauce for pizza, though fresh cherry tomatoes are used to make the pie the Neapolitans call Al Fileto.

THE TOPPINGS

I love the taste of fresh, meaty, fennel sausage on pizza. Unfortunately, many places use what I call sausage pellets or sausage droppings, which are not worth the calories or the fat grams. Chris Bianco makes his own sweet sausage to use as a topping. But even if your local pizzeria doesn't make its own sausage, it can buy it locally from a butcher. I find the best sausage is irregularly shaped and chunked. Small rounds can be okay, as can long oblong pieces of sausage, but avoid the pellets. The best pizzerias also use fresh mushrooms and roast their own peppers. Before you order, ask if the mushrooms are fresh and if the peppers are roasted in-house. All pepperonis are not created equal. Hormel's Grande pepperoni has a much cleaner taste than regular pepperoni. Mario Batali makes his own pepperoni at Otto, and it's the best pepperoni pizza I have ever tasted. Clams are a fantastic topping for pizza, as long as they're fresh and used judiciously.

BALANCE

The best pizzas achieve a kind of harmonic and textural balance. It's a balance shared by all great dishes. What contributes to that balance? The right combination of tastes and textures. The puffy, chewy and just salty enough crust should play off the oozy, creamy mozzarella and the acidic sweetness of the tomato sauce. I like all my toppings to be used in moderation. This means I like discrete areas of sauce and cheese on my pizza. I like my mozzarella fresh and my sausage chunked and sweet and fennelly. I like my pizza sauce made with uncooked fresh tomatoes and a little salt.

Pizza Cognition Theory

Sam Sifton

Sam Sifton edited my stories for the Dining Section of the New York Times *for two years. Though Sam has now moved on to the Culture desk he is a passionate and opinionated pizza lover.*

THERE IS A THEORY OF COGNITIVE DEVELOPMENT THAT SAYS CHILDREN learn to identify things only in opposition to other things. Only the child who has learned what is not brown, the theory holds, can discern what is "brown."

Pizza naturally throws this theory into a tailspin. The first slice of pizza a child sees and tastes (and somehow appreciates on something more than a child-like, mmmgoood, thanks-mom level), becomes, for him, pizza. He relegates all subsequent slices, if they are different in some manner from that first triangle of dough and cheese and tomato and oil and herbs and spices, to a status that we can characterize as not pizza.

You cannot teach a child what pizza is, this explanation of pizza cognition asserts, by providing him with oppositional ingredients or styles. The love of pizza simply doesn't work that way. Invariably, if a child's first slice of pizza comes from a deep-dish Chicago pie or is a slick, chewy, pillow of Sicilian or a half-hour-guaranteed-delivery cardboard Frisbee or a frozen French-bread travesty, semolina-dusted "Creole" or sweet pineapple and plastic ham "Hawaiian" pie, then, well, that is pizza to him. He will defend this interpretation to the end of his life.

Is this an unfair assertion? Perhaps. Learned behaviors and tastes can be, after all, unlearned. Thus are colts broken and prisoners released from jail. And, in any event, the question of what makes a slice of pizza "good" or "right" is so loaded with cultural baggage as to make it almost meaningless. One might as well ask: Which is the better painting, Picasso's *Guernica* or David's *Marat*? Who was the better baseball player, Reggie Jackson or Thurman Munson? Good pizza is simply good pizza, in a hundred different ways, for thousands of different reasons.

A brief definition of terms, then, so that you may understand what pizza is in New York City: it is, in essence, Neapolitan, a thin-crust pie, lightly slathered with a tomato sauce that one might describe, depending on mood, as herb-infused, sprinkled with mozzarella, a fine mist of Parmesan. No more. Toppings—pepperoni, sausage, lardo, artichoke hearts, onion, roasted peppers, hunks of garlic—are optional. No bad pie is made good by the presence of toppings.

A pizza's crust should be very close to pliant. Conversely, it should approach crackly; it should yield to the teeth with a dissolving crunch. The sauce should be neither salty nor overly sweet, and the presence of herbs in its flavor—oregano, basil, black pepper, let's say—should neither overwhelm nor be entirely absent. They should balance, a perfect triangle of salt, acidity, sweet. That is pizza in New York City. All else—however delicious, however redolent of wood smoke or sweet clams or new traditions or old—is not.

Who measures up? There is Fascati Pizza. I learned so as a child, standing there in the heat of its oven, a long shadow away from the rise of the Brooklyn Bridge, eating slices after long afternoons spent riding a skateboard. This was pizza. And when you get right down to it, there is no other.

Fascati Pizza 80 Henry Street, Brooklyn, NY, 718-237-1278.

OWNER-OCCUPIED PIZZA

After eating pizza in twenty states, Italy and Canada, I have come to one inescapable conclusion: The best pizza is made in places where a pizzaiolo/owner shows up every day. Why have I concluded this? Making great pizza requires the pizzaiolo to make adjustments every night. Fresh dough is a living thing. The yeast action in the dough changes daily because that's what yeast does. Weather—specifically temperature and humidity—affects the dough. The cheese, whether it's made in house or not, is going to change every night. One day the mozzarella is a little wet, the next day it might be drier. The oven's heat and intensity also change every night with wood- and coal-burning ovens because the fire is made fresh daily. Even the sauce changes every day, because each can of tomatoes has a different sugar content.

With so many variables, adjustments have to be made daily, and it's not realistic to expect even the most dedicated employees to make these adjustments as needed. Chris Bianco says, "I can teach just about anyone to make one great pizza. The trick in this business is to figure out how to make great pizza night in and night out, when the ground is constantly shifting under your feet."

I arrived at the owner-occupied theory after looking at the pizza men in Chapter 17: The Keepers of the Flame. Domenico DeMarco of Di Fara has been making pizza every day in his little corner slice place in Midwood, Brooklyn, for more than four decades. Ten years after opening Pizzeria Bianco, Chris Bianco is still making pizza night in and night out. Bianco is so serious about his pizza-making responsibilities that when he's not there, he closes the place. John Sorrano still cooks for three hours every night in one of his three Punch pizzerias in Minneapolis. As Sorrano points out, "Pizza makers have it even rougher than bread bakers. Once a bread baker makes up his dough he puts it all in the oven at the same time. When we're making pizza for ten or twelve hours a day, the dough is changing every minute, and we have to account for those changes when we make the pizza." More often than not, Totonno's Lawrence Ciminieri can be found making pizzas at the original Totonno's in Coney Island. And even though there are now three other Totonno's in New York City and Westchester that Ciminieri doesn't cook in, every month the pizzaiolo in each location returns to the Coney Island mothership for a refresher course. Ciminieri's mother, Cookie, also does her part to ensure high-quality pizza in the other locations. She is a demanding pizza perfectionist, and woe to any Totonno's pizzaiolo who makes a less-than-exemplary pie for a Totonno's regular.

What suffers when a pizzeria is not owner-occupied is consistency. That's why the pizza can be sensational one night and merely good the next at many of the best pizzerias around the world. Pizza requires constant vigilance and adjustments to make it great every night. That vigilance and the ability to recognize the adjustments that have to be made on a daily basis can best be supplied by an owner.

SONG TO DECENT PIZZA

Roy Blount Jr.

*When Roy Blount Jr. was a guest on my radio show, he recited
two of his infamous food poems, about fried chicken and oysters.
He was clearly holding out on me, because he never mentioned
the following pithy pizza verse.*

Yes, pepperoni, tomato, cheese

Onions, peppers. But over all these

(And yes, oregano, yes, and 'shrooms)

An underlying factor looms:

Pizza's founded on its crust.

Do not foist upon me just

Some slack, doughy, gummy basis

For my sauce and all. There are no cases

Of edible pizzas—and I've had a lottom—

That aren't al dente on the bottom.

From *Soupsongs/Webster's Ark*

Perfect Pizza

Jeffrey Steingarten

Jeffrey Steingarten (Food Critic of Vogue*) and I have eaten hundreds of slices of pizza together. What follows is an updated version of a hilarious pizza yarn Steingarten spun in his own book,* It Must Have Been Something I Ate.

THE DULL GRAY, SNUB-NOSED GUN WAVERED IN MY TREMBLING hand. The laser sight projected a blazing red dot onto my prey. I held my breath and squeezed the trigger. Ah! It was even worse than I had feared!

My gun is exceedingly cool. It is a Raynger ST-8 noncontact thermometer made by Raytek of Santa Cruz, California. From several feet away, you point it at anything you wish and pull the trigger, and it instantly tells you the temperature of that thing within a tenth of a degree. My gun goes up to one 1,000° Fahrenheit! Sure, it cost way too much. Yes, I should have used the money to upgrade my footwear instead, or have a makeover. But everyone turns green with envy when I demonstrate my ST-8, especially men and boys, girls maybe a little less.

I have recently been going around New York City, taking the temperature of the best commercial pizza ovens, plus my own ovens at home, gas and electric, and my array of barbecue grills. Do you go through phases when you simply can't get pizza off your mind? I certainly do—and more often than I would care to admit to anybody but you. As you may have guessed, I am going through such a phase right now, a pretty serious one, though I have hopes that I will soon pull out of it. For I feel I am at long last ready to hoist my pizza-making to an entirely new level. I believe I am close to a pizza breakthrough for the American home.

Here's the idea. Pizza is a perfect food. From Elizabeth David to Marcella Hazan, all gastronomes agree. It is high on my list of the hundred greatest foods of the world. Though it is the most primitive of breads—a flatbread baked on stones heated by a wood fire—pizza is today made in pretty much its primordial form on 61,269 street corners in America. In New York City at least, it is still typically handmade, from scratch. Flour, water, yeast, and salt are kneaded into dough, given plenty of time to rise, patted and stretched into a circle, and baked to order in a special oven. A Neolithic bakery on every block—do you find this as astonishing as I do?

I have made thousands of pizzas at home. I have boldly faced the challenges that fate has thrown at me and overcome most of them. The most important thing about pizza is the crust. Toppings are secondary. (Both at home and in restaurants, cooks who don't know how to bake a good pizza crust become wearily creative with their toppings; they aim to distract us from their fundamental failings, the way poor bread bakers add cilantro and dried cherries to their mediocre loaves.) Over the years, I have spent hours in renowned pizzerias trying to learn their methods. I have experimented with a hundred types of dough and by now have pretty much got it right. I'll give you the recipe later.

And yet my pizzas are not perfect, not even close. There are two perfect pizzas. One is Neapolitan. Pizza was not invented in Naples, nor probably in Italy. But around 1760, when tomatoes replaced lard and garlic as the principal pizza condiment, Naples—both the nobility and the poor—went mad for this ancient flatbread, and devised the greatest pizza in the world. It is about ten inches in diameter and ¼-inch thick, with a narrow, charred, puffy, sauceless rim, crisp but tender and light; it is made with about seven ounces of dough prepared with soft flour; and it is most often topped, very lightly, with tomatoes, garlic, oregano, and olive oil (this is the *pizza marinara*) or with tomatoes, olive oil, mozzarella, and a leaf or two of basil (this is the *pizza Margherita*, named in 1889 for the visiting queen of Italy and notable for the red, white, and green of the Italian flag). The mozzarella is usually made from cow's milk, sometimes from water buffalo's milk. In Naples, pizza toppings are not cooked in advance—only by the heat of the pizza oven.

The other perfect pizza is Neapolitan-American. Pizza came to the New World just before the turn of the twentieth century with the arrival of immigrants from Naples. Though Gennaro Lombardi, at 53½ Spring Street, was granted the first license to bake pizza, issued by the city of New York in 1905, his justifiably proud yet fair-minded descendants reveal that Neapolitan bread bakers in New York had been making pizza with their surplus dough for at least the previous ten years. In my experience, the perfect Neapolitan-American pizzas are made in New York City and in New Haven, Connecticut, at the towering Frank Pepe's Pizzeria and Sally's Apizza. (For all I know, the three other cities where Italian immigrants predominantly settled—Providence, Philadelphia, and Boston—are unheralded treasure troves of pizza, but I have never heard anyone brag about them.[1]) Lombardi's reopened several years ago, at 32 Spring Street, where the oven could be repaired by the one company in Brooklyn that still knows how. Through both anecdotal evidence and photographic proof on the walls of today's Lombardi's, we know that Gennaro Lombardi taught both Anthony "Totonno" Pero and John Sasso the art of pizza; these men would gain metropolitan and, yes, nationwide renown with their own pizza places, John's Pizzeria on Bleecker Street and Totonno's in Coney Island.

The mystic hand[2] of evolution somehow transmuted the true Neapolitan pizza of 1889 into the perfect Neapolitan-American pizza of today, which is 14 to 18 inches in diameter, rimmed with a wide, puffy, charred circumferential border; heavier, thinner, crisper, and chewier than the Neapolitan original; made with high-protein bread flour; and topped with lavish quantities of cooked tomato sauce, thick slabs of fresh cow's-milk mozzarella, olive oil, and most often—36 percent of the time—pepperoni, an innovation of the 1950s and still America's favorite topping, for which there is little excuse. The perfect Neapolitan-American crust is about ³⁄₁₆-inch thick. Viewed in cross section, the bottom ¹⁄₃₂-inch is very crisp and nearly charred. The next ³⁄₃₂-inch is made up of dense, delicious, chewy bread. And the top ¹⁄₁₆-inch is slightly gooey from its contact with the oil and sauce. The outer rim is shot through with huge and crunchy bubbles. *This is the crust I have been after for as long as I can remember.*

Serious pizza places here and in Naples have brick ovens fueled either by wood or, in New York City and New Haven, by coal. Yes, coal—large hunks of shiny, blue, bituminous coal. Authentic Neapolitan pizzas take from 80 to 120 seconds to bake, authentic Neapolitan-American pizzas maybe five minutes. Mine take fourteen minutes. It seems obvious that what stands between me and perfect pizza crust is temperature—real pizza ovens are much hotter than anything I can attain in my own kitchen. Lower temperatures dry out the dough before the outside is crisp and the topping has cooked.

I have confirmed all this with my new Raynger ST-8. At the reasonably authentic Neapolitan La Pizza Fresca Ristorante on Twentieth Street, for example, the floor of its wood-burning brick oven measures 675°F; the back wall (and presumably the ambient air washing over the pizza) pushes 770°F, and the domed ceiling 950°F. The floor of Lombardi's Neapolitan-American coal oven soars to an amazing 850° measured a foot from the inferno, less under the pizza itself. My ST-8 and I have become inseparable.

I have tried a wide variety of measures to reach such breathtaking temperatures. Laypersons may possibly feel that some of these measures are desperate. I own a creaky old restaurant stove with a gas oven that goes up to 500°F, no higher. The hot air is exhausted through two vents in back. What if I blocked the vents with crumpled aluminum foil and kept the hot air from escaping? Would the oven get hotter and hotter and hotter? No, this experiment was a failure. As I could have predicted if I had had my wits about me, the oven's thermostat quickly turned down the flame as soon as the hot air I had trapped threatened to exceed 500°F.

How to defeat the thermostat? More than once, I have skillfully taken apart my stove and then needed to pay the extortionate fees of a restaurant-stove-reassembly company. This time, I had a better idea. Way in the back of the oven you can see the thermostat's heat sensor, a slender rod spanning the opening to the exhaust vents. How, I wondered, could I keep this bar artificially cold while the stove tried harder and harder to bring up the temperature and in the process exceed its intended 500°F limit? I folded together many layers of wet paper towels, put them in the freezer until they had frozen solid, draped them over the temperature sensor with the oven set to high, shoveled in an unbaked pizza, and stood back.

The results were brilliant, especially in concept. My oven, believing incorrectly that its temperature was near the freezing point, went full blast until thick waves of smoke billowed from every crack, vent, and pore, filling the house with the palpable signs of scientific progress. Yes, the experiment had to be cut short, but it had lasted longer than the Wright brothers' first flight. Inside the oven was a blackened disk of dough pocked with puddles of flaming cheese. I had succeeded beyond all expectations.

And not long afterward, I slid a raw pizza into a friend's electric oven, switched on the self-cleaning cycle, locked the door, and watched with satisfaction as the temperature soared to 800°F. Then, at the crucial moment, to defeat the safety latch and retrieve my perfectly baked pizza, I pulled out the massive electrical plug and, protecting my arm with a wet bath towel, tugged on the door. Somehow, this stratagem failed, and by the time we had got the door open again half an hour later, the pizza had completely disappeared, and the oven was unaccountably lined with a thick layer of ash. I feel that I am onto something here, though as with the controlled use of hydrogen fusion, the solution may remain elusive for many years.

Then came the breakthrough. The scene was the deck of my Southern California house. The occasion was the maiden voyage of my hulking, rectangular,

black-steel barbecue, which has an extravagant grilling area measuring 18 by 30 inches. I had built my inaugural fire, using hardwood charcoal and wood chunks; hours later, a thick steak would go on the grill, but for now I was just playing. At some point, I closed the massive hood and watched the built-in thermometer, as the temperature climbed to 550°F. And then it struck me. Why not double the fuel, the wood and the charcoal? Why not 650°F? Why not 750°F? Why not pizza?

I dashed into the kitchen and prepared my excellent recipe for pizza dough. It must be understood that this was not to be the popular "grilled pizza" introduced by Joanne Killeen and George Germon at their Al Forno restaurant in Providence, Rhode Island, in which the dough is placed directly over the fire. My barbecue grill was to be used only for its ability to generate great amounts of heat.

As the pizza dough was completing its mandatory three-hour rise and one hour's refrigeration, just as the sun was setting over Charles A. Lindbergh Airport, I built a massive fire using eighteen pounds of hardwood charcoal, two bulging bags that filled the firebox to overflowing. In 45 minutes, when gray ash had covered the charcoal, I lowered the hood and watched the thermometer climb to 600°F —and go no further! Where had I gone wrong? I opened all the air vents and the large front door that lets you add fuel and remove ashes. Huge volumes of oxygen flowed in, and bingo! The needle climbed past the 700°F red line and into uncharted territory. Using oven mitts, I fitted a thick round baking stone onto the grill, waited for advice from my ST-8, slid a raw pizza onto the stone, and lowered the hood.

This is when I learned that a pizza stone can get much hotter than the air around it if you put it directly over fire, causing the bottom of the pizza to burn to a crisp before the top is done. I also learned that when your ST-8 noncontact thermometer tells you that the barbecue grill has reached 900°F, the electrical cord of the rotisserie motor you slothfully left attached to the bracket on one side will melt like a milk-chocolate bar in your jeans pocket or, more aptly, like the huge plastic all-weather barbecue cover you just as carelessly left draped over the shelf below the grill.

These were mere details, for victory was mine. And it can be yours as well. If you scrape the fiery coals to either side of the baking stone, taking care not to singe your eyebrows again, you can reduce the stone's temperature to the ideal

650°F while keeping the air temperature directly over the pizza near the perfect 750°F or even higher. Use all the hardwood charcoal you can carry, and between pizzas, add more to maintain the heat. Just before you slide the pizza onto the stone, throw some wood chips or chunks onto the coals to produce the aromatic smoke of a wood-burning oven near the Bay of Naples. And in the light of day, feel no regrets that you have burned the paint off the sides of your barbecue and voided the manufacturer's limited warranty.

This remains my favorite and best way of making pizza. Although the procedure is tricky, three out of four of the pizzas that emerge from my barbecue are pretty wonderful—crisp on the bottom and around the very puffy rim, chewy in the center, artfully charred here and there, tasting of wood smoke.

Very little time had passed, however, before I became uneasy and discontented once again. How could I complacently feast while others went without? Very few American families possess my monstrous barbecue. How could I bring my pizza breakthrough to the average American home?

It was time to exhume my Weber Kettle, which without a moment's hesitation or research, I knew to be the most popular charcoal grill in the country. As I had long ago discovered that the Weber Kettle (which lacks a mechanism for raising and lowering the fuel or the grill, admits only a trickle of oxygen when the cover is closed, et cetera, et cetera) is of extremely limited use for cooking, I had exiled it to the garage, where it held two 50-pound bags of French bread flour, the gems of my collection, off the moist concrete floor.

I filled the Weber to the brim with hardwood charcoal, let the fire go for a half hour, plopped on the baking stone, and put on the cover. The internal temperature barely reached 450°F, and the baking stone even less. I dumped ten pounds of additional charcoal into the center, fired it, produced a conflagration measuring 625°F, with the stone at an even higher temperature, and in no time at all had achieved a pizza completely incinerated on the bottom and barely done on top. Despite the vast amounts of ingenuity that I brought to bear in half a day of exhaustive tests, I simply could not get the Weber Kettle to heat the air above the baking stone to anywhere near the desired heat. The Weber is simply not wide enough for enough of the heat to flow up around the baking stone and over the top of the pizza. Once again, the Weber proved itself incapable of producing gastronomic treasures. Back into the garage it went.

By all means, experiment with your own charcoal grill. Like me, you will not regret the hours and days spent on backyard exploration. And to forestall the obloquy to which you may be subjected if the results are not good enough to eat, remember to make a double dose of dough and to preheat the oven in your kitchen as a backup. Indoor pizzas can still be awfully good. Meticulous instructions follow.

[1] Author's note: Though the population of Providence, Rhode Island, remained quiet, the voices of several Philadelphians were raised, recommending Tacconelli's.

[2] Author's note: As there used to be two seriously authentic Neapolitan pizzerias within taxi distance of my house—Gemelli and Pizza Fresca—one could set side by side a direct descendent of the original pizza next to its American cousin and, alternately chewing and thinking, ruminate on the process of evolution and wonder how one became the other. This I did several times. Nothing to report. Gemelli was destroyed on September 11, 2001.

AUTHOR'S UPDATE: In Europe you can buy several Italian-made models of small, electric, countertop pizza ovens. Norwegian food writer and friend, Andreas Viestad, bought me one in Oslo and brought it to Manhattan. Meanwhile, I acquired a large and heavy transformer to step up our 115-volt electricity. The oven is bright red and round, measures between eleven and twelve inches in diameter, and has a hinged top like a waffle iron and a thin, heated baking stone on the bottom. It's capable of temperatures of over 800°F. Because of the rudimentary construction and the single, incomprehensible thermostat, you need considerable practice, but after a while, you can produce excellent pizzas. It works best with Neapolitan-size pizzas—seven ounces of dough, about eleven inches in diameter—which is how I've recently adapted my recipe, whether I bake the pizzas in the oven or in my little red toy.

After visiting Chris Bianco in Phoenix (as I hope you will learn elsewhere in this book, Chris makes the finest pizza in the United States and, in all frankness, the world), I've been making pizza only with canned Italian tomatoes rather than sauce, leaving more juice in the hand-squished tomatoes than I've called for in my recipe. I've also copied Chris's practice of scattering about six ¾-inch cubes of mozzarella over the pizza (instead of thin slices).

NEAPOLITAN-AMERICAN PIZZA

2 lbs. (about 6½ c.) flour, half all-purpose unbleached and half bread flour, both preferably King Arthur brand (see note)

1⅛ tsp. SAF instant yeast or 1½ tsp. active dry yeast

1 tbsp. plus 1 tsp. salt

3¼ c. cold water

6 tbsp. extra-virgin olive oil, plus a few teaspoons more to oil the measuring cup and plates used to hold the rising dough

½ c. cornmeal or semolina

1½ c. tomato sauce (a good recipe follows), or crushed, drained canned plum tomatoes

(empty a large can into a strainer set over a bowl and squeeze the tomatoes with your hand, using only the solids left in the strainer)

½ lb. fresh cow's-milk mozzarella, cut into 12 slices

1½ tsp. salt (or 3 tbsp. grated Parmesan)

SPECIAL EQUIPMENT: an electric mixer suitable for kneading dough; a thick ceramic baking stone, round or square, at least 14 inches across; a wooden peel (a flat paddle for transferring unbaked breads and pizzas) or a rimless baking sheet

IN THE MIXER BOWL, stir together the flours, yeast and salt. Pour in the water and stir vigorously with a wooden spoon until the ingredients come together into a shaggy dough. Mount the bowl on the mixer and attach the beater (not the dough hook—this dough is too wet for conventional kneading). Mix on slow speed for about a minute, then increase the speed to high and beat for three and a half minutes, scraping down the beater and bowl halfway through.

Here is a good way to tell when the dough is properly developed. With well-floured fingers, pull off a piece of dough about the size of a walnut and roll it in flour. You should now be able to stretch it with the fingers of both hands into an unbroken sheet at least three inches across.

Scrape and pour the dough onto a heavily floured work surface. (The only way to handle dough as moist and soft as this is to keep your fingers, countertop and the dough itself very well floured; whenever it sticks to the counter, use a metal pastry scraper or a long, wide knife or even a paint scraper to detach the dough without pulling and tearing it more than you have to.) It will spread into an irregular blob. Fold the far end over to the near end so that half the floured underside covers the rest of the dough. Let it rest for about ten minutes.

With a dough scraper, divide the dough into four equal pieces. (Each will weigh about 14.5 ounces, should you have an accurate electronic scale, as I do.) Shape each piece into a smooth ball. Place three of the balls on well-oiled, eight-inch plates, generously dust their tops with flour, and cover loosely with plastic wrap. Put the fourth ball into an oiled, one-quart glass measuring cup and cover tightly with plastic wrap. Let everything rise at warm room temperature until the balls have doubled in volume, which should take between three and four hours.

With this proprietary and surely patentable method, the markings on the side of the one-quart measuring cup will tell you when the ball inside, and by inference the three others, have doubled in volume, from one-and-a-half cups to three. Now refrigerate all four balls of dough— for a minimum of one hour, an ideal of three hours, and a maximum of twenty-four hours.

At your own risk and following the procedure described in this article, prepare your outdoor grill to achieve a temperature of 750°F, regardless of the warranty. Clear an area in the center of the coals and place a heavy baking stone over it.

Alternately, preheat your oven for at least an hour to its maximum temperature, 500 or 550°F, with your baking stone inside. In a gas oven, the baking stone goes right on the metal floor of the oven, in an electric oven, on the lowest shelf.

Set the peel on a level surface and dust with about 2 tablespoons of cornmeal. Take one or more of the balls of dough (now disks) from the refrigerator. On a well-floured surface, pat one into a neat, 8-inch circle. Now stretch its rim all around (the center will take care of itself) by draping the dough over your fists, knuckles up, and passing it from hand to hand and revolving it, keeping most of the dough resting on the counter—until the circle of dough reaches a diameter of about 12 inches. With your fists still under the dough and held apart, quickly bring the circle of dough over to the peel, plop it down, and pull it into a neat circle between 12½ and 13 inches across.

Put a heaping quarter-cup of tomato sauce or crushed, drained canned tomatoes in the center of the pizza and spread with the back of a wooden spoon, but only to within 1½ or 2 inches of the rim. Sprinkle with freshly ground pepper. Arrange three slices of mozzarella over the tomatoes. Sprinkle with a generous 1½ teaspoon salt (or 2 teaspoons of grated Parmesan) and 1½ tablespoons of olive oil. Shake the peel back and forth to see that the pizza is not sticking to the peel. Bake immediately: Open the oven door, place the leading

NOTE: I have called for King Arthur flour because it is of good quality, and widely available in supermarkets and at (800) 827-6836. Flours differ widely in their ability to hold water, which depends largely on their protein content. (Protein also determines the ideal mixing time.) If you use the flour I use, your results should be similar to mine. The combined protein level of these two flours is 12.27%; if you especially like a particular bread flour having about 12.27% protein, by all means substitute it for both King Arthur flours. If your preferred flour has more or less protein, increase or decrease, respectively, by a few tablespoons the amount of cold water you add. King Arthur also sells inexpensive plastic rising buckets marked on the side in quarts and liters.

edge of the peel just short of the far edge of the baking stone and at about a 45° angle to it, and by a combination of jerking and pulling the peel towards you, evenly slide the pizza onto the stone. This will be difficult at first, child's play with practice.

Bake for ten to fifteen minutes (rotating the pizza after seven minutes so that it will bake evenly) until the rim of the pizza is very well-browned, the topping is bubbling and the cheese is golden-brown, and the underside is crisp and charred here and there. Cut into sections with a long scissors or a pizza wheel.

Tomato Sauce

¼ c. extra-virgin olive oil

1 3-inch onion, finely chopped

4 cans (28 oz. each) whole Italian plum tomatoes

1 head of garlic, cut in half crosswise, any loose outer papery skin removed

2 tbsp. coarsely chopped fresh herbs (basil, oregano, marjoram) or
2 tbsp. dried herbs

2 tsp. salt

freshly ground black pepper

HEAT THE OLIVE OIL in a 4- to 5-quart saucepan and gently cook the chopped onion in it until just translucent. Empty the tomatoes into a large strainer set over a 2- to 3- quart bowl. Squish the tomatoes with your hands until no large pieces remain. This should be quite enjoyable. Empty the tomato solids in the strainer into the saucepan. Add 1½ cups of the tomato water and stir in all the other ingredients except the pepper. Bring to a snappy simmer, cook for about twenty minutes, and remove from the heat. Add about 16 grindings of pepper. When it cools, the sauce should be very thick. Makes one quart.

Pizza Burn

Sid Kirchheimer

This minitreatise on pizza burn is taken from The Doctors Book of Home Remedies II *(Bantam Books, 1995).*

BITE INTO A SLICE OF STEAMING HOT PIZZA AND . . . *yow!* That nasty burn you get on the roof of your mouth could make you consider take-out Chinese next time.

It's an agonizing encounter: Searing-hot cheese meets the tender parts of your upper palate. What you can expect are a blistering lesion, moderate pain that lasts for about a week and sometimes a loosened piece of flesh that hangs down from the roof of your mouth. The symptoms are so typical that this condition has made it into the pages of authoritative medical journals as—what else?—"pizza burn."

But actually, pizza is only one of the hot foods that can burn. The tissue on the roof of your mouth is only millimeters thick. Just about any food or drink that retains heat well—any melted cheese dish, many soups and sauces, beverages like tea and hot chocolate, even *hot* hot-fudge topping—can damage that tissue and cause swelling. Until recently, these other culprits have been bit players in this

oral drama. Pizza was the main villain. But now, in the age of the microwave, any hot food can produce a sneak attack.

So here's what to do if you singe your mouth.

- **Ice it.** "Put an ice cube in your mouth immediately to neutralize some of the tissue reaction," suggests Fred Magaziner, D.D.S., a spokesdentist for the Academy of General Dentistry and host of "Open Wide—A Look at Dentistry," a Baltimore TV talk show about dental care. "Besides lessening some of the pain, it will reduce the chance of any additional swelling and irritation. That's why it's also a good idea to never bite into pizza without a cold drink handy."

- **Gargle with salt water.** "I recommend frequent saltwater rinses—every hour or so if you can manage," says Bernard Dishler, D.D.S., a dentist in Elkins Park, Pennsylvania. "Make your own rinse of ½ teaspoon of salt mixed with eight ounces of warm water to promote the healing process."

- **Avoid "sharp" foods.** That means sharp in taste and in edges. "Spicy foods, particularly Italian, will increase the pain from an existing pizza burn and may trigger infection," says Allen R. Crawford, Jr., D.M.D., a dentist in Macungie, Pennsylvania. "You'll also want to avoid potato chips and other foods with sharp edges, which will aggravate the lesion."

- **Head for the drugstore.** "A product called Orabase, which is available over the counter, is a pectin ointment that sticks to wet tissue to protect the lesion from the heat you eat—particularly spicy foods," says Dr. Magaziner. Apply Orabase directly on the burn to protect as well as heal.

- **Drink plenty of milk.** "Milk provides a mild coating that protects the lesion slightly," adds Dr. Crawford.

- **Let microwaved foods "sit."** Foods prepared in microwaves cook unevenly, so the outside and inside may be different temperatures, says Dr. Magaziner. "Most people get burned because they don't do what you're supposed to do with microwaved food." And what should you do? "Let the food sit in the microwave for two minutes after the buzzer rings before you eat it," advises Dr. Magaziner.

Pizza Ratings

ALL PIZZA IS NOT CREATED EQUAL. Most places that sell by the slice use commercial aged mozzarella, gas ovens, inexpensive sausage and canned mushrooms. On the other hand, almost all of the whole-pie establishments I write about use fresh mozzarella, fresh fennel sausage, high-quality canned tomatoes for their sauce and either coal- or wood-fired brick ovens. So the only fair thing to do is to judge slice and whole-pie places using different standards. True Neapolitan pizza, which is breadier and doughier than regular pizza (and never crisp), must also be judged within its own context.

In the case of slices and standard pies, an exemplary slice of pizza should have discrete sections of cheese and sauce and a puffy, chewy crust that is crisp and thin but not too thin, with lovely air bubbles popping up on the edges. Most pizza these days has a barely visible layer of sauce—it's as though the sauce has gone into exile.

There is a different aesthetic involved in making pizza by the slice, though guys like Domenico DeMarco blur the line between the two. Finally, when it comes to slices, proximity rules. On a rainy night, when the kids are restless and your brain is screaming "PIZZA!" a mediocre slice from the shop down the street beats a superior slice from way across town. New Yorkers especially are loathe to travel far for a slice of pizza. This kind of slice sloth is the result of having at least one very fine slice choice in every neighborhood.

I have devised dual rating systems for slices and whole pies. The whole-pie scale ranges from two to four whole pies. Likewise, the slice scale ranges from two to four slices. Pizza that would have received a one-slice or -pie rating simply is not worthy of inclusion in the book.

PIE RATING SCALE

A fine neighborhood pie

An excellent pizza

Pizza lovers will swear that eating this pizza is a religious experience.

SLICE RATING SCALE

A good, solid neighborhood slice

Worth a one mile or twenty minute detour

A transcendent slice

NOTE: In location listings, the first address and phone number are for the original location visited and rated.

CHAPTER
2

*Pizza
in Italy*

NAPLES: PIZZA AT ITS SOURCE

THE PIZZA POLICE, DEDICATED TO THE PROPOSITION THAT authenticity is everything, tell us that you cannot judge or taste pizza properly without having eaten it in Naples. Pizza wasn't invented in Naples (there have been flatbreads with toppings for thousands of years), but it is the place where pizza became popular, and where this perfect, simple food burrowed itself deep into the consciousness of Neapolitans of every class and neighborhood. Naples, they say, is where the modern pizza-eating rituals first flowered.

In 1830 the world's first pizzeria, Antica Pizzeria Port'Alba, opened its doors in Naples, and an industry was born. Antica Pizzeria Port'Alba is still in business, by the way. Fifty-nine years later a pizzaiolo named Raffaele Esposito was invited to the Italian royal palace to make three pizzas for the visit of King Umberto and Queen Margherita of Savoy. The queen was apparently no dummy when it came to politics, so she declared her favorite pizza to be the one with the colors of the Italian flag: red (tomato), white (mozzarella cheese) and green (basil). Thus, *pizza Margherita* was born.

Right around the time Esposito came up with the Margherita, Italians started coming to America by the millions, driven by the prospect of improving their standard of living. According to author Pamela Sheldon Johns, five million Italians made their way to America by the turn of the twentieth century, 80 percent of them from the south of Italy. Thus it was almost inevitable that a Neapolitan immigrant named Gennaro Lombardi would open the first pizzeria in America—on Spring Street in lower Manhattan in 1905.

Every food writer and historian worth his or her pizza crust has made the pilgrimage to Naples to taste pizza at the source. When I went, I was armed with clippings from many of the illustrious "foodies" who had gone before me—David Downie, Alan Richman and Jeff Steingarten, all of whom are represented in *A Slice of Heaven*. To bolster my credibility and to guide me through that stunningly beauti-

ful city, I persuaded Maurizio DeRosa to come with me. Maurizio is a Neapolitan native and the former owner (along with his mother and brother) of the now defunct DeRosa, the only Neapolitan restaurant ever given three stars by Ruth Reichl (see page 166) during her stint as restaurant critic for the *New York Times*. We stayed at his mother's in the Vomero section of Naples, and set out to eat at the fifteen best pizzerias in the city. I actually would have gone to more, but Maurizio assured me that fifteen pizzerias in five days would be his limit. What did we find? Well, I hope Maurizio doesn't banish me from Italy for saying this, but what I found is that the Neapolitan *culture* of pizza is in many ways more interesting than the pizza itself.

PIZZA PILGRIMAGE

As the plane touched down in Rome, I had a disturbing thought: What if Neapolitan pizza wasn't as good as the pizza I most love in the States: Chris Bianco's and Totonno's and Sally's and Pepe's in New Haven? What if I showed my true provincial food colors once again? How could I face my purist foodie brethren, who claim that food is always best eaten in its place of origin? How could I face my Naples host, Maurizio DeRosa, who is an unabashed Neapolitan pizza champion, the keeper of the wood-burning flame as it were? He had graciously offered to take me to Naples on a pizza-eating expedition or exploration. We were going to eat in Rome for a day, and then head down to Naples to stay at his mother's apartment in the Vomero section of the city.

We deplaned in Rome, rented a car and headed to one of Rome's legendary pizzerias, Da Baffetto, recommended to me by many of the best Italian-influenced chefs in the States, including Mario Batali and Todd English. I wanted to try the place, but Maurizio disdained Roman-style pizza—that of the thin, crisp crust—and wanted to get to Naples. As he parked the car in a lot, he fired the first shot. "If you ever had a choice and you ordered a Roman pie instead of a Neapolitan pie, I would say, 'You are sick.'"

Keeping that in mind, we arrived at Da Baffetto, only to find that it was closed for lunch. A nearby shopkeeper told us the son of the owner of Da Baffetto had a pizzeria, Bel Paino, just around the corner, and he was open for lunch. We sat down and ordered a Margherita and a marinara. When they arrived at our table a few minutes later, Maurizio took one look at the ultrathin, crisp crusts and said, "Take a good look at these, and remember what they look like and taste like. Never forget it. This is not pizza."

I actually liked it, but wasn't about to tell Maurizio that I thought the crust was crunchy and offered a nice counterpoint to the creamy melted mozzarella. We then hit two other Roman pizza variations: the *pizza bianca* ("white" pizza,

with no tomato sauce) at Il Forno di Campo de' Fiori (a crisp yet pliant flatbread made with sea salt and rosemary), and pizza by the meter at a bakery recommended by our friend, Italian food maven and food radio host Arthur Schwartz. I liked them both, but Maurizio dismissed each with a wave of his hand. "You may like them, Ed, but they're nothing special."

As we walked back to the car I thought, "Can it get any better than this? Four kinds of pizza—all of which I thought were pretty good—and I haven't even unpacked my bags." I was so psyched to get to Naples that I barely noticed the torrential rainstorm that accompanied us all the way down the autostrada.

Around fifty kilometers from Naples, Maurizio started rhapsodizing about pizza in his native city. "You put it in your mouth, and you go *wow*, now you have something—layers and layers of flavor coming at you in waves. Our pizza is like a soufflé, the dough is like a volcanic explosion in your mouth. Our pizza is like . . . heaven." I looked over at him and realized that he'd gotten so excited about the subject that his hands were completely off the steering wheel as he gesticulated for emphasis. Also, Maurizio and I couldn't figure out how to turn the windshield wipers on. I began to worry if we were even going to make it to Naples.

We arrived at Maurizio's mother's house around 8:00 P.M. Rita, a tiny woman (and a legendary Neapolitan chef) with a warm smile and sunken, expressive eyes, asked if we were hungry. I was full, sickeningly full to be exact, but Maurizio suggested we have his local pizzeria deliver a couple of pies to begin our quest. "It's not the best, but it's still better than anything you can get in New York." Maurizio's brother Bruno, a trained chef who cooked with his mother at DeRosa before moving back to Naples four years ago, called in the order. A half hour later, the pies arrived. The crusts were thicker than crackers and bready, and the toppings were reasonably sparse without being demure. The pizza had a lovely smoky flavor. The crust was not crisp, but that could have been the result of steaming in the delivery boxes. I liked it, more than my neighborhood slice place to be sure, but the pizza wasn't transcendent. I didn't dare tell Maurizio though, for fear he'd send me back to New York on the next plane. I went to bed, full of Roman street food, Neapolitan pizza and dread.

The next day we started our pizza hunt at L'Europeo, a trattoria and pizzeria located in a commercial district just off the water in one of the ancient parts of Naples. Before we made it to the restaurant, I tried a Neapolitan street pizza that I saw many people eating while they walked. The pizzas are sold from heated boxes in front of these trattorias, and they come right from wood-burning ovens. The one I got was fresh, doughy and very tasty. Trying to fit in, I folded it in thirds, the way I had been told Neapolitans eat pizza on the go, and walked as I ate.

Maurizio, Bruno and I arrived at L'Europeo, and Bruno alerted the owner to what I was doing. Alfonso Mattozzi was among the warmest and most gracious restaurateurs I have ever met or seen in action. He brought us two pizzas, a Margherita and a marinara, and they were not just good, they were astounding. The lip, what the Italians call the *cornicione*, was puffy and almost two inches high. The crust was light, ethereal and cloudlike. The San Marzano tomatoes were sweet, and the melted *mozzarella di bufala* was creamy and slightly tart. "See, Ed," Bruno said with a wry smile, "good pizza should melt in your mouth."

As we talked about the pizza, pointing at its features, holding it up to get a better look at the crust, rolling our eyes at the flavor and texture, an elegant-looking man at an adjoining table chimed in. "I have lived in Naples my entire life," he said, "as have two generations of my family before me, and I can tell you that the pizza you are eating is one of the best in Naples, and therefore anywhere in the world." Mr. Mattozzi introduced this man, a Neapolitan shipping magnate named Mr. Grimaldi. He was dressed in a custom-tailored, three-piece suit, and had chosen to dine today on pizza from L'Europeo. "The great province of Naples has the longest and best pizza-making tradition in the world. But pizza is everywhere in Naples, so I am very careful about where and when I eat it. I'm trying to think of ten pizzas I would finish here. There's here, maybe Lombardi, Ettori, Ciro a Margelline, Cafasso." He stopped, falling way short of ten. "Even here, for a few months after Mr. Mattozzi lost his pizzaiolo, he went through four or five people, and the pizza was no good."

Our discussion became quite heated and animated. Soon Mr. Mattozzi, his newfound pizzaiolo and the restaurant's oyster shucker, a toothless elderly man dressed in a fisherman's sweater, joined in the discussion. Maurizio said, "The frame [the crust] should have holes, like great bread. It should be thin in the center but not too thin. When you bite into it, it should melt in your mouth. All the elements should come together when you are in the hands of a great pizzaiolo." The oyster-man waved his hand dismissively at Maurizio. Bruno translated with a chuckle: "He says that you are talking about pizza as it were a work of art. Michelangelo was an artist. Now *he* had hands. This is just food. There is only one thing that makes things taste good: hunger. The best chef is hunger." It was obvious that Neapolitans care a great deal about pizza and could talk about it for hours on end, the same way New Yorkers could talk about pastrami, or Parisians about baguettes.

The rest of the food at L'Europeo was absolutely delicious: eggplant parmigiana made with smoked mozzarella that was nothing like the stuff we eat at American pizzerias; pasta with potatoes and basil and onions; focaccia with cured meats. Signore Mattozzi even had his pizzaiolo fry up some pizza dough just to illustrate how light it is. Sprinkled with powdered sugar, it tasted like the best *zeppóle* I could imagine. It practically floated off the plate. Signore Mattozzi said, "Put your finger on one of the holes. It will spring back." To illustrate, he put his knife on one of the holes and depressed it. It sprung back immediately. "That is the sign of good Neapolitan pizza dough," said Maurizio.

Over the next five days we went to just about every pizzeria that either Maurizio or Bruno knew to be good, fifteen in all. Our test pizzas were a Margherita and a marinara. Sometimes we would augment those two with a specialty. At Lombardi's, for example, we had a very fine pizza made with lard.

We went to Da Michele, where they deviate from Neapolitan pizza orthodoxy by offering three sizes of pizza. It didn't matter. All three sizes tasted the same. We went to Brandi and ate pizza surrounded by Japanese and even a scattering of Americans. We went to Trianon and Lombardi's (Steingarten's favorite), Ciro a Mergellina, and 165-year-old Port'Alba and Cafasso, an off-the-beaten-path spot that famed cookbook writer and Italian food expert Faith Willinger had recommended. And we went to Di Matteo, where President Clinton ate while attending the G7 economic summit in 1999. And guess what? The pizzas at virtually every place we went to tasted eerily similar. They all baked for less than two minutes in a 700°F, wood-burning oven. They all had a very high lip, at least two inches. The crusts were all slightly bready, with a taste-enhancing charred flavor. There wasn't a crisp crust in the lot. They all used locally sourced mozzarella, *fior di latte*, which not one pizzeria made on its own. *Mozzarella di bufala* was available upon request for a little extra money.

The canned tomatoes were not drained, and this, combined with the rather large splash of oil (sometimes olive oil and sometimes sunflower seed oil!) and the moisture given off by the cheese, made for wet pizzas that occasionally bordered on swampy.

Although occasionally underbaked with a resulting gummy crust, the pizzas were all very tasty. But . . . with the possible exception of the pizzas at L'Europeo, none were exceptional enough to have me swearing off Pepe's or Sally's or Totonno's.

On the second-to-last night, we ate at a bustling trattoria and pizzeria, Da Ettore. We had memorable pasta with langoustines and some very fine pizza with a crust that at least approached crispness. When Maurizio went to the bathroom, Bruno whispered, "You see, Ed, there just isn't that much variation between pizzerias in Naples. The difference between the best and worst isn't all that great. In Naples, pizza is pizza. We are proud of it but, as you have seen, there are many places to get real Neapolitan pizza in Naples."

On our last day in Naples, Maurizio and I went back to L'Europeo. We had two pizzas: a Margherita and one with arugula and prosciutto. Both were fantastic; fresh tasting, yeasty crust and not too wet. We also had fabulous fried zucchini flowers stuffed with ricotta, incomparable foccacia topped with thin slices of pork

belly that melted in our mouths and the best *pasta e fagiole* (pasta with beans) I'd ever had. We were taken care of with grace and charm by Mr. Mattozzi. I realized that I loved just about everything about Naples—its people, its sights, the food—everything, that is, but the pizza. I couldn't bring myself to tell Maurizio. It would break his heart. So as we left Naples on the way to the Rome airport, I merely nodded when Maurizio said, "Now you see, Ed, what I have been talking about all these years. Now I know you understand about our pizza. You are on your way to having a Neapolitan heart and soul."

PIZZA IN NAPLES

Here are names, addresses and phone numbers of all the places I ate pizza in Naples—plus brief reviews.

- **Antica Pizzeria Brandi,** steps off Via Chaia, on a tiny side street called Salita S. Anna di Palazzo, 081-416-928. The only restaurant in Naples where I heard English spoken. Brandi is a charming, multilevel tourist trap. The pizza here is solid if unspectacular, but mighty pricey.
- **Antica Pizzeria Port'Alba,** 18, Via Port'Alba, 081-45-9713. The pizza I had here was from the heated case in front of the pizzeria. Surprisingly tasty, easy to fold and not wet at all. The man who sold it to me indicated he wanted to come back with us to New York.
- **Ciro a Mergellina,** 18/21, Via Mergellina, 081-681-780. A fancy-pants pizzeria right on the water. The pizza had nice charred spots on the crust, but it had a puddle in the center. Good fried seafood and pasta with clams here.
- **Da Ettore Ristorante e Pizzeria,** 56, Via Santa Lucia, 081-764-04-98. A boisterous trattoria where the food and the waiters are the star attraction. The only pizza I had in Naples that could be described as crisp. The pasta with langoustines was smashing.
- **Da Michele,** 1/3, Via Cesare Sersale, 081-553-92-04. One of the classic Neapolitan pizzerias. The only place I saw in Naples that had more than one size of pie. Fine crust, cheap oil, wet pie.

D'Auria, 81/83, Via Simone Martini, 081-579-4711. D'Auria delivered three pizzas to Maurizio's mother's house the night we arrived in Naples. The pizza was classic Neapolitan pizza, though by the time it arrived in the boxes, the crusts had been steamed into oblivion. Mr. D'Auria has apparently won many pizza-making contests in Naples. The same can be said of almost every pizzeria I ate in. I think they have pizza-making contests every week.

Di Matteo, 94, Via dei Tribunali, 081-455-262. Very fine pizza on a charming, narrow Neapolitan street. Smoky, well-cooked crust and not too wet. This is where President Clinton ate pizza when he was in Naples for the G7. Just mention his name, and they'll offer you a Clinton souvenir—a simulated passport with Clinton's photo on it.

Gorizia, 29, Via Bernini, 081-578-2248. Another, fancier pizzeria/ristorante in the Vomero. The pizza had a very high lip and a very light crust. The rest of the food was fairly standard Neapolitan fare.

Il Pizzaiolo del Presidente, 120/121, Via Tribunali, 081-21-09-03. Next door to Di Matteo. The Presidente in the title is, yes, our man Clinton. The gentleman who owns Il Pizzaiolo is the brother of the owner of Di Matteo. He decided to capitalize on the Clinton connection as well. He also showed us his grottolike dining room, where he claimed resistance fighters hid during World War II.

L'Europeo di Mattozzi, 4, Via Marchese Campodisola, 081-552-1323. My favorite pizza in Naples, and my favorite all-around restaurant as well. The pizza melts in your mouth, and the pasta with peas and potatoes is the ultimate Italian comfort food.

Lombardi a Santa Chiara, 59, Via Benedetto Croce, 081-552-0780. It was jammed when we ate lunch here. We ordered a Margherita and a pizza with *lardo* (cured pig fat). The Margherita was undercooked with a doughy crust. The lardo pie was delicious, although I'm sure my cardiologist and my wife would have disapproved.

Pizza e Contorni, 27, Via Giuilio Cesare, 081-593-8740. I had my first street pizza at this minichain, on our way to L'Europeo for the first time. Street pizza in Naples is remarkably good. It's made in wood-burning ovens and then placed in a heated box outside the restaurants. As a result, it dries out, which to my way of thinking is a good thing.

🍴 **Pizzeria Cafasso,** 156/158, Via G. Cesare, 081-239-5281. Food writer and Italian food expert Faith Willinger, whom I know and respect, touts this pizzeria in an out-of-the-way, nondescript Neapolitan neighborhood. We didn't have any pizza here that was worth the trouble of finding it. It was good, don't get me wrong. It just wasn't distinctive or special.

🍴 **Trianon,** 42-44-46, Via Pietro Colletta, 081-553-9426. Gorgeous multilevel pizzeria. We sat downstairs surrounded by vintage photos. The pizza was actually quite good if a little soupy.

PIZZA IN ROME

🍴 **Antico Forno Marco Roscioli,** 34, Via dei Chiavari, 06-68-75-287. Very good pizza by the meter that makes a perfect walking lunch (or even a walking appetizer on your way to lunch somewhere else).

🍴 **Da Baffetto.** See page 318.

🍴 **Dal Paino,** 34, Via del Parione, 06-68-135-140. First-rate crisp, thin-crusted pizza, made by the son of the owner of Da Baffetto. It may not be pizza to a Neapolitan, but anybody else would be very happy eating it. The fried and stuffed zucchini flowers were a tasty treat, too.

🍴 **Il Forno di Campo de' Fiori,** 22, Piazza Campo de' Fiori, 06-68-806-662. I was crushed when we went by Il Forno the first time and it was closed for lunch. Thank God I prevailed on Maurizio to come back at 4:30, when it reopened. Both the pizza bianca and the pizza with tomato sauce are positively addictive. It is virtually impossible to limit yourself to one piece of each. 🍕

CHAPTER
3

Old Pizza

ANCIENT PIE

How far back does pizza go? A long way, more than a thousand years. According to Ed Behr in his *Art of Eating* newsletter, "The written record of the word pizza, in the sense of focaccia, goes back to the Codex Cajetanus of the year 997." Evelyne Slomon in *The Pizza Book* says even before that Plato gave an account of pizza in his *Republic*: "They will provide meal from their barley and flour from their wheat and kneading and cook these . . .

IL PIZZAIUOLO.

they [the cakes] will also have relishes—salt . . . and of olives and cheese; and onions and greens." It's a bit of a stretch, but the idea of Plato waxing philosophical about pizza is a delicious notion. Behr goes on to say that "pizza is an alternation of the Greek word *pitta,* which was introduced to southern Italy during the Byzantine conquest of the sixth century." Slomon says, "The name [pizza] comes from a southern Italian corruption of the Latin adjective *picea* (peechia), which described the black tar-like coating underneath the placenta, a pie made of the finest flours, a topping of cheese mixed with honey, and a seasoning of bay leaves and oil." The first pizzas, as we would recognize them today, were white pies, made with lard.

In the 1700s, King Ferdinand IV built a pizza oven for his wife, Maria Carolina, sister of Marie Antoinette. According to Behr, in the 1850s Emmanuelle Rocca wrote in a book called *The Customs of Naples,* "The frequenter of the pizzajuolo is a careless youth who has no other occupation or who is occupied simply by sitting from eleven to three, provided with a strong stomach and a little money." That pretty much fits the description of my friends and me in high school.

Rocca goes on to say, "The most ordinary pizzas, called *coll'aglio e l'oglio,* have for condiments oil, a scattering of salt, oregano, and finely cut up cloves of garlic. Others are covered with grated cheese and seasoned with lard and then some leaves of basil. To the first, tiny fish are often added; to the second, thin slices of mozzarella. Sometimes slices of ham are used or else tomato, mussels, etc." The tomato, called a golden apple, or *pomodoro* in Italian, was brought back from the new world in the mid-sixteenth century. Slomon says that Neapolitans were initially scared of the supposedly poisonous tomato, but by the eighteenth century they were putting it on pizza and pasta.

Maybe the most prescient pizza observer was nineteenth-century French author Alexandre Dumas. In a travel essay he wrote that "the pizza is a kind of schiacciata which is made in St. Denis; it is round in shape and made with bread dough. At first glance it looks like a simple food, but examined more closely, it seems complicated."

A Brief History of Pizza in America

ONCE UPON A TIME, AROUND THE TURN OF THE LAST CENTURY, pizza in America was an inexpensive peasant food, made *casalinga* (home-style) by southern Italian immigrant women in their kitchens. Adverse economic conditions had forced four million southern Italians to come to America by 1900. Descendents of all the seminal American pizza makers indicated their ancestors learned to make pizza by watching relatives make it at home.

In 1905 Gennaro Lombardi applied to the New York City government for the first license to make and sell pizza in this country, at his grocery store on Spring Street in what was then a thriving Italian-American neighborhood. In 1912 Joe's Tomato Pies opened in Trenton, New Jersey. Twelve years later, Anthony (Totonno) Pero left Lombardi's to open Totonno's in Coney Island. A year later, in 1925, Frank Pepe opened his eponymous pizzeria in New Haven, Connecticut. In 1929 John Sasso left Lombardi's to open John's Pizza in Greenwich Village. The thirties saw pizza spread to Boston (Santarpio's in 1933) and San Francisco with the opening of Tommaso's (1934), followed shortly thereafter with additional openings in New Jersey (Sciortino's in Perth Amboy in 1934 and the Reservoir Tavern in Boonton in 1936). In 1943, Chicago pizza was born when Ike Sewell opened Uno's. What did New York, New Haven, Boston and Trenton have in common? Factory work available to poorly educated southern Italian immigrants. Pizza at this point was very much an ethnic, poor person's food eaten by Italians in the urban enclaves in which they had settled.

The mainstreaming of pizza into American life began after World War II, when American GIs stationed in Italy returned home with a hankering for the pizza they had discovered overseas. In 1945, one of these returning soldiers, Ira Nevin, combined his eating experiences during the war with the know-how he had gained repairing ovens for his father's business to build the first gas-fired Bakers Pride pizza oven. These pizza ovens allowed retailers to bake pizzas quickly, cleanly, efficiently and cheaply. Armed with a little knowledge, a Bakers Pride oven and a by-then ubiquitous Hobart Mixer, aspiring pie men were ready to go into business.

Between 1945 and 1960 pizzerias began sprouting up all over the country. Most were owned by independent operators—some Italian, some Greek—but all of them American. People were either making their own mozzarella, or buying fresh mozzarella from a local purveyor. They were originally making their own sauce from fresh tomatoes, but at the very least they were making it from canned tomatoes. Dough was made in-house. Toppings were made in-house or locally.

The pizza-eating habit spread quickly to workers on their lunch hour, families looking for a cheap and satisfying meal out and bar habitués looking for a food chaser for their alcohol. It is no coincidence that so many pizzeria/bars opened up after the end of Prohibition in 1933. And unlike other classic American foods such as hot dogs, meat loaf, ham sandwiches and hamburgers, pizza was a perfect communal food. In fact, it was meant to be shared. There were no slices in most places, so you needed a group to order and eat a pizza. The group could be coworkers, teammates on a ball team or a family.

Many of the seminal pizzerias started as taverns, which could be frequented only by adults or kids accompanied by adults. At Vito & Nick's in Chicago, there's still a sign that greets you, saying, "No one under 21 is allowed in unless accompanied by adults." Lots of seminal pizzerias have "tavern" in their names: Reservoir Tavern in Boonton, Star Tavern in West Orange, Top Road Tavern in West Trenton. Jimmy DeLorenzo told me that the original DeLorenzo's in Trenton had a dance floor that made it the best place to meet girls in the city at the time it opened in 1936. Sociologists talk about the need for third places in every culture, the one place people can gather besides work and home. It seems to me that pizzerias were a third place in many Italian-American communities.

The pizza at most of the early American pizzerias was thin-crusted and *casalinga* in style. This kind of pizza is still being made all along the Jersey Shore at places such as Pete and Elda's/Carmen's in Neptune and Vic's in Bradley Beach, on Long Island at Eddie's in New Hyde Park, and in Chicago at the afore-mentioned Vito & Nick's. I've eaten at many of these pizza taverns in researching *A Slice of Heaven*. The pizza tends to be very good, it's always made by hand and it tastes great as long as you don't overanalyze it. It's true that none of this pizza is as good as the classic coal-fired pies that were coming out of the ovens in New Haven and New York and even Trenton before they changed over to gas. But that doesn't matter. This pizza was honest, handmade food that brought people together. Pizza is, after all, the ultimate populist, minimalist food.

What changed the pizza-scape in this country forever was the proliferation of chains. Pizza Hut started in Wichita, Kansas, in 1958; Little Caesar's emerged in 1959 and Domino's in 1960 (both in Michigan); and Papa John's opened in 1989 in Indiana. None was started with the idea of making the great home-style pizza the founders grew up with. If you go to each of the websites, you find that they all started as, first and foremost, a business proposition.

The chains made pizza a commodity. Though they still made pizza by hand, they used sauce and cheese and dough made in a central location and shipped to each city and location. Pride in the pizza-maker's craft disappeared. Chain pizza shops sold cheap, communal food with a fun image. Independents couldn't com-pete on price. At House of Pizza and Calzone in Brooklyn, former owner John Teutonico told me that when a Domino's opened a couple of blocks away, he knew his business was in trouble. "How can I compete with this?" he asked, show-ing me a flyer offering a large pizza with two toppings for $10.00. Teutonico and his partner sold the business in 2004.

The chains produced a chain reaction (pun intended). The independent pizza makers were and are being driven out of business. Between 1960 and 2000 the number of independents decreased markedly while the number of pizza chain outlets increased exponentially. As a result, many people had their first exposure to pizza in a chain restaurant. The Pizza Huts of the world became the pizza taste standard bearer in their minds. Even chain pizza tastes eminently satisfying, espe-cially if you've never had the real thing.

But the chains haven't won the war. I found there are still hundreds of independents selling good, honest, handmade pizza all over the country, and it's these pizza makers that I've tried to identify and celebrate in this book. I'm sure I haven't hit them all, and for that I apologize. Please let me know about the ones I've missed. No matter where you live you can find them. And you don't have to be a food critic to be able to taste the difference. The best pizza has the taste of great handmade food; it's the taste of love and family and community, and it's the taste we all should seek out no matter what we want to eat. The chains are not going to go away, but that doesn't mean we have to eat at them if we have a choice. And in most places we do have a choice. We might have to pay a little more for a pie, but what we get in return is a better-tasting pizza made by hand, with love and perhaps with a local ingredient or two.

The last time I went to Pizzeria Bianco, a young man with a short haircut and a baseball cap on backwards was leaving the restaurant as I was talking to owner/pizzaiolo Chris Bianco. "Are you the owner?" the young man asked Chris. "I am," Chris answered. "Well, I just want to tell you that your pizza rocks. It's way better than Pizza Hut." After he left, Chris smiled and said, "I guess that's progress."

THE PIZZA BELT

YOU'VE HEARD OF THE CORN BELT AND THE RUST BELT. BUT WHAT about the Pizza Belt, the part of America that gave birth to what Jeffrey Steingarten calls Neapolitan-American pizza. The Pizza Belt starts in Philadelphia and runs through Trenton and the rest of New Jersey. It extends throughout New York, Long Island and New Haven and ends in Boston. Think of it as the Interstate 95 belt, with a few detours along the way.

It was in New York that Neapolitan immigrant and grocery store owner Gennaro Lombardi was granted the nation's first license to sell pizza in 1905. Lombardi's, in turn, spawned Totonno's in 1924 and John's in 1929 and, in an apparently unrelated move, Patsy's in East Harlem in 1933. Joe's Tomato Pies opened in Trenton in 1910, followed by Papa's Tomato Pies in 1912. New Haven was next, where a Neapolitan immigrant Italian bread baker named Frank Pepe opened his eponymous Pizzeria Napoletana in 1925, followed in short order by Paul's Apizza in 1932, State Street Apizza (now called Modern Apizza) in 1934 and finally Sally's in 1938 (founded by Frank Pepe's nephew, Salvatore Consiglio). In Philadelphia, Salvatore and Chiarina Marra opened Marra's in 1927. The Tacconelli family started baking bread in their Port Richmond neighborhood in the 1920s, though they didn't start making pizza until 1946. Similarly, in East Boston, Francisco Santarpio baked bread at his eponymous bakery until Prohibition ended in 1933, when he took over the adjoining storefront and began serving pizza. Seven years before that, Anthony Polcari opened Pizzeria Regina in Boston's North End.

Why did all these pizzerias start in the same thirty-three year period? What did they have in common? Did Frank Pepe work at Lombardi's before moving to New Haven? Here's what we do know. There was a tremendous wave of southern Italian immigration in the late nineteenth century. These immigrants all came in through Ellis Island, and then fanned out along the Eastern

Seaboard looking for work among relatives, neighbors and friends who had come from the same area in Italy. New York, of course, was where they landed, so it made sense for a certain number of them to look for and find work there. Trenton had hundreds of thousands of manufacturing jobs and a burgeoning Italian-American community called Chambersburg. New Haven had many factories (including Colt Industries), as well as a plethora of fishing and port-related jobs. Philadelphia (South Philly) and Boston (East Boston and the North End) both had fast-growing Italian-American communities with thriving commercial centers.

What can we conclude from all this? That the development of America's pizza culture closely followed southern Italian immigration patterns. If the southern Italians had come into this country through Duluth, Minnesota might have been known as the Land of a Thousand Pizzas.

American Pizzeria Timeline

Here's the American Pizzeria Timeline, which includes only two non–Pizza Belt entries, Tommaso's and Uno's:

1905   **Lombardi's,** on Spring Street in New York City, is granted the nation's first license to sell pizza.

1910   **Joe's Tomato Pies** opens in the Trenton, NJ, Chambersburg neighborhood.

1912   **Papa's Tomato Pies** in Trenton opened by Papa, who learned his trade at Joe's.

1924   Anthony (Totonno) Pero leaves Lombardi's and opens **Totonno's** in Coney Island, NY.

1925   **Frank Pepe** opens on Wooster Street in New Haven, CT.

1926   **Pizzeria Regina** opens in Boston's North End.

1929   John Sasso from Lombardi's opens **John's** on Bleecker Street in New York's Greenwich Village.

1929   **Marra's** opens in Philadelphia, PA.

1931   **Eddie's** opens in New Hyde Park, Long Island (Nassau County), NY.

1932   **Paul's Apizza** opens in East Haven, CT.

1933   **Santarpio's** starts serving pizza in East Boston, MA.

1933   Patsy Lancieri opens **Patsy's** in East Harlem, NY.

1934   **State Street Apizza** (now Modern Apizza) opens in New Haven, CT.

1934   **Sciortino's** opens in Perth Amboy, NJ.

1935   **Tommaso's** (originally Lupo's) opens in San Francisco, CA (not in the Pizza Belt).

1936   **Reservoir Tavern** opens in Boonton, NJ.

1936   Original **DeLorenzo's** opens in Trenton, NJ, on Hudson Street.

1938   Salvatore Consiglio, Frank Pepe's nephew, opens **Sally's** on Wooster Street in New Haven, CT.

1943   **Uno's** opens in Chicago, IL (not in the Pizza Belt).

1946   **Tacconelli's** begins serving pizza in the Port Richmond section of Philadelphia, PA.

CHAPTER
4

*New York
Pizza*

New York, New York: Center of the Pie Universe

NEW YORK IS THE KING OF PIZZA CITIES. OH, YES, THERE ARE other pretenders to the pizza crown. Naples has its adherents, those who champion that beautiful city's high-lipped, slightly wet pies made in gorgeous wood-burning ovens. Chicagoans love their deep-dish pizza, and it is in fact a mighty tasty casserole, but one kind of pizza does not make a strong enough case for designating a city pizza royalty. New Havenites proudly point to the gorgeous, asymmetrical pies that come out of the coal-fired ovens of Sally's and Pepe's. Those are righteous pies indeed, but, again, you have to be able to show some pizza breadth. Pizza *variety* is why New York City sits comfortably on its pizza throne.

Let's start with classic Neapolitan-American pies, made in coal-fired brick ovens with fresh mozzarella. New York has Lombardi's, which opened the first licensed pizzeria in America, in 1905. On page 87, we get an inside look at the original Lombardi's from chef, pizzaiola and writer Evelyne Slomon. Lombardi's pie man Anthony (Totonno) Pero opened his own shop, Totonno's, in Coney Island, Brooklyn, in 1924 and his descendants are still turning out masterful pies there today. Patsy Lancieri opened a similar place, Patsy's, using the same kind of oven in 1933 in East Harlem, and it, too, is still around. Other whole-pie places utilizing coal-fired brick ovens include the Patsy's minichain, Grimaldi's, Arturo's, Angelo's and Bella Via. The array of New York pizzerias named Patsy's, Grimaldi's, Totonno's, John's, Nick's and Angelo's is confusing even to the most esteemed pizzaologists among us. To our rescue comes Eric Asimov of the *New York Times*, who follows each of the twisted branches of the New York pizza family tree (page 63).

Then there's the New York City whole-pie culture that utilizes gas ovens. Estimable pies come out of the ovens of Denino's in Staten Island, Mario's in the Bronx, and Nick's Pizza in Forest Hills, Queens, and the Upper East Side of Manhattan. In fact, Nick Angelis makes a pie with so much char and chew and pliancy in his high-tech gas ovens that he has me rethinking my allegiance to coal- and wood-fired pizzas.

Interested in individually sized, Neapolitan-inspired pies that come out of a wood-burning oven? New York has those, too, starting with La Pizza Fresca in the Flatiron district, Celeste on the Upper West Side, Naples 45 in Grand Central for commuters in need of a good pizza fix, and Caserta Vecchia and Franny's in Brooklyn, just a tunnel or bridge away from lower Manhattan.

New York is the home of the slice, as well. Want a slice made with *mozzarella di bufala*? Head to Di Fara in Midwood, Brooklyn, to sample Domenico DeMarco's wares. Need just a good crisp-crusted slice with fresh or aged mozzarella? Go to Louie and Ernie's in the Bronx, Joe's Pizza at Carmine and Bleecker in the Village, Sal and Carmine's on the Upper West Side, Nunzio's or Joe & Pat's in Staten Island, or even Patsy's in East Harlem for a coal-fired, brick-oven slice. New York is also the home of scores of slicerias with Ray in the name. Interestingly, on page 105 William Geist tells us that the truly original Ray is actually named Ralph.

Sicilian pizza aficionados who crave a square, slightly oily slice baked in a pan can head to L & B Spumoni Gardens in Brooklyn, or Rizzo's or Rose and Joe's Italian Bakery in Astoria, or even the grandma pie at Maffei at 22nd Street and Sixth Avenue in Manhattan.

Or maybe, just maybe, you want a designer pie. New York has those, too. Try the focaccia stuffed with *robiola* cheese and truffle oil at Thirty One in Queens or Da Ciro in Manhattan, or the pie topped with Manila clams at Otto, or the fontina cheese, pancetta and egg pie at Franny's, or one of Todd English's oddly shaped but addictive pies at Olives. If you've got a hankering for grilled pizza, you can't do much better than Vinnie Scotto's pies at Gonzo. And if you're one of those Roman snobs who wants your pizza by the meter, the aforementioned Thirty One has that as well.

If you want multicultural pizza, go to Flushing, where, as *Los Angeles Times* reporter Geraldine Baum points out on page 117, Tony Sala turns out a mean pie topped with kimchi. If kimchi isn't your ideal pizza topping, perhaps you want to have an Indian-style pie made with curry powder and coriander at Famous Pizza in Jackson Heights.

There's a reason that every other city has pizza restaurants with names like Escape from New York, Big Apple Pizza and Manhattan Slice. They want to offer their customers a slice of the real thing. But it's just a come-on. To enjoy New York pizza in all its forms, you've got to come to New York.

NEW YORK'S PIZZA FAMILIES

Eric Asimov

Eric Asimov, now Wine Columnist for the New York Times, *shows just what a terrific reporter he is in this updated version of a story he wrote for the* Times *in 1998.*

NEW YORK PIZZA IS A PHRASE SYNONYMOUS WITH GREATNESS, YET for years New Yorkers could find the genuine article in only a few isolated spots. But since the mid-1990s, pizza lovers have rejoiced: the true New York pie returned to stay.

I'm not talking about the typical by-the-slice pies congealing in neighborhood display windows as they await reheating, and certainly not about the sodden boxes delivered to the door. I'm talking about classic New York pizza: pies cooked quickly in extremely hot ovens, generally coal-fired, until the thin crust achieves a gloriously charred, smoky crispness. The dough is prepared daily; the mozzarella is real, not packaged; tomatoes are the best quality, and toppings are simple and used in moderation—no pineapple or Thai chicken. The pizzas are cooked to order and almost never sold by the slice.

As recently as 1990, the classic pizza was on the endangered list, treasured as an artifact of old New York but bypassed by a culture that preferred its pizzas fast, cheap and delivered. Just a few pizza landmarks, most famously John's Pizzeria on Bleecker Street, Patsy's Pizza in East Harlem and Totonno's Pizzeria Napolitano in Coney Island—all presided over by rival clans—zealously preserved the traditions. Disciples were required to make pilgrimages to these hallowed halls for a taste.

Today, those three families, plus a latecomer to the game, are almost entirely responsible for the pizza renaissance in New York. The landmarks have been joined by a new set of great names: Grimaldi's under the Brooklyn Bridge;

Lombardi's on Spring Street; Nick's on the Upper East Side and in Forest Hills, Queens, as well as Rockville Centre, on Long Island; and, most recently, Angelo's on West 57th Street and on Second Avenue near 55th Street. The landmarks have themselves branched out. There are now John's, Patsy's and Totonno's in many Manhattan neighborhoods.

What's more, as people have been drawn to the classic pizzerias, they have also gained a new appreciation of top-of-the-line pizzas of many styles. Di Fara in Midwood, Brooklyn, is a by-the-slice place that offers pizzas made with artisanal care. Pizzerias that use wood ovens and follow the classic Neapolitan formula have proliferated. Small chains such as Pintaile's offer excellent though idiosyncratic pizzas, while more renowned restaurateurs such as Mario Batali and Joe Bastianich at Otto offer their own equally idiosyncratic versions.

Why the renaissance? It's driven by the same sense of renewed connoisseurship that gave rise to the boom in microbrewed beers and to the search for the best breads. And as with the ponds of microbrews measured against oceans of Budweiser, it's easy to forget that the number of classic pizzerias amounts to no more than a leaf of fresh basil in a sea of canned tomato sauce. Not much volume but great significance.

At its highest level, pizza-making is a labor-intensive, artisanal craft requiring dedication and training. The coal ovens, more than twice as hot as the gas oven at the corner pizzeria, demand an apprenticeship to master their intricacies. Good pizza makers, or "stick men," are artists, shifting and moving the pies within the oven as they cook, equalizing the effects of hot spots. The ovens are also subject to stringent environmental regulations and to regular inspections.

Ferreting out the freshest mozzarella cheese, building relationships with tomato suppliers and sausage makers, starting dough fresh each day, rather than in advance, being willing to jettison ingredients past their prime—all this takes rare dedication when it's so much easier to buy long-lasting, factory-made mozzarella or to make a week's supply of dough and freeze it.

The determination to make pizza the hard way seems to come from being born and bred into a pizza-making tradition. New York pizza did not exist before

1905, when Gennaro Lombardi, a Neapolitan immigrant, began to sell pies in his grocery store in Little Italy. Lombardi's was by most accounts the first New York pizzeria, and Mr. Lombardi, who hired and trained a series of other immigrants, became the sturdy tap root of a tree of family and acquaintances that would go on to define great New York pizza.

The legendary pizza makers—John Sasso of John's, Patsy Lancieri of Patsy's and Anthony (Totonno) Pero of Totonno's—are all said to have learned their craft at Lombardi's brick-walled coal oven. A century later, their descendants, including Lombardi's grandson, are fueling the expansion. New York's pizza dynasties are now in their third and fourth generations, and counting.

Yet, a lot of the energy has come from new blood, the Angelis-Tsoulos clan, which joined the pizza pantheon just a decade ago. In 1994, Nick Angelis, the son of a Greek pizza maker who learned the art in Naples, opened Nick's Pizza in Forest Hills, Queens. It is dedicated to preserving the tradition of New York's great pie men. Paradoxically, he uses a new kind of gas oven that can achieve the high heat necessary for the best pies. No matter. It's hard to imagine a better crust than Nick's: blackened and barely crisp, glistening and golden, with a faintly smoky flavor. The crust is matched by the other ingredients: pure, creamy mozzarella, delicious roasted peppers, terrific sausage. Since then, Mr. Angelis has opened a second branch in Rockville Centre, Long Island, a third on the Upper East Side and is considering a fourth in the financial district.

Meanwhile, Nick Tsoulos, Nick Angelis's brother-in-law, seeing how well Mr. Angelis was doing, decided to get into the business, too. He made an arrangement with the owners of the East Harlem Patsy's to use that name and in 1995 opened Patsy's Pizza at 509 Third Avenue, near 34th Street. The smooth, blackened crust is light and crisp, and if it lacks that classic smoky flavor, the toppings at least are very good: mellow mozzarella and excellent sauce made of plum tomatoes. The five other Patsy's that have since opened in Manhattan vary somewhat in quality, but the standard is generally high.

In 1998, the clan combined forces and opened Angelo's at 117 West 57th Street, named after Mr. Angelis's father and run by Nick and John Pashalis,

Mr. Angelis's cousins. The pizzas are excellent, very much like the Patsy's pies. A second Angelo's has since opened at 1043 Second Avenue near 55th Street.

Not surprisingly, these new pizzerias have heightened tensions among old-line pizza dynasties, which regard one another with all the sunny warmth of rival boxing promoters. Yet, faced with newcomers, they band together with a universal sneer at Mr. Angelis and Mr. Tsoulos as imitators.

More serious is the battle over the name Patsy's. The original Patsy—Patsy Lancieri—died in the 1970s, and his widow sold the East Harlem pizzeria to longtime employees in 1991, to the chagrin of Patsy Grimaldi, her nephew, who opened a Patsy's in Brooklyn in 1990. He got even angrier when the Tsoulos Patsy's began to open in Manhattan. Finally, in a fit of independence—not, he insists, through any legal coercion—he changed the name of his pizzeria to Grimaldi's. Nor is there any love lost between the East Harlem Patsy's and all the others.

If the mantle of Patsy Lancieri were awarded on quality alone, Grimaldi's, at 19 Old Fulton Street, near Front Street, under the Brooklyn Bridge, would win hands down. The crust, bready and dense, is excellent, and the fragrant tomato sauce, the fresh mozzarella and the home-roasted peppers are spectacular.

Mr. Grimaldi himself, though still an owner, takes a less active role these days. The pizzeria is now run by a company, Patabbe Inc., which opened a Patsy Grimaldi's in Scottsdale, AZ, in 2003, and is planning a Grimaldi's in Garden City, NY, in the fall of 2004. Of Mr. Grimaldi, another partner, Frank Ciolli, said, "He may not be there but he's there."

And after a long down period, the original Patsy's, in a picturesque storefront in a remnant of an Italian neighborhood at 2287-91 First Avenue, near 118th Street, is once again making top-of-the-line pizzas, with perhaps the best crust in the city, impossibly thin, light and crisp.

The other pizzerias, too, have their up and down periods. The original John's, at 278 Bleecker Street, once epitomized New York pizza. Its crust was just crisp enough, with a wonderful smoky flavor, creamy mozzarella and perfectly spiced tomato sauce. There was no excess. Sadly, John's is in decline, living off of

New York's Pizza Family Tree

MOST TRUE NEW YORK PIZZAS, baked in intensely hot ovens, can be traced to Gennaro Lombardi.

Gennaro Lombardi: Opened Lombardi's, perhaps the first pizzeria in the United States, in 1905.

John Sasso: Opened John's Pizzeria in 1929, after being trained by Gennaro Lombardi.

Augustine and Patrick Vesce: Sasso's nephews. Took over John's in 1947.

Pete Castellotti and Bob Vittoria: Sasso's grand-nephews. With Pete's wife, Madeline, took over John's in the mid-1970s.

Pete Jr. and Lisa Castellotti: Sasso's great-grand-nephew and -niece. Share ownership of three John's in Manhattan with the previous generation since the 1980s.

Anthony (Totonno) Pero: Opened Totonno's in Coney Island in 1924, after being trained by Gennaro Lombardi.

Jerry Pero: Anthony's son. Took over Totonno's in the 1940s.

Cookie and Joel Ciminieri: Jerry's niece and her husband. Took over Totonno's in the 1980s, and opened two branches in Manhattan and one in Yonkers.

Lawrence Ciminieri: Cookie and Joel's son. Has managed Totonno's since 1994.

Gennaro Lombardi: Grandson of the original Gennaro. Opened a new Lombardi's in 1994 in Manhattan.

Pasquale (Patsy) Lancieri: Opened the original Patsy's in East Harlem in 1933, after, some say, working with Gennaro Lombardi.

Patsy Grimaldi: Nephew of the original Patsy. Opened his own place, now called Grimaldi's, in Brooklyn, in 1990. Patsy Grimaldi also learned by watching Jerry Pero at Totonno's.

John Brecevich and Frank Brija: Employees of Patsy Lancieri. Bought the original Patsy's in 1991.

Angelo Angelis: Opened Pizza Chef, a successful pizzeria in downtown Brooklyn, in the 1960s.

Nick and John Angelis: Angelo's sons. Operate Nick's Pizza in Forest Hills (1994), Rockville Centre (1997) and the Upper East Side (2003). Nick Angelis also observed Patsy Grimaldi's operation.

Mirene Angelis and Nick Tsoulis: Angelo's daughter and son-in-law. They licensed the Patsy's name from John Brecevich and Frank Brija, and opened six Patsy's Pizzerias in Manhattan in the 1990s.

John and Nick Pashalis: Angelo's nephews. Trained with Nick Angelis, and opened two Angelo's in Manhattan.

tourist dollars and a reputation as old as the eight-by-ten glossies hanging on its walls, rather than off of excellent pizza.

Lombardi's, at 32 Spring Street, was opened in 1994 by old Gennaro Lombardi's grandson and namesake, and diners there revel in tradition. The handsome brick-and-stucco dining room is adorned with old photographs, and though it's inconsistent, when you eat the pizza on a good day, the crust is gloriously light and thin, crisp yet elastic, and you feel you are devouring history. What's more, Lombardi's also serves great clam pizza, a style original to New Haven that is a worthy departure from New York traditions.

Totonno's, the third of the old New York institutions, offers a slightly different style of pizza, whether at its simple bastion in Coney Island or its duded-up Manhattan quarters, at 1544 Second Avenue, near 80th Street, and at 462 Second Avenue near 26th Street. The crust is puffy, bready rather than thin. I'm not the biggest fan of this style, but its partisans love it. Totonno's also opened a Yonkers branch in late 2003, situated incongruously in a Holiday Inn.

Ultimately, in the pizza-making stratosphere, it may be nitpicking to quarrel over whose mozzarella is the freshest or whether the Totonno's pie is better than the thinner Patsy's crust. But it is awfully nice to have so many choices.

THE STATE OF THE SLICE

Ed Levine

I wrote this story for the New York Times *in 2002, before I ever thought about* A Slice of Heaven. *Many friends and colleagues called to congratulate me and to inform me in no uncertain terms that I had missed their pick for best slice.*

WHAT'S THE BEST WAY TO SET NEW YORKERS TO BICKERING? Ask where to find the best slice of pizza in the city. No subject starts a battle faster—not bagels or hot dogs or chopped liver, not even the primacy of the Rangers or the fastest route to JFK. Pizza, introduced to New York in 1905 by Gennaro Lombardi, who saw it as a way to use up the day-old bread in his Spring Street grocery store, has long been the affordable, satisfying food of choice for peripatetic New Yorkers of every age, sex, race and class.

Slices of pizza, that is. Mr. Lombardi's descendants serve only whole pies at their pizza shop, and now no groceries. The Pero family, which established Totonno's pizzeria in Coney Island in 1924, does the same. John Sasso of John's Pizza, which opened on Bleecker Street in 1929, famously put a sign in the window: "No Slices." Indeed, of all the seminal New York pizzerias, only Patsy's on First Avenue near 118th Street in East Harlem sells pizza slices, as it did when it opened in 1933.

But the pizza slice is ubiquitous on New York streets. The metropolitan region has some 2,750 pizzerias, according to the yellow pages. Mario Batali is about to open Otto at 1 Fifth Avenue [it's of course now open], where he will serve thin, crisp pizza inspired by the Sardinian flat bread called *carta da musica*, and he dreams of opening a slice place on Eighth Street with a window that opens onto the street. At the newly opened Ápizz on the Lower East Side, Frank DeCarlo is making pizza in a wood-burning stove and selling it by the foot or the inch, in rectangular slices.

When did pizzerias first start serving slices, and not pies? Patsy's may or may not have been the first. Giovanni Brecevich, the current owner, has a photograph that he says was taken in the 1950s, showing the pizzeria's distinctive white shelved slice box on the sidewalk in front. Louie and Ernie Ottuso served slices at Louie and Ernie's pizzeria in East Harlem as early as 1947; they moved the business to the current site in the Throgs Neck section of the Bronx in 1959. Nunzio Trivoluzzo served slices at his pizzeria in South Beach, Staten Island, when he opened in 1943.

Many experts trace the slice's widespread popularity to the end of World War II, when non-Italian veterans returning from service in Italy began to crave the sliced pizza they had enjoyed there. (In New York before the war, pizza was considered strictly an ethnic food.) But John Brescio, an owner of Lombardi's, also credits the proliferation of mixers from the Hobart Corporation, which introduced its first commercial machine in 1927 and a larger heavy-duty version in 1955. "With the Hobart mixer," Mr. Brescio said, "it was a lot easier to make a lot of pizza."

Another factor that probably spurred the postwar pizza boom was the move away from coal and wood ovens and toward gas-fired pizza ovens made by the likes of Bari, Blodgett and Bakers Pride. Those ovens were much easier to install, and cheaper, and they burned cleaner fuel more efficiently—all important in the high-volume slice business.

Of course, if the origin of the New York slice is a bit murky, the fact that New Yorkers love the things is not in doubt. Slices are cheap, almost always $2 or less. They are convenient, with a pizzeria seemingly on every block. And they are often filling, thanks to the thick blanket of cheese that covers most pizza-by-the-slice sold these days. (Many pizza lovers credit the Ray's Pizza shop at Avenue of the Americas and 11th Street with popularizing the half-pound slice, though Columbia University students often cite the gigantic slices at Koronet, at Broadway and 112th Street, as the original good-value portion, at nearly fifteen inches long.)

But the desire for lots of oozing cheese has obscured many other important characteristics of a fine slice of pizza, some pizza cognoscenti say.

"All that cheese takes pizza from being a bread item to being a vessel for its toppings," says Ed Schoenfeld, a restaurant consultant with offices in Brooklyn. "It's like getting all corned beef and no rye bread."

That's not to mention the quality of the cheese itself. So-called "pizza cheese" has become the norm on slices. But just what is pizza cheese? It's a low-moisture mozzarella, very occasionally blended with provolone. You can say this about it: It melts well.

The best pizzerias in New York wouldn't dream of using an inferior mozzarella. Before pizza was a New York tradition it was a Neapolitan one, says Arthur Schwartz, a host on radio station WOR and the author of *Naples at Table*. In Naples, he says, "they use either buffalo mozzarella that's made from the milk of water buffalo or cow's milk mozzarella on their pizzas."

John Tiso, who now owns Louie and Ernie's in the Bronx with his brother Cosmo, uses a full-cream mozzarella made in Wisconsin by the Grande Cheese Company. "I tried using something else once, and I hated it," he said. "The only mozzarella I'll use is full-cream Grande." The cheese comes in large blocks that Mr. Tiso grinds himself. Other top pizzerias like Nunzio's on Staten Island use full-cream mozzarella made by Polly-O, a cheese company based in New Jersey and owned by Kraft Foods.

But though buffalo mozzarella imported from Italy has been available in New York for some time, it is simply too expensive to be used regularly by any but one pizza-by-the-slice man: Domenico DeMarco, at Di Fara Pizza in Midwood, Brooklyn. Mr. DeMarco uses three parts buffalo mozzarella to one part mozzarella Grande on his majestic pies.

"Of course it's more expensive," says Mr. DeMarco. "But for me it's important to get the flavor you can only get from buffalo milk mozzarella." He also dusts his pizza with freshly grated *grana Padana*, a slightly salty and hard cow's-milk cheese from Italy.

Other top slice purveyors, like both Nunzio's and Joe & Pat's on Staten Island, top their finished pizzas with a touch of pecorino Romano. But Michele Scicolone, an author of *Pizza: Any Way You Slice It*, calls that sacrilege. "Romano cheese has no place on Neapolitan pizza," she says.

Ms. Scicolone has a problem with the fresh cow's milk mozzarella sold by many fancy food stores all over the country. "Fresh mozzarella is softer and very gloppy when it melts," she said. "It can wet the whole pizza down."

Still, one recent trend in the slice business has been the "premium" slice made with fresh mozzarella. Giuseppe Vitale, who runs two Joe's pizzerias in Greenwich Village, serves such a slice. "People want fresh ingredients," he said with a shrug.

Directly beneath the thick padding of pizza cheese on most New York slices can be found a dollop of sauce, too often a canned and ready-made "pizza sauce." "Most of the time it's gummy and oversweetened and lacks the straightforward good taste of good tomatoes, olive oil, garlic, salt and pepper, well cooked," says Mr. Schoenfeld, the consultant. Imported canned Italian tomatoes, preferably San Marzanos, are the proper base for the sauce, he believes.

Nunzio's and Di Fara both use San Marzano tomatoes. Nunzio's adds fresh basil and a sprinkling of black pepper to the sauce.

"That's how my dad made it, and he learned from Nunzio, so that's how we make it," says Concetta Whiteaker, an owner.

Other pie men, like Joe Pasquale of Joe & Pat's, use California tomatoes grown from the seeds of San Marzanos. Mr. Vitale of Joe's has even had some success with canned cooked tomatoes from Spain.

"The fact is," he says, "every case of tomatoes I get has a slightly different flavor." Mr. DeMarco at Di Fara blends fresh tomatoes and canned San Marzano tomatoes in his sauce.

Then there is the crust, that centrally important component of the New York slice, crisp though pliant enough to bend, with a few bubbles in the dough. As Ms. Scicolone put it, "Bubbles mean the dough has been hand-formed and cooked at a high temperature." Remember how John Travolta, as Tony Manero in *Saturday Night Fever,* folded one slice around another in the opening sequence? The scene can be understood primarily as a paean to the perfect pizza-slice crust. (For anyone who might have forgotten, the movie was set in Bay Ridge, Brooklyn.)

The best pizzerias make their dough every day from high-gluten flour, water, yeast and a little salt. They also serve their pizzas plain, although toppings are another hotly contested subdivision of the pizza debate.

"I've only made one Hawaiian pizza in my life," says Mr. Vitale. "One of the regular customers was eight months pregnant and told me she had a craving for Hawaiian pizza. So I bought a can of pineapple and made one for her. But that's the last time."

The final variable in any credible pizza-slice discussion is heat, and particularly the kind of oven used to cook, or reheat, the slice. When pizza was introduced to New York in the early 1900s by Gennaro Lombardi, it was made in a coal-fired brick oven used to bake bread. Places like Lombardi's and John's and Totonno's still make their whole pies in ovens like that. Patsy's in East Harlem is currently the only place that makes slice pie in a coal-fired brick oven. Lawrence Ciminieri of Totonno's has tried to use his own coal-fired brick oven to make and reheat slices, but he says they "stuck to the floor of the oven because the cheese overflowed."

The most common slice ovens are gas-fired models made by Bari, in business in lower Manhattan since 1950 under an immense Italian flag. (Joe's and Nunzio's, however, use ovens from Bakers Pride of New Rochelle.) The stone bottoms of the Bari ovens, which retain and distribute heat evenly despite the constant opening and closing of the oven door, help ensure the crispness of the pizza.

Of course, pizza is no longer the exclusive province of Italians. Kosher pizzerias have cropped up in the Midwood section of Brooklyn and on the Upper West Side of Manhattan. Greeks have opened pizzerias in all five boroughs, making a Greek-style pizza with a highly seasoned sauce that finds echoes in the cornmeal-crusted pizzas served at the Two Boots mini chain. Italians now share the Arthur Avenue neighborhood in the Bronx with Albanians, and while Tony & Tina's, a pizzeria there, serves decent if not great pizza, it has fabulous bureks—multilayer savory pies made with spinach, cheese and ground beef. And for the increasingly South Asian population in Jackson Heights, Queens, two Famous Pizza shops offer pizza with curry powder and jalapeño toppings. By the slice.

Manhattan Pizza: Minichains

PATSY'S AND ANGELO'S | As Eric Asimov points out in his story on New York pizza families (see page 63), both the Patsy's minichain (six locations and counting) and the two Angelo's are owned by relatives of Angelo Angelis, the elder statesman of the family that is playing a crucial role in upholding New York pizza values and tradition. Mr. Angelis should be very proud of what he's wrought at Patsy's and Angelo's. Seven of the eight locations use a coal-fired brick oven (only the Third Avenue and 34th Street location was forced by the city to install a gas oven). The rest of the formula is consistent: fresh mozzarella; superb sweet fennel sausage from the esteemed Frankie Cappezza of the Corona Heights Pork Store; simple sauce of canned and strained tomatoes; and a consistent charred crust that has a properly thin layer of crunch on the top and bottom that gives way to a softer, slightly bready interior.

These eight pizzerias make pizza I'm happy to eat any time, pizza I wholeheartedly recommend to out-of-towners looking for a slice of New York heaven. And if there were a Patsy's or an Angelo's in every town in America, it would speak volumes about the strides we're making as a pizza-loving country. 🍕

> **NOTE:** Because these pizzerias are not owner-occupied, there can be times when the pizza coming out of these ovens is not up to Mr. Angelis's standards. I'm afraid this is an inevitable by-product of multiple locations.

Patsy's:
61 West 74th Street (between Columbus Avenue and Central Park West), New York, NY, 212-579-3000.
1312 Second Avenue (between 69th and 70th Streets), New York, NY, 212-639-1000.
206 East 60th Street (between Second and Third Avenues), New York, NY, 212-688-9707.
509 Third Avenue (between 34th and 35th Streets), New York, NY, 212-689-7500.
318 West 23rd Street (between Seventh and Eighth Avenues), New York, NY, 646-486-7400.
67 University Place (between 10th and 11th Streets), New York, NY, 212-533-3500.
RATING:

Angelo's
117 West 57th Street (between Sixth and Seventh Avenues), New York, NY, 212-333-4333.
1043 Second Avenue (between 54th and 55th Streets), New York, NY, 212-521-3600.
RATING:

PIZZA AND ORGANIZED CRIME

PIZZA AND ORGANIZED CRIME share a long and storied history. In the 1930s Al Capone decided he wanted his piece of the burgeoning pizza-industry pie. He forced neighborhood pizza parlors to purchase only his mozzarella cheese, which was made in a mob-controlled plant in Fond du Lac, Wisconsin.

More than fifty years later Rudy Giuliani made a name for himself as a federal prosecutor with the famed Pizza-Connection case. Giuliani prosecuted organized-crime figure Salvatore Catalano and twenty-two other defendants of Sicilian descent, who from 1979 through 1984 imported 1.6 billion dollars worth of heroin into the United States and then laundered the proceeds through pizza parlors throughout the country. In the course of an eighteen-month trial one defendant died, and another was murdered. After six days of deliberation all but one of the defendants were convicted. Who was Giuliani's star witness? None other than Joe Pistone, otherwise known as Donnie Brasco.

In July 2004 the *New York Daily News* reported that the mob-linked CasaBlanca Restaurant and Pizzeria in Queens went on the market after a drop-off in business due to the prosecution of alleged Bonanno-family boss Joseph Massino. "Owner Alfred Altadonna, a reputed Bonanno soldier who worked sixteen-hour days making pizzas at the Maspeth eatery, has decided to pack it in because of poor health and declining business due to Massino's racketeering trial, which played out for several weeks in federal court. All [Altadonna] wanted to do was run a restaurant," his lawyer Arthur Goldstein lamented.

Mr. Giuliani found himself in the midst of mob-related pizzeria controversy in 2004 when he recommended the restaurant Da Nico to Republican delegates visiting New York for the Republican convention. According to the *New York Times*, "When word surfaced that a list of top-10 New York restaurants included Da Nico, a reputed Mafia hangout, it threatened to embarrass organizers of the convention. But as it turned out, convention officials had already taken the kind of decisive action that would have made Don Corleone proud: they made the list disappear."

Manhattan Pizza: Uptown

(North of 42nd Street)

⊞ ANGELO'S | See page 74.

⊞ BRIO FORNO | Brio Forno is one of those generically sleek restaurants on New York's tony Upper East Side that I would have never walked into without a nudge from Simon Dean, one of the managing partners of the terrific Italian fish restaurant Esca. (Full disclosure: I am writing a book with Esca partner/chef Dave Pasternack.) He said, "Ed, I just wandered into Brio Forno with a friend, and we had a terrific pizza and an even better calzone." He didn't tell me about the stunning photos of gorgeous women that greet you from the wall as you walk in the door. Stunning photos of gorgeous women enhance the pizza-eating experience every time.

The other thing you notice at Brio Forno is the colorful, geometrically shaped pizza oven tucked into the corner. The pile of hardwood stored right beneath the oven indicates that Brio's oven is the real, wood-burning deal. I sat down at the counter right in front of the oven because I wanted to observe the pizzaiolo in action. I ordered a Margherita and a calzone and watched Andreas Rinaldi, who learned to make pizza in his native Buenos Aires (see Robb Walsh's piece on Buenos Aires pizza on page 300), do his thing. He stretched the dough for the Margherita first, and carefully put some *fior di latte* imported from Naples on top of the finest-quality imported La Valle tomatoes. He used the same dough for the calzone, which he filled with the *fior di latte*, ricotta, *prosciutto cotto* (roast ham) and champignon mushrooms. A few minutes later Rinaldi slid them out of the oven and onto plates. The pizza was very fine, with a crisp, chewy, slightly blackened crust. The sauce was clean tasting; the mozzarella just creamy enough. It would have been a perfect pizza if the outer rim had just puffed up a little more. The calzone was almost too hefty to eat, but was tasty and substantial.

I asked Brio chef Massimo Carbone about his pizza: "There are no secrets to making good Neapolitan pizza. We use Caputo double-zero flour from Italy. It costs twice as much as American flour, but you really need it to make this style of pizza. The La Valle tomatoes are the best tomatoes to use for pizza. Even Mario Batali (see page 288) uses them. The *fior di latte* comes from Italy in two-kilo bricks. It's right for the pizza, but we use *mozzarella di bufala* for the Caprese salad. The oven comes from Italy. We use hickory and oak. The pizzas cook for only three minutes because they are baking at seven hundred degrees. Our customers are half neighborhood people, and half Italians visiting or staying in the city for a while. They appreciate what we do. We make them happy. There is one thing I won't do for anyone, however. We won't put pineapple on our pizza."

Brio Forno
135 East 61st Street (between Lexington and Park Avenues), New York, NY, 212-980-2300.
RATING: ⊗ ⊗ ⊗

CELESTE | At his friend Maurizio DeRosa's urging, Celeste chef Giancarlo Quadalti set out to make authentic Neapolitan pizza in the gorgeous wood-burning oven installed in the corner of his restaurant. A year later, DeRosa concluded that New Yorkers didn't want the real thing. "It was too wet for people. People would take napkins and blot the pizza to absorb the moisture. We were devastated. We would look and suffer in silence."

But after an appropriate mourning period, Quadalti made the necessary adjustments. Now Quadalti drains the tomatoes just the way many American pizzaioli do. As a result, Celeste's pizza is probably not authentically Neapolitan, but it is quite delicious and Italian in conception. That means they use double-zero Italian flour, imported canned tomatoes (drained) and excellent cow's-milk mozzarella, imported from Maspeth, Queens. The crust is a little crisper than any I found in Naples, but trust me, Giancarlo, that's the way we like it. I usually have either the Margherita or a marinara (made with tomato sauce and anchovies here), but sometimes I get crazy and order the one with prosciutto and arugula. It doesn't matter what pizza you eat at Celeste. They're all delicious. After devouring your pie, it is imperative that you have gelato for dessert at Celeste. They're all made by the mad-genius gelato maker, Gino Cammarata, from the tragically shuttered restaurant Bussola. If you're with a group, have the "porcini mushroom" ice cream, made with hazelnut ice cream and chocolate sauce in the shape of, yes, a porcini mushroom.

Celeste
502 Amsterdam Avenue (between 84th and 85th Streets), New York, NY, 212-874-4559.
RATING:

🍴 JOHN'S PIZZERIA | See page 84.

🍴 MIMI'S PIZZERIA | My friend Bob first put me on to Mimi's, but he's so finicky about his pizza slices that he claimed it should be included in the book only if I mentioned that Mimi's quality depends on who's making the pizza. I think that's a bit much (but I love him for saying it), so I'll just report that Mimi's makes a mean slice of pizza, with a chewy crust and too much cheese. Some people think they go a little light on the sauce, but I for one don't really miss it. Neither, apparently, does Paul McCartney. According to Mimi's lore, a few years ago McCartney himself called up and asked that ten Mimi's pies be delivered to Newark Airport for him and his entourage to enjoy.

Mimi's Pizzeria
1248 Lexington Avenue (between 84th and 85th Streets), New York, NY, 212-861-3363.
RATING:

🍴 NAPLES 45 | See page 332.

🍴 NICK'S PIZZA | See page 348.

PATSY'S | See page 74.

PATSY'S PIZZERIA AND RESTAURANT | Patsy's is the only pizzeria left in a century-old Italian neighborhood that once was a hotbed of pizza activity. The adjoining restaurant has tablecloths and a full Italian menu. The slice space has a gorgeous oven, a simple white box that holds the slices, a soda machine and one chair that is nearly always empty. The slices are small, with just enough cheese and the great smoky crust that comes only from a coal-fired brick oven. The pizza at the full-service Patsy's restaurant next door has been inconsistent in recent years. My last pie was pretty good, though it was made with aged mozzarella. There was a disquieting sign in the window at the time: "Pie Man Wanted." Eric Asimov was at Patsy's more recently than I, and, based on what he wrote (see page 63), they must have found their man (or woman).

Patsy's Pizzeria and Restaurant
2287-91 First Avenue (between 117th and 118th Streets), New York, NY, 212-534-9783.
RATING: 🍕🍕🍕🍕 (slice joint)   🍊🍊🍊🍊 (full-service pizzeria restaurant)

SAL AND CARMINE'S | I've begged and I've begged, but to no avail. I told Sal and Carmine my wife had a broken leg. They wouldn't budge. They wouldn't deliver. I've had the following imaginary conversation with Sal and Carmine many times. "But Sal," I plead, "you make one of the best slices in Manhattan. I mean, it's not even close. I love your charred crust, your sauce, your full-cream mozzarella. Do you know how many of your slices I've eaten in the past twenty-four years?" I do a quick calculation. "Fifteen hundred. I've eaten fifteen hundred of your slices and if you used fresh mushrooms instead of canned, that number would have easily doubled." No dice on the fresh mushrooms and no dice on the deliveries.

Sal and Carmine's
2671 Broadway (between 101st and 102nd Streets), New York, NY, 212-663-7651.
RATING: 🍕🍕🍕

SULLIVAN STREET BAKERY | See page 108.

T & R PIZZA | A former boss of mine, Art Weiner, couldn't believe I didn't know about T & R. "It's just a real solid New York pizza place, and it's a few blocks from your house. Now that you're Mr. Food, you've gotta try a slice there." Art was right. At T & R, the slices have crisp, pliant crusts even after reheating, and the sauce-to-cheese ratio is just about perfect. They even make a creditable white pie at T & R, topped with fresh garlic and ricotta. I don't know that T & R is worth a trip from other neighborhoods, but fans of Vinnie's on the Upper West Side looking for a lighter slice should check it out.

    WARNING: A post-8:00 P.M. foray can be problematic, because the owner goes home and the nighttime pizza guys inevitably undercook the pie.

T & R Pizza
411 Amsterdam Avenue (between 79th and 80th Streets), New York, NY, 212-787-4093.
RATING: 🍕 🍕 🍕 (for the daytime pizza)

TOTONNO'S | See page 353.

Manhattan Pizza: Downtown

(South of 42nd Street)

DA CIRO | See page 124.

FAMOUS BEN'S PIZZA | Daniel Young, who writes about pizza in the south of France on page 304, is one of my pizza compadres. When he wrote for the *New York Daily News* he was the best pizza writer and reporter in the country. He has perfect pizza pitch. So when he told me about a couple of the specialty slices at Ben's, I had to go, even though it had already been a six-slice day. Per Danny's instructions I ordered two slices of what Ben's calls a Palermo Pizza. It looked ugly and unattractive, but it tasted great, with seasoned breadcrumbs and a sweet onion sauce atop Sicilian dough. I also ordered the No-Cheese Square, a deliciously oily Sicilian slice made with a heavily herbed sauce and no cheese. I could have done without all the dried oregano, but it was pretty fine anyway. One other slice, a square slice with fresh mozzarella, caught my eye, and though I was red-zoning it at ten slices in one day, I ordered one anyway. The fresh mozzarella barely covered half of the slice, and presented a lovely creamy contrast to the sweet sauce and crunchy crust. Danny Young, you're the man.

Famous Ben's Pizza
177 Spring Street (at the corner of Thompson Street), New York, NY, 212-966-4494.
RATING: 🍕 🍕 🍕

GONZO | Vinnie Scotto grew up in Brooklyn, and spent his formative pizza-eating years eating excellent slices at Vesuvio, L & B Spumoni Gardens and Krispy Pizza. He then learned how to make grilled pizza at its source, with

George Germon at Al Forno in Providence, Rhode Island. So it's no surprise that Scotto's own spin on grilled pizza at his New York restaurant, Gonzo, combines the best of two pizza worlds. His pizza is so fine that I don't feel compelled to travel to Providence as often as I once did. Scotto's grilled pizza is cracker thin and less oily than Germon's, and it's just as addictively light and delicious as the ones at Al Forno. His sparse toppings are full of vivid, intense flavors and are perfect foils to the crunchy crust. Vinnie told me he has one hundred different pizzas on his computer at the restaurant, and though I haven't tasted them all, I haven't had a bad one yet. His Margherita is unconventional, topped with fresh tomatoes, Bel Paese and Romano (Scotto doesn't use mozzarella on any of his pizzas, but uses mozzarella and tomato salad as a topping in the summer). I'm crazy about his spicy cauliflower, topped with caramelized onions, Bel Paese, Romano and ricotta cheese, and about the Siciliano, brushed with a Sicilian tomato sauce, topped with eggplant caponata and cumin-scented ricotta along with the Bel Paese and Romano. Even the bizarre-sounding, carb-lethal mashed-potato-and-corn pizza, which Scotto serves in the summer when he can get fresh sweet corn, is absolutely delicious.

Gonzo
140 West 13th Street (between Sixth and Seventh Avenues), New York, NY, 212-645-4606.
RATING:

JOE'S PIZZA | Giuseppe Vitale, who owns Joe's with his father-in-law, Pino Pozzuoli, mastered the art of doughmaking at the G&G Bakery in Brooklyn. He is a slice purist; no heroes or pasta are served in his restaurants. Mr. Vitale says his motto is "pride, knowledge and ingredients." It's worth it to have both a regular slice and a fresh mozzarella slice here, just to taste the difference. They both have superbly crisp crusts.

Joe's Pizza
7 Carmine Street (at Avenue of the Americas), New York, NY, 212-255-3946.
RATING:

🍴 JOHN'S PIZZERIA | Eric Asimov correctly and sadly reported the decline in quality at the original John's location in Greenwich Village. They use canned pizza sauce and commercial aged mozzarella when they could walk down the street to the terrific Faicco Pork Store and buy fresh mozzarella and good Italian canned tomatoes (they do in fact use Faicco's sausage). That said, the pizza is still better than you can find at 95 percent of the pizzerias in this country.

There is also a John's Pizzeria in the theater district that's located in an old church. I like the idea of a church of pizza. It's huge, seating perhaps two hundred people, and they have three coal-fired brick ovens to meet demand. The pizza in the church is incredibly inconsistent. I've had terrific pies with a fine charred crust, and lousy pizza with uncooked dough.

The most consistent of the three John's locations is at East 64th Street. It's not easy to find (it's on a side street), but the last two pies I've had there have been fine New York pizza specimens: puffy and chewy crust, fresh mozzarella and a simple sauce of decent canned tomatoes that have been strained.

John's Pizzeria

278 Bleecker Street (between 6th and 7th Avenues), New York, NY, 212-243-1680.
RATING: 🍊 🍊 🍊

260 West 44th Street (between Broadway and 8th Avenue), New York, NY, 212-391-7560.
RATING: 🍊 🍊 🍊

408 East 64th Street (between York and 1st Avenues), New York, NY, 212-935-2895.
RATING: 🍊 🍊 🍊

🍴 LA PIZZA FRESCA | See page 331.

🍴 LOMBARDI'S | Lombardi's is the pizza mothership in this country, as Evelyne Slomon points out in her superb and succinct pizza history of the world, her sadly out-of-print *Pizza Book*. It was at the original Lombardi's, across the street from its current location, that Neapolitan immigrant Gennaro Lombardi

first began selling pizza in his grocery store in 1905. These cheese pies, made by Lombardi and a friend, Anthony Pero (who would later open Totonno's), were wrapped in paper and tied with a string, and sold to Italian laborers who would take them to work. Pero left in 1924 to open Totonno's in Coney Island, but Lombardi's remained open, selling pizza and more elaborate Italian food until 1984. Ten years later, John Brescio (also known as Hollywood John, according to a photo hanging in the current Lombardi's), teamed with Gennaro's grandson Gerry and reopened Lombardi's in 1994, with the aid of a young New York pizzaiolo named Andrew Bellucci. Andrew turned out to be a fugitive from justice, but I'll let Eric Asimov tell that story on page 98.

Bellucci was a first-rate pizzaiolo. His pies, baked in a coal-fired brick oven used for bread that Brescio and company had come upon when they were looking for space for the new Lombardi's, were absolutely sensational. The coal imparted the desirable charred flavor that can't be gotten any other way. The crust was puffy and chewy, the mozzarella creamy and fresh, and the sauce was a minimalist's delight. Being a serious pizzaologist, Bellucci also took a page out of Frank Pepe's book and made New York's first clam pie. It wasn't Frank Pepe's, but it was pretty darn fine. Critics declared it pizza heaven, and even though Bellucci ended up in the hoosegow, Lombardi's was a shoo-in for Comeback Pizzeria of the Year award. Then came the inevitable backlash: whispers of parbaked crusts during peak periods, soggy and underbaked pies and substandard mozzarella. Internet food sites such as Chowhound were rife with critical comments about Lombardi's.

I've eaten at least a hundred pizzas at Lombardi's over the last ten years. I've had less than exemplary pies on occasion, soggy crusts and all, and yet I can say that on a good day, Lombardi's pizza is as good as you'll find anywhere. I say that as someone who had a small pie there recently that had virtually no puff, no lip, and was all sog, and as someone who realizes that Lombardi's makes its clam pies with way too many rubbery topneck clams.

So here's my recipe for getting the most out of Lombardi's. When you order your pies make them large, even if you're by yourself (you won't regret it in the morning). The small pies do not bake as well. Specify that you want your crust chewy and puffy. If you order a clam pie, ask them to go very light on the clams. And if your pizza does come with a flat, soggy crust, send it back. Think of it as a steak that's been overcooked. If you follow these simple instructions, you will get your slice(s) of heaven at the oldest pizzeria in America.

Lombardi's

32 Spring Street (between Mott and Mulberry Streets), New York, NY, 212-941-7994, www.lombardispizza.com.

RATING: ⊛ ⊛ ⊛ ⊛ (on a good day)
⊛ ⊛ ◖ (when they're making too many pies)

TEL CANAL 6-9866

RAVIOLI A SPECIALTY

Home Cooking

Lombardi's

Restaurant

Pizzeria

OPEN FROM 9 A. M. TO 5 A. M.

53 SPRING STREET
NEW YORK CITY

LOMBARDI'S: A PIECE OF PIZZA HISTORY... THE LEGEND ENDURES

Evelyne Slomon

Evelyne Slomon is chef/co-owner of Nizza La Bella in Albany, California. She also wrote the seminal Pizza Book. *The following piece was originally published in the magazine* Pizza Today, *where she is a contributing editor. She is currently at work on a new pizza book.*

MAKING THE GREAT COMEBACK IS AN EVENT USUALLY ASSOCIATED with the likes of legendary sports figures, entertainers and movie stars. But in this case, pizza is the game, and the legend is Lombardi's. In the present-day pizza universe, which has grown so large and diverse, the name Lombardi's may not ring a bell to most. But to the rarefied pizza intelligentsia and—most of all—to the cognoscenti of traditional New York–style pizza, Lombardi's pizza was just one of those local treasures that—like the old Brooklyn Dodgers—was gone but not forgotten. Alas, the Dodgers may never return to Brooklyn, but I'm happy to report that Lombardi's is back! This isn't just any old pizzeria re-opening its doors—this is Lombardi's, the first pizzeria in the United States. And the Lombardi story is quite a tale indeed. Recently, Gennaro (Gerry) Lombardi, grandson of the original, sat down and spun the yarn for me once more about how the pizza biz got started in New York City. It's a wonderful piece of pizza history, so here goes.

Gennaro Lombardi came to the United States from Naples when he was 14 years old. A baker by trade, he came to the New World for more opportunity and that is exactly what he found. At first he worked nights as a baker in Brooklyn and days in the grocery store below his flat, in return for room and board from the store owner. Despite his tender age, Lombardi was already quite a dynamic and enterprising young man. Observing how difficult it was to make any money in the grocery trade, Lombardi thought he might help increase revenues by baking off some pizzas and some extra loaves of bread at night at the bakery to sell the next day at the grocery store. The grocery stores of Little Italy were a far cry from the modern food factories that we are now accustomed to. In those days, most of the *business* was conducted on credit or through barter; very little money ever passed hands. For example, prized staples like imported canned tomatoes, olive oil and macaroni were sold in tiny quantities. A can of tomatoes would be opened and sold by the individ-

·LOMBARDI'S *in* 1905·

ual tomato, dried pasta was sold by the handful, and olive oil was vended by the tea cup. These imported products were luxuries to the poor Italian immigrants who were eking it out in the city. Lombardi saw the possibility of expanding upon the available market by selling pieces of pizza along with loaves of bread to the many factory workers who worked in the nearby Soho section of New York City.

The first pizzas Lombardi pre-baked at the bakery in Brooklyn were the thin Neapolitan kind. He would carefully wrap them in paper and cardboard and stack them up before tying them into a neat bundle. The next morning, they were displayed in a wooden showcase on the counter. There was no oven to reheat them, but there was an old pot belly stove that served as an adequate warming device. The pies were sold by the piece and not by the slice. The price depended on the pocketbook; 2 or 3 cents was a reasonable price for a factory worker, while a penny might be all a local could afford. Portion size was based on how much and to whom it was being sold. Gerry says that times were so tough, "According to some of the old timers, the poorest of the poor used to sneak in to eat the discarded pieces of crust."

Lombardi's little venture proved to be successful. With the local factory workers now buying pieces for lunch and the neighborhood families lined up out the door on meatless Fridays, the addition of pizza to the grocery store did indeed boost sales. Lombardi's next break came when the aging store owner made him the offer to take over the business and purchase the building it was housed in. This was an offer that young Lombardi could not refuse. At the ripe age of 17, Lombardi became a landowner and entrepreneur. He struggled with the grocery business for a few more years, and carefully assessed that the bread and bakery market had become very tight with lots of competition from existing and incoming bakeries and from mobile bread carts hawking loaves throughout the streets. For Lombardi the choice was simple—his craft may have been bread baking but his second nature was pizza. His new venture, taking its inspiration from the pizzerias of his native Naples, would be a legitimate enterprise. Lombardi acquired his official business license to open and operate the first pizzeria in New York City at 53½ Spring Street in 1905.

The first pizzeria was a no-frills kind of place. Lombardi had a big baker's-style coal oven built into the store, he added a few tables and chairs, and continued to sell the imported staples of tomatoes, olive oil and macaroni—all of which he also used in the pizzeria. The menu was simple, with only one kind of pizza—tomato and mozzarella. In those days there were no such toppings as pepperoni, mushrooms, peppers and the like. Pizza was pure and simple: imported San Marzano tomatoes, handmade local mozzarella and a superb baker's crust. Rustic peasant home-style pastas like spaghetti with garlic and oil, or with marinara sauce, or pasta *e fagiole* (with beans), or *con ceci* (with chickpeas) rounded out the menu. On special occasions, Lombardi's offered a huge calzone, resembling a charred puffed pillow stuffed with soft creamy ricotta and large enough to feed an entire family. Wine was provided from the barrels of friends' and family's local basement wineries. The pizzeria was nearly a twenty-four hour operation, with business hours from 7:00 A.M. until 4:00 A.M. daily.

Lombardi's became much more than just a pizzeria to the neighborhood, it somehow rose above that mere distinction and became the great equalizer of the Little Italy community. Like its Neapolitan predecessors, Lombardi's was first and foremost a simple place of the people. Here, all social stratums were leveled and people of all kinds frequented the pizzeria. At night, the party goers, high rollers, and personalities like the famous opera star Enrico Caruso would frequent the place. During the day, housewives, children, neighbors and street urchins would drift in and out or sit out front, to keep up on the local gossip and news. Lombardi's was *the* Italian social hangout. Lombardi became a successful man, and with that success came responsibilities. Known as Don Gennaro, he became a very powerful member of the community and was especially active in caring for those in need.

Lombardi's served as the first stop in the New World for many young men immigrating from Naples. In return for sponsorship, and room and board (upstairs from the store), these men worked in the pizzeria. Lombardi taught them the trade and they generally stayed 2 to 3 years with him before going off and starting their own pizzerias. Some of his most famous followers included Anthony Pero of Totonno's in Brooklyn, and John Sasso of John's on Bleecker Street in Manhattan. "Most of them," according to Gerry, "after they left my grandfather's, went off on their own all over the rest of the country." Could it be that Lombardi's actually helped seed the first generation of pizza makers in America?

What was pizza-making like in those days? The pizzaiolo was considered a rare breed—an individual of almost heroic stature who considered the craft of pizza-making a calling. Signore Lombardi best summed it up in a quote from a 1956 *New York Times* article, when he fondly patted his old coal oven and said, "This is what made me a man today." In the beginning—certainly for the first 40 or so years, there was no mechanization involved in the production of pizza. There were no dough mixers, no grinders, no refrigeration, and the old coal ovens demanded lots of attention. The daily pizza-making was not for the meek or weak, it was a physically demanding operation. The day would begin early in the morning when the dough would be mixed by hand and kneaded on a giant table by four or five men with arms so muscled that they could barely bend them. After fermentation, the dough was shaped and stored in wooden boxes, ready to be turned into pizza. The ovens had to be cleaned and stoked by shoveling a pile of coal into the chamber. If a local source of mozzarella cheese was not available, the pizzaiolo would frequently have to go through the chore of working fresh curd in 180-degree water, to make the cheese that would end up on the pizza. There was no mixer to knead the dough, no distributor to call for shredded mozzarella cheese, no flick of the switch for the oven to heat up, and no refrigeration to hold the ingredients.

Gennaro Lombardi created the original authentic New York–style pizza. While New York–style pizzas have proliferated from coast to coast, this version is still practiced by only a few honest devotees of the true style—just as it was made nearly a century ago. The procedure is simple and is still adhered to by grandson Gerry in the current reincarnation of the famed pizzeria. The dough must be soft as a baby's bottom and smooth as silk. This type of dough is far too delicate to be tossed; it should be stretched over the fists until it is just the right thickness—which is really, really thin. Then the cheese goes down on the crust (Apparently this order was a bone of contention between father and son. Lombardi senior always put the cheese down first, while junior insisted on putting the sauce down first; grandson Gerry uses either method depending on his fancy.) The cheese, sliced at ¼ inch thick, is never shredded and it must be fresh mozzarella—not the low-moisture brick type favored by today's modern pizza makers. The sauce, which must be made of San Marzano or similar-quality tomatoes that are naturally sweet, utilizes whole tomatoes that are crushed by hand, resulting in a light semi-chunky tomato sauce. Ladles are not used to apply sauce on these pies. Instead, a large flat spoon is employed to puddle the sauce in spots on the pizza and then to spread it around. Seasonings consist of dried oregano, fresh basil (when available) and fresh garlic—thinly sliced or chopped. (Garlic was called *essence* by the old timers—it still reads that way on Lombardi's menu.) Grated Romano cheese, dusted over all is another essential element of this classic style. With a generous drizzle of pure Italian olive oil, the pie is ready to bake. The secret of a coal oven is the dry, dry bake the pie gets, which makes the crust incredibly light and delicately crunchy. The coal lends a nice smoky finish to the overall flavors. Coal-oven pizza is characterized with a slightly charred crust—if there isn't enough char on the crust, it is considered underdone to the connoisseur of authentic New York–style pie. The crust has a light and puffy collar (outer rim) that is no larger than 1½–2 inches wide, while the crust at the center of the pie must be no thicker than ¼ of an inch. The cheese and sauce fuse together into a molten mass and the pie is ready to be eaten as soon as your mouth can stand it.

This New York classic is sold only by the whole pie. The pie's uneven, handmade characteristics and distinct character do not lend themselves to the slice trade. (Even today, slice operations still offer *traditional* or *classic* New York–style pizza by the whole pie only.) That's it—nothing more or nothing less. Toppings such as sausage didn't come along until the 1950s, when other toppings like meatball, pepperoni, mushroom, peppers and onions also became popular.

The golden years of Lombardi's continued until after World War II, then things changed, and the pizzeria began to ebb. There are many socio and economic reasons for the decline of the pizzeria prototypes. The typical traditional pizzeria was an Italian social club that functioned in closely knit urban Italian neighborhoods. After WWII, there was a great exodus from the old neighborhoods out to the suburbs. Different ethnic groups moved into the old neighborhoods, and the cultural as well as economic balance shifted. In New York, for example, Chinatown began spilling over into Little Italy. The factories of Soho shut down and moved to New Jersey and other surrounding industrial areas, leaving many of the loft buildings standing empty, while others were torn down. Pizza was becoming popular beyond its Italian ethnic roots, and a new market was evolving.

The fast pace of New York City life called for a new breed of pizza to be born. Pizza entrepreneurs took on the challenge—just as Lombardi had done years before when he sold pieces of pizza to local factory workers. In the old-time

traditional pizzeria, pizza was sold only by the whole pie. It took time to make the pie . . . and time to sit down and eat. Whole-pie pizza just couldn't compete with the more modern fast-paced lunch items like sandwiches. Not until some pizza entrepreneurs came up with the idea of making perfectly round large slice pies and selling them by the slice at lunch. How did they draw the customers? Simple. They put on a show. The gimmick was to place a pizzaiolo in the window to artfully toss pies for the lunchtime audiences. That bit of showmanship drew crowds and sold lots of slices. Thus, another New York tradition was born.

A whole industry grew up around the pizza business: distributors, equipment and products. The coal-oven monsters were quickly replaced with convenient gas-deck ovens. The business was no longer a tradition passed down from father to son, and fell out of the hands of families. Other ethnic groups took over old pizzerias and things really began to change. By the late 1960s and early 1970s there were only a handful of the old-style traditional coal-oven pizzerias left. It seemed that modern times had passed by these old dinosaurs of pizza. Few Italian families now residing in the suburbs made it back to the old neighborhood on a regular basis to patronize the traditional pizza parlors. With the proliferation of thousands of mediocre pizza places all over the city, and the profusion of the chains like Pizza Hut and Domino's on the national scene, the old pizzerias seemed nearly faded, forgotten and certainly under-appreciated. Sadly, Lombardi's became a victim of the times and the pizzeria closed its doors in the early part of the 1970s.

Grandson Gerry Lombardi re-opened Lombardi's a few years later in the mid-1970s. In this reincarnation, the old coal oven, which had begun to collapse from the vibrations of the ancient subway line running beneath, was covered over. Gerry set about to create a very urbane and formal Italian restaurant. It was during this time that I met Gerry, and he began to unfold his family's story through interviews. It seemed such a shame to me that all that great tradition would wind up lost forever. When I asked Gerry why wouldn't he consider opening a pizzeria again, he replied, "People don't know what that kind of pizza is anymore. They only know junk. They think pizza is junk food." Even though I didn't agree with him—and told him so—I had to admit, despite my predictions to the contrary, that the current state of pizza in the late 1970s made me acutely aware of exactly where he was coming from in his thinking. Lombardi's stayed open for almost a decade, until health problems and the general toll of restaurant-related stress caused Gerry to close the restaurant for good in the mid-1980s.

But the ghost of Lombardi's would not leave him in peace. The name and the legend continued to endure, continued to be mentioned, written about in books, newspapers and magazines and spoken about in radio interviews. And the question remained—why not reopen? According to Gerry, "Enough was enough already." But he eventually gave in and decided, "What the heck, let's do it again!"

Because the old oven had collapsed in the original site of the first pizzeria at 53½ Spring Street, Gerry decided to find another location in an old bakery (32 Spring) just a few doors down the block. Their coal oven was of a similar vintage as the Lombardi's oven, but still in good working condition. The bakery site was small, with little refrigeration and kitchen space, but the distinct flavor of Old Little Italy permeated the place; it was just right for the re-incarnation of Lombardi's Pizzeria. Gerry, along with his wife Josephine and his other partner, Joan Volpe, breathed some life into this little old store.

They carefully removed the old tiles from the crumbling face of the old Lombardi oven and restored them to the face of the current oven. The decor of the store is simple, using the charm of the old building, the storefront window is stacked with colorful cans of tomatoes and olive oil like in the original place and classic old-style pizzeria booths line one side of the tiny dining room. The walls are sandblasted natural brick, and there is a mural on the wall that is more reminiscent of a Botticelli than of the ubiquitous Mount Vesuvius that adorns most pizzerias. Admittedly, stepping into this store is a bit like entering the pizza twilight zone. The walls are lined with old photos of the original Lombardi's and of the cast of characters that made up that universe. A combination of Placido Domingo and Frank Sinatra puts you into the mood, and, of course, the aroma of pizza seductively wafts through the air. Just like the original Lombardi's, this is a no-frills kind of place with plain wooden tables, no tablecloths, no fancy china, water glasses for wine and old-fashioned metal cake stands that act as pedestals for when the pie is brought to the table.

Although the oven is not visible from the main dining area, anyone can walk back to where the action is. Looking at the setup here it's hard to imagine that this pizzeria was only opened in December of 1994. It seems more like 1894! In a cramped area the head pizzaiolo, Andrew Bellucci, originally from Two Boots Pizzeria in New York, whips out the pies. Andrew, who manages the back of the house, worked hard on recreating that old Lombardi magic along with grandson Gerry Lombardi. To his credit, Andrew may have been the final straw to break the camel's back in convincing Gerry to finally get back into the pizza business.

The menu features the justifiably famous pizza, with a few appetizer specials such as fresh *mozzarella di bufala*, beefsteak tomatoes, coal-oven-roasted red peppers and a dish of baked clams with mozzarella and pancetta. The generous house salad is a crisp mélange of mesclun greens, wild mushrooms, fresh tomatoes and red onion. The pies come in two sizes: a small 14-inch with 6 slices and a large 18-inch with 8 slices. There are two special pies that are most definitely not traditionally Lombardiesque. They are Gennaro's (grandson Gennaro's) Fresh Clam Pie, which consists of fresh top-neck clams, garlic, oregano, parsley, pecorino Romano, black pepper and extra-virgin olive oil. There is also an amazing Pizza Bianca that consists of a rich mixture of mozzarella, ricotta impastata, pecorino Romano, garlic, black pepper, extra-virgin olive oil and fresh basil. As for the rest of the toppings? They are all pretty classy and with pedigrees to boot. The house-made meatballs are the old-fashioned kind; the sausage is Esposito's; the pepperoni is Hormel's; the pancetta is Citteria's; the red peppers are roasted in the coal oven; the mushrooms are a mixture of cremini, shiitake and oyster; the onions are red; the fresh tomatoes are beefsteaks; the sauce tomatoes are San Marzano; the olives are kalamatas; the ricotta is locally made impastata; the mozzarella is fresh from Brooklyn; and the anchovies, well the anchovies are—imported anchovies packed in olive oil! Fresh garlic and fresh basil round out the pizza-topping palette. The calzone is a work of art—crisp and charred on the outside and oozing with creamy ricotta and mozzarella on the inside. What you won't find at Lombardi's is the super trendy. You won't find any Thai-chicken or Mexican-style toppings here. Lombardi's makes pizza the old fashioned way—with the right stuff.

The service is friendly and efficient; Gerry Lombardi still knows how to run a classy restaurant, even if it is only a humble pizzeria. The prices range from $10.50 for a small to $12.50 for a large pie. Add $3.00 for 1 additional topping; $5.00 buys 2; $6.00 buys 3; and so on . . . $20.00 buys a bit of everything! (Topping prices are the same for both size pies.) You can select from 15 different beers to drink with your pie—a wine license is pending—or you can finish it all off with an espresso or cappuccino. The house doesn't accept credit cards. Lombardi's operates 7 days a week opening daily at 11:30 A.M. to 11:00 P.M. Monday through Thursday, to 12:00 P.M. Friday and Saturday, and until 10:00 P.M. on Sundays. Ever since Lombardi's opened its doors, they've been a resounding success. New York has welcomed them back with open arms. Newspapers, magazines and television reporters have been descending upon the humble little store in droves. I guess you could say that the re-opening of Lombardi's has been noticed. As for the customers; they love it. The place does as much business as it can handle. Gerry is opening up another dining room next door that will double the current seating capacity.

Gerry Lombardi is a congenial, soft-spoken man who just happens to have pizza running through his veins. He is so natural about the whole thing, so unpretentious—it just flows from his fingertips. Everyone has their part here, Joan takes care of the books and Josephine watches over the matriarch of the pizza dynasty, Ruth Lombardi, the 82-year-old widow of Gennaro Lombardi junior. There is definitely a spirit to this place, and a comfortable sense of order that comes with experience. This man, Gerry Lombardi, knows a thing or two about pizza. During my last visit to Lombardi's, one dark and chilly November afternoon, as I sat in the pizzeria talking pie with Gerry and listening to his recounts of the old days, snowflakes lightly dusted the old street outside. For a moment, I could imagine Spring Street circa 1905—the ghosts now filing in and out of the pizzeria—possibly still stealing leftover crusts of pizza. Perhaps one of the ghosts was Enrico Caruso storming into the pizzeria, tearing off a makeshift tablecloth while exclaiming, "I come here to eat pizza, not to eat tablecloths!" Perchance it is Don Gennaro himself who still hovers over the place—I think he does.

TOO HOT OUT OF THE KITCHEN

Pie Man Told World About His Pizza, Not His Past

Eric Asimov

Eric Asimov broke the story in May 1996 about the previous life of Andrew Bellucci, the original pie man at the reopened Lombardi's, in the New York Times. As you are about to read, I was one of many people unaware of his past. Bellucci was released from prison after paying his debt to society, but I have not been able to track him down. Let's hope he's making pizza somewhere.

NOBODY EVER DOUBTED THAT ANDREW BELLUCCI WAS A PIE MAN. In fact, he was a pizza fanatic's dream. Possessed with the desire to create the perfect pizza pie, obsessed with the history and lore of pizza, and blessed with the hustler's gift of gab, he seemed like a man destined to inspire a pizza renaissance.

He appeared on television and in newspapers and magazines after his pizzeria, Lombardi's, opened at 32 Spring Street in SoHo in late 1994. He told his story to anybody who would listen, about how in New York pizza annals, the name Lombardi is to Ray what in the steak business Peter Luger is to Tad. He explained how the original Lombardi's was opened in 1905 by Gennaro Lombardi, an Italian immigrant who not only introduced pizza to New York City, but trained the men who went on to open such other fabled coal-oven pizzerias as Patsy's of East Harlem, John's of Bleecker Street and Totonno's of Coney Island.

He recalled how he had prevailed on the grandson of Gennaro Lombardi, also named Gennaro, to advise him on historical accuracy. Together, he said, they decided to build the new Lombardi's in an old bakery a block from the original Lombardi's.

Food critics loved his story. More important, they loved his pizza. Famous chefs were equally charmed, making pilgrimages to Lombardi's to study Mr. Bellucci's methods, which he was happy to demonstrate.

But it will be some time before Mr. Bellucci, 32, has another chance to twirl a pie for the public. To the astonishment of his admirers, Mr. Bellucci pleaded guilty last year to 54 counts of fraud, accounting for hundreds of thousands of dollars embezzled from the New York law firm of Newman Schlau Fitch & Lane, where he was an administrator in the late 1980s, before he started making pizzas. He surrendered to federal authorities earlier this month and entered the Federal Correctional Institution in Otisville, NY, to begin a 13-month sentence.

To those who thought they knew Mr. Bellucci, the news was like being hit in the face with an anchovy pie.

"I'm shocked," said Ed Levine, a food writer who featured Mr. Bellucci in his weekly Fox-TV News segment "New York Eats" shortly after Lombardi's opened. "He was like a pizzaologist. He never gave me any indication that there were some fundamental character flaws. It just seems incongruous."

"You're kidding," said Nancy Silverton, an owner of Campanile restaurant and La Brea Bakery, both in Los Angeles, who had visited and cooked with Mr. Bellucci at Lombardi's, giving him pointers on baking bread. "He was so sweet to all of us. I fell in love with that clam pie. He Fed-Exed me like six clam pies."

But as Mr. Bellucci begins his prison term, it's clear that embezzlement was only the grandest scheme in a pattern of deceit that has recently characterized his life.

He claimed to be the owner of Lombardi's, but in fact he was just a young and aggressive hired hand whom the reclusive real owners, Gennaro Lombardi and Joan Volpe, did not discourage from acting as a spokesman. Without the authority of his bosses, he spoke to reporters of franchising the Lombardi name, of opening a chain of pizzerias.

"He never stole anything," Mr. Lombardi said. "He was just interested in his picture in the paper, telling stories and in delusions of grandeur, of Lombardi's all over the country. He was claiming all the credit himself, but I had to go back behind the counter and teach him how to make a pizza!"

There were also little lies. Mr. Bellucci, whose family is from New Jersey, told people that he had grown up in the Bronx, presumably to attach himself to the pizza-making tradition of Arthur Avenue. He said he was writing a book about pizza.

"He was a charming guy, humble, trying to make a go out of it, bring back a tradition," said Todd English, the chef at Olive's, an acclaimed Boston restaurant. Mr. English, who had visited Mr. Bellucci, said, "He was very sincere."

Put together, Mr. Bellucci seemed desperate to receive recognition and credit. Had he not been, Mr. Bellucci might not have been arrested. He had been sought by federal agents since 1990, when the law firm had told the authorities of their suspicions. But the agents did not find him, even though he had been cooking pizzas at two restaurants in the East Village, Two Boots and Three of Cups. In fact, a notation on the arrest warrant in 1994 said: "F.B.I. investigation indicates that defendant has fled to France."

Not too long after that, the news coverage of Lombardi's began.

"One day, one of our partners saw him on television," said Philip Schlau, a partner at the law firm and who has since retired. "He was touting his pizzeria. It was incredible that he would have the gall to do that!"

The law firm notified the authorities, who moved to arrest him.

"We were working," Mr. Lombardi said. "It was lunch hour. These two men came in and ordered a pizza, identified themselves as F.B.I. agents, and took him away."

Many of his acquaintances cannot understand why Mr. Bellucci would let himself be photographed knowing he was wanted for a crime.

"To have his face plastered everywhere in New York: he seemed to love it," Ms. Silverton said. "That doesn't make any sense."

For his part, Mr. Bellucci said in a telephone interview from prison that since leaving the law firm in 1990 he had lived in New York and paid his taxes, and so did not realize that anybody was looking for him. "To be honest, I didn't give the matter too much thought," he said.

While neither Mr. Bellucci's Legal Aid lawyer, Cary A. Bricker, nor the United States Attorney's office will discuss the case, there are indications that drugs may have played a role. When Mr. Bellucci was released on $75,000 bond after his arrest in March 1995, it was stipulated that he be tested regularly for drugs, and his sentencing recommends that he undergo drug counseling in prison. Mr. Lombardi says he suspected that Mr. Bellucci was using drugs.

"I saw these mood swings, and I wasn't sure," Mr. Lombardi said. "I saw abusive behavior and foul language."

Mr. Bellucci emphatically denied using drugs. "This is something that happened quite a while ago," he said. "What I'm interested in now is putting out good food, that's what I'm about. I was wrong."

He said his victims were just a law firm, an insurance firm and a bank. "It's not exactly like sticking up an old lady," he said.

After his arrest and release from custody, Mr. Bellucci continued to work at Lombardi's and to live rent-free in a small apartment owned by Mr. Lombardi at 53 Spring Street.

Now, Mr. Lombardi acknowledges sounding paternal about Mr. Bellucci, proud of his pizza-making accomplishments and bitter about his betrayal.

"I do have paternal feelings, because he's a pie man," Mr. Lombardi said, rolling out his greatest accolade. He said that he had offered to appear with his family at Mr. Bellucci's sentencing in hopes of helping him avoid a prison term. He said he had been prepared to guarantee Mr. Bellucci a job, even offering to open another pizzeria to be called Bellucci's, but that Mr. Bellucci never informed him of the sentencing date.

"He could be a good kid, if he just listens to me!" Mr. Lombardi said. "I thought Andy was the guy who was going to carry the name for me. But I didn't know he was going to turn on me. He's just a hustler who conned me."

Lombardi's has carried on, even thrived since Mr. Bellucci's departure. Still, Mr. Lombardi said, he would save a place for the prodigal son: "I feel sorry for him, but I'll still help him if he comes to me."

Mr. Bellucci, who said he plans on making pizza again after his release, said that he was close to Mr. Lombardi at one time but that now, "Jerry wouldn't be able to make a batch of dough if his life depended on it."

While Mr. Bellucci's words often turned out to be lies, nobody questioned the quality of his pizzas.

"He was very cheflike, unlike a lot of pizza makers in pursuit of the perfect pizza," Mr. Levine said. "That was what he was all about. At least, that's what I thought he was all about."

🍴 LAZZARA'S PIZZA | I love thin-crusted Sicilian pizza, so until I discovered Lazzara's I found myself spending a lot of time on the N train heading out to Rizzo's in Astoria. Lazzara's is up a flight of stairs, a sure sign of quality in my experience. A Lazzara's slice is a crispy, thin-crusted square of pizza with mozzarella barely covering half its surface. Note: Lazzara's slices are petite, so order three or four for a satisfying lunch; it's impossible to eat just one.

Lazzara's Pizza
221 West 38th Street, upstairs (between Seventh and Eighth Avenues), New York, NY, 212-944-7792, -7793 and -7794.
RATING: 🍕 🍕

🍴 MEZZOGIORNO | Mezzogiorno opened in 1987, and was something of a wood-burning oven pizza pioneer in its Soho neighborhood. In recent years, each time I walked past its floor-to-ceiling windows I would ask myself, "Why did I stop going here?" The answer became clear as soon as I walked through the door one Saturday afternoon to research Mezzogiorno for this book. The maître d', wearing a shirt with a one-story-high collar, was trying to explain to a young couple why they couldn't have the table they wanted in a restaurant that was at most a third full. I stopped going to Mezzogiorno because they treat people they deem of insufficient social stature as though they were Sicilian day laborers walking into a lunch haunt of Milanese industrialists. The high-collared man seated me immediately, and the waiter took my order shortly thereafter. I was seated right next to the wood-burning pizza oven, which is painted blue with a face carved out of its opening. I asked the waiter where the mozzarella came from. He told me it was made by a man in the neighborhood who delivers it fresh every day. The Margherita arrived. It had a thin crust with just enough height around the edges, with blobs of mozzarella, coarse tomato sauce, a few basil leaves and, inexplicably, three olives in the center. The pizza was excellent, the mozzarella creamy, the sauce unseasoned and the crust a few degrees north of cracker-thin. The waiter came over and recited the specials of the day. Clearly

he was expecting me to order more food. I succumbed to the pressure and ordered a salad with pancetta, a poached egg and frisée. It arrived a few minutes later, a meager collection of undressed ingredients. That Sicilian laborer feeling immediately came over me again. I vowed never to return, since there are a whole lot of other places in this town to get pizza.

Mezzogiorno
195 Spring Street, New York, NY, 212-334-2144.
RATING: ✿ ✿ (for the pizza; no pies for the attitude)

🍴 PIZZA SUPREMA | If you find yourself headed to Madison Square Garden for a Knicks or Rangers game or a concert and you have fifteen minutes or less to get something to eat, Pizza Suprema is the answer to your prayers. A mere two blocks from a Garden entrance, it looks like a generic pizzeria. Don't be fooled. The regular slices have a crisp crust, a fine if overly sweet sauce and a little too much cheese. Have one regular slice and one slice of the marinara pie—a Sicilian slice coated with marinara sauce containing flecks of fresh onion, then sprinkled with just enough Romano cheese to give the whole thing a pleasant tang. The Sicilian crust is thick but surprisingly light, with enough oil to keep it moist. If you're still hungry (and I don't think you will be) get a Roman slice, basically a stuffed slice with a crisp crust filled with sausage, pepperoni, ham and cheese. After your stop here, you can go the Garden totally sated, armed with the knowledge that you won't have to spring for the absurdly expensive hot dogs.

Pizza Suprema
413 Eighth Avenue (at 31st Street), New York, NY, 212-594-8939.
RATING: 🍕 🍕

🍴 RAY'S PIZZA | Forget the Famous Original Ray's, One and Only Ray's of Greenwich Village, Ray Bari or any other pizzeria with Ray in its name. This Ray's Pizza is the original Ray's Pizza in New York. It's somehow fitting that it was opened

in 1959 and is still owned by a guy named Ralph. Ralph makes a first-rate slice with a crispy crust, not-too-sweet tomato sauce and fresh mozzarella. If you want one of the slices laden with so much white pizza cheese that it needs an industrial-strength plate to properly hold it, go to one of the zillion other pizzerias with Ray in its name. If you want a high-quality slice of pizza, then come here.

Ray's Pizza
27 Prince Street (between Mott and Elizabeth Streets), New York, NY, 212-966-1960.
RATING: 🍕🍕

You Can Call It Ray's, but Expect a Lawsuit to Go

William Geist

This piece by former New York Times *columnist William Geist was origi-*
nally published in the Times *more than seventeen years ago. Remarkably, today*
there are more pizzerias than ever in New York with Ray or Ray's in their names.

"Hello, Ray's Pizza," said the woman answering the telephone.

"May I please speak to Ray?" she was asked.

"Ray?" she replied. "Oh, Ray. Ray cannot come to the phone. . . . You know,
there is no Ray, really. . . . Nobody is Ray."

It had been hoped that talking to Ray himself might straighten out this
whole Ray's pizza imbroglio.

Now, Rosolino Mangano has decided to do something about it himself. Mr.
Mangano, who opened his first Original Ray's Pizza at 1073 First Avenue—and
went on to open nine additional Original Ray's—said yesterday that he has filed
a lawsuit to enjoin the multitudinous and mounting number of Ray's pizza parlors
in Manhattan from using the good name of Ray.

This would apparently include, but would not be limited to: Ray's Pizza,
Original Ray's, Ray's Original, Famous Ray's, Ray's Famous, Famous and Original
Ray's, the One and Only Famous Ray's, Real Ray's and so on.

"Something had to be done," said Mr. Mangano, who said all of these Ray's
are troubling to New York's vast pizza-eating community.

"You get into a cab and say 'Take me to Ray's pizza,'" complained the manager of one Ray's, "and you'll never get to our place. The cab stops in half a block
at the first Ray's."

"It is unbelievably confusing," said Nelson Birgene, having a pepperoni and mushroom slice yesterday at the Ray's on Seventh Avenue at 53rd Street. "This one is called 'Famous' and 'Original Ray's,' so I figured I was covered." But his companion, Cheryl Koehler, said she was surprised to find that it was not at all like her favorite Ray's on Madison Avenue.

Managers of Ray's complain about receiving each other's mail, phone calls and deliveries. "We get their complaints too," said Joe Bari, who owns three Ray's parlors. "They say they ate at our other place and it was lousy, and we say, 'That's not our Ray's.'"

"It's bad when they put the health code violations in the paper," said another manager, "and people think it's our place that has the filth and the roaches. We say: 'Wrong Ray's.'" Most of the Ray's in New York—those in the business say there are dozens—are unrelated, yet most seem to have certain characteristics in common. Virtually all claim to be the first Ray's. Also, they all claim that theirs is the best Ray's pizza available at any price and that the other Ray's are ruining their reputation. And none seems to have a real Ray.

Mr. Mangano can't recall why he chose the name of Ray when he opened his Original Ray's in 1964, but he has fond memories of the day, as do most New Yorkers who have opened their own Original Ray's over the years.

"We had to take a stand on Ray's pizza," Mr. Mangano said. One of his competitors replied that this was about all Mr. Mangano's Ray's pizza is good for: standing on it. This is typical of the sort of sniping that goes on in the teeming community of Ray's pizza operators.

"How can he sue when I own the trademarks?" claimed Mr. Bari, who said he holds rights in New York State to the terms "Ray's," "Original" and "Famous" insofar as they relate to round, edible objects of dough, tomato sauce and mozzarella cheese. He said that he sued two places using the name "Famous Ray's," but tired of the long legal process and the large legal bills and is not pursuing it.

"We were the first Ray's," Mr. Bari claimed, recalling the opening of his Ray's at 76th Street and Third Avenue in 1973. Informed that Mr. Mangano claimed to have opened in 1964, Mr. Bari retorted, "Maybe, but we made Ray's a famous name in pizza."

Why Ray? Why not Guido's or Benito's or Giuseppe's famous and original pizza? "Ray is a nice name," said Mr. Bari. "If our restaurant was named Michelle's, the whole city would be full of Michelle's pizza."

"None of these other people even have a real Ray behind Ray's pizza," scoffed Mr. Bari. "We have Ray Bari." Who is Ray Bari? "Well," said Mr. Bari, "there is no Ray Bari, as such. But we have the name. We were the first pizza place to put a last name on Ray."

"We were actually the first Ray's," said Anthony Salvatore, manager of Ray's Pizza on Prince Street in Little Italy, which claims to have opened in 1959. "We don't have to say 'Famous' or 'Original.' We leave that to the Johnny-come-latelys. I get tired of answering questions about whether we're the same as the ones here and there.

"And we have something none of them have," he said. "We have a Ray."

And who might this Ray be? "The owner," he said, proudly, "Ralph Cuomo."

Ray's owners say that not only are new Ray's opening, but that some named Bob's and Phil's and Jim's are changing their names to Ray's to profit from the name recognition.

"The frightening thing," said Mr. Bari, sounding concerned, "is that someday all pizza will be Ray's pizza. Think about it."

STROMBOLI PIZZERIA

Ed Norton

Ed Norton is a fine young actor and a pizza aficionado. How did I find this out? Ed Norton and I have a mutual friend, screenwriter Brian Koppelman (see page 255). Brian asked Ed for his take on pizza, and here's what he e-mailed me about Stromboli's.

ADD $250 A MONTH TO THE RENT of any hovel within walking distance of this silver counter. Just the right amount of cheese; lots of sauce, both spicy and sweet; big slice but not unwieldy and never heated to scalding, a rare consideration in callous times; run day in day out by a father and son who know their regulars, what could be better; even the name is satisfying, say it—Stromboli's. Say no more. That's New York pizza.

 STROMBOLI PIZZERIA

112 University Place (between 12th and 13th Streets), New York, NY, 212-255-0812.
RATING: 🍕 🍕 (my rating, not Ed Norton's)

SULLIVAN STREET BAKERY | Sullivan Street Bakery proprietor

Jim Lahey learned how to make pizza bianca at the famed Il Forno Campo de' Fiori in Rome. He learned so well that I'm hard-pressed to say which is better. His plain pizza bianca has a crisp exterior crust and just the right amount of sea salt and fresh rosemary. Atkins advocates will want to stay away from Lahey's divine potato-

and-rosemary pizza, which has gorgeous browned slices of paper-thin potatoes and just enough fruity olive oil on top of a light, thin crust. His wild-mushroom pizza and onion pizza is as earthy a slice as I've come across. If you insist on some kind of tomato flavor on your pizza, have Lahey's tomato pizza, topped with a pesto-and-tomato sauce. In season I can't resist the fresh artichoke pie, and I never seem to be able to leave the store without a zucchini slice, topped with bread crumbs and a little bit of pecorino Romano cheese. Lahey's room-temperature pies are so fine that I promise you won't even miss the mozzarella.

Sullivan Street Bakery

73 Sullivan Street (between Broome and Spring Streets), New York, NY, 212-334-9435, www.sullivanstreetbakery.com.
534 West 47th Street (between Tenth and Eleventh Avenues), New York, NY, 646-442-2394.
RATING: 🍕 🍕 🍕 🍕

TOTONNO'S | See page 353.

Brooklyn Pizza

⊞ CASERTA VECCHIA | The owners of Caserta Vecchia, the D'Amato family, just celebrated the fiftieth anniversary of its involvement in the pizza business in New York. Maddalena Carusone, grandmother of two of Caserta Vecchia's owners, Rina and Marilyn D'Amato, is sometimes referred to as the Amelia Earhart of the New York pizza business. She just may have been the first woman commercial pizzaiola in New York. After opening a couple of conventional by-the-slice places in New York (Dino's in Queens is still open and operated by the family), the D'Amatos decided to open Caserta Vecchia, a more authentic, whole-pie place. They built a beautiful Neapolitan wood-burning oven and opened the doors in November of

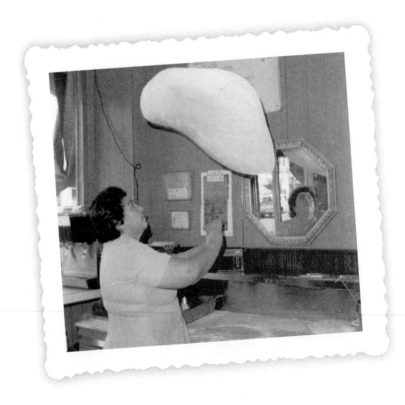

2002. Eight days later a fire destroyed much of the restaurant. Undeterred (how could a family with an Amelia Earhart–like figure at the helm be deterred by a fire?), they rebuilt the place and reopened four months later, in February 2003. The original pizzaiolo, Alfonso Carusone, Rina's uncle, decided to hang up his pizza paddle. Shockingly, the D'Amatos for the first time went outside the family for a replacement: Vittorio Tagliafierro. Vittorio had been making pizza in Italy for thirty-five years, and it turns out the pizza is better than ever at Caserta Vecchia. The crust is crisper and chewier than before, and the ingredients remain the same: imported *fior di latte* from Italy, Italian tomatoes, Italian pizza flour. My last Margherita there was too crisp for Naples, but perfect for New York, and the marinara and the *quattro formaggio* were both exemplary. The spirit of pizza's Amelia Earhart lives on at Caserta Vecchia.

Caserta Vecchia
221 Smith Street (between Baltic and Butler Streets), Brooklyn, NY, 718-624-7549.
RATING:

DI FARA PIZZA | See page 345.

FRANNY'S | What do you get when you cross a culinary-school grad (with an impressive restaurant cooking pedigree) with a sustainable-agriculture advocate who mixes a mean cocktail? Franny's, a restaurant where, according to its press kit, artisanal pizza meets sustainable agriculture. What does that mean, exactly? It means that chef Andrew Feinberg and his wife and restaurateur partner, Francine Stephens, are making fabulous pizzas using ingredients raised or grown with an eye to sustaining every part of the food chain: the farmers, the land and the consumers.

I am a huge supporter of sustainable agriculture, but if Feinberg weren't turning out some of the best, most seriously delicious pizza to be found anywhere in this country, I wouldn't be writing about Franny's. Feinberg's pizzas have a slightly chewy and just-charred-and-crispy-enough crust that is ethereally light. In fact, I hope that as time goes on Feinberg will figure out a way to give his crust a little more body and heft without sacrificing lightness. He uses very fine mozzarella from Lioni in Brooklyn, excellent San Marzano canned tomatoes, and pepperoni and dried sausage that he makes and cures in a room downstairs at the restaurant. Though his pies have ingredients that go well beyond the usual, they are the very model of post-modern, minimalist pizza. Barely melted fontina cheese, house-cured pancetta (Italian bacon) and a sunny-side-up egg make a fabulous combination that McDonald's might consider emulating for its breakfast menu. Feinberg's clam pie takes the Pepe's classic to new heights by adding capers and a touch of cream that gives the whole pie a gorgeous and sumptuous brown sheen. Feinberg and Stephens have just started on their Chris Bianco–like, pizza-sustainable-agriculture odyssey (hard as it is to believe, Feinberg had never made a pizza in a restaurant before opening Franny's), and those of us lucky enough to go along for the ride are in for a treat.

Franny's
295 Flatbush Avenue (at Prospect Place), Brooklyn, NY, 718-230-0221.
RATING: ⊗ ⊗ ⊗ ◖

GRIMALDI'S | When Patsy Grimaldi owned and operated the Grimaldi's under the Brooklyn Bridge, it was one of the truly great pizzerias in this country and the very definition of an owner-occupied pizzeria. Grimaldi used mozzarella and sausage made by Frankie Capezza at the Corona Heights Pork Store, and he lovingly presided over every pie that came out of his gorgeous coal-fired brick oven. Grimaldi eventually sold much of the business to Frank Ciolli, though he stayed on as a sometime consultant. The pizza is not as consistent as it once was, but it still can be very good. The crust is often flat, and the sausage and mozzarella are no longer made by Mr. Capezza. After your pizza, it is required that you walk down the street to the Brooklyn Ice Cream factory for some of the nation's best ice cream (the spectacular view is gratis).

The Hoboken, New Jersey, Grimaldi's makes a very fine pie, although occasionally I've had pizza there with a bready, too-thick crust. Again, this may all come under the heading of hair-splitting, as I have never left either of the above-mentioned locations unsatisfied.

My favorite Grimaldi's at the moment is in Scottsdale, Arizona. Frank Ciolli's son Joseph lovingly presides over a Latino pizza-making crew who are creating impressive, sparsely topped pies with pliant, slightly chewy crusts. As *A Slice of Heaven* goes to press, Joseph Ciolli is about to open a Patsy Grimaldi's in Chandler, Arizona. Who knows, maybe Arizona is on the verge of becoming America's next great pizza destination.

Grimaldi's

119 Old Fulton Street (between Front and Water Streets), Brooklyn, NY, 718-858-4300, www.grimaldis.com.

RATING: ◉ ◉ ◖

133 Clinton Street (at 2nd Street) Hoboken, NJ, 201-792-0800.

RATING: ◉ ◉ ◉

4000 North Scottsdale Road (one block south of Indian School Road), Scottsdale, AZ, 480-994-1100. (This branch is called Patsy Grimaldi's Pizzeria.)

RATING: ◉ ◉ ◉ ◖

HOUSE OF PIZZA AND CALZONE | In most New York pizzerias, calzones are an afterthought. The pie men just take some pizza dough and bake a pocket filled with mozzarella, ricotta and sausage. But at House of Pizza and Calzone in Carroll Gardens, it's the calzone you see most people devouring. Why? Because HPC is to calzones what Peter Luger is to steak. This is the definitive calzone to be had in New York.

The calzones at HPC are fried, not baked. The dough is slightly sweet, but not so sweet that you think you're eating a *zeppóle*. These golden-brown, half-moon beauties are filled with creamy ricotta and full-cream mozzarella. Smack dab in the middle of the calzone are two bites of ham. The effect is the same as eating a *pain au chocolat*. Just when you're wondering where the ham is, say four bites in, it magically appears on your tongue.

There are also, in fact, fine, crunchy, thin-crusted Neapolitan slices to be had here. And the Sicilian is far superior to your local pizzeria's. But in a city as calzone-challenged as New York, we all should do our part to preserve this last bastion of real calzonedom by ordering a calzone here.

House of Pizza and Calzone
132 Union Street (between Columbia and Hicks Streets), Brooklyn, NY, 718-624-9107.
RATING: 🍕🍕🍕

> NOTE: House of Pizza and Calzone has just been sold. The new owners swear they're not going to change anything. We'll see.

L & B SPUMONI GARDENS | L & B Spumoni in Bensonhurst is a beachfront kind of pizzeria, only there's no beach within half a mile of the place. In good weather, everyone sits outside at L & B (there is an inside dining room that serves a complete southern-Italian/American menu), and it's the only pizzeria I know of in New York City that has its own parking lot.

L & B started in 1939 when Ludovico Barbati drove around Brooklyn in a horse-drawn carriage selling spumoni, a southern-Italian frozen treat that's sort of a cross between ice cream and a milk sherbert. After the war, two of Barbati's sons went into the business and they decided to expand the spumoni business into Sicilian pizza, which Barbati's father had taught his son and grandsons to make. An L & B Sicilian slice is topped with a remarkably modest amount of mozzarella, making it an anomaly among Sicilian pizzerias. The slices look heavy, like most Sicilian slices, but are reasonably light. That's because they're proofed twice, once before they're dressed, and once after, when they sit next to the hot ovens on racks. They have regular Neapolitan-American slices at L & B as well. I've just never had occasion to order one. Two L & B Sicilian slices and a spumoni is my idea of a fine and filling South Brooklyn lunch. Ludovico's son Louie says succession plans have already been made at L & B. "We're going to keep doing what we're doing and keep it in the family."

L & B Spumoni Gardens
2725 86th Street (at West 11th Avenue), Brooklyn, NY, 718-372-8400,
www.spumonigardens.com.
RATING: 🍕🍕🍕

SAM'S RESTAURANT | When you walk down the two steps to get

into the time warp that is Sam's, the first thing you notice is the following sign: "Toilet First $2.00." All right, so it's not the most welcoming signal you could see walking into a pizzeria. But I've used the facilities here before ordering on a number of occasions, and I've never been charged. Sam's has been making terrific pizza in the once almost-exclusively Italian neighborhood of Carroll Gardens for nearly seventy-five years. Settle into one of the red Naugahyde booths with the red tablecloths covered in plastic and place your order with Mario Migliaccio, who has been the face of Sam's for as long as I can remember. The oven, converted from wood to gas in 1965, still turns out very fine Neapolitan pies with an interesting twist: The cheese is on the bottom and the sauce is on top. The thickish, chewy crust is excellent, with just the right amount of char on the bottom. The cheese is plain, unadorned and made in the neighborhood, and if only Mario would put less cheese on his pizza, Sam's pies would make it into the Brooklyn Pizza Hall of Fame on the first ballot. I don't have to add that the Brooklyn Pizza Hall of Fame is probably the highest honor a pizzeria can attain.

Sam's Restaurant
238 Court Street (between Baltic and Kane Streets), Brooklyn, NY, 718-596-3458.
RATING: ◉ ◉ ◉

NOTE: Besides terrific pizza Sam's also sells, according to another sign on the front door, fifty-pound bags of calcium chloride rock salt. Maybe it's for the sidewalk when it snows. I don't think it's used in the pizza.

TOTONNO'S | See page 353.

QUEENS PIZZA

BELLA VIA | Salvatore Pollito is a pie man, no two ways about it. Ten years ago he opened a solid sliceria in Queens. Then, when he felt he had mastered the art of the slice, he decided to tackle coal-fired, brick-oven pizza, inspired by his many trips to Totonno's and Patsy's. He has done that successfully at Bella Via, which with its brick walls and big windows is one of the more cheerful pizzerias I have come across. Pollito had a local guy build the oven at Bella Via, and tucked it into the back of the place in full view of the salivating patrons, who watch as he turns out beautiful pies. Sal uses low-moisture, slightly aged mozzarella, Italian tomatoes and fine locally sourced sausage on his pies. His crust is fairly thin, bready and soft, and doesn't have much chew to it.

Bella Via
47-46 Vernon Boulevard (at 48th Avenue), Long Island City, NY, 718-361-7510.
RATING: ⊗ ⊗ ⊗

FORNO ITALIA | The first time I tried to have a pizza at Forno Italia, the place had been reduced to rubble by a complete renovation. I worried that the wood-burning pizza oven I had heard so much about would not be part of the new restaurant. I needn't have worried. What makes Forno Italia's pizza so good is the gorgeous oven, a skilled pizzaiolo and the house-made mozzarella, which is so good that the proprietors wholesale it to other Italian restaurants and pizzerias in the know. The pies are individual Neapolitan-style beauties, with a chewy, puffy crust that is pretty swell. I usually have the Margherita here, but I've always been tempted to order the Southern pizza, topped with spicy sausage and American and Swiss cheeses. It ain't exactly authentic, but I bet it's tasty.

Forno Italia
43-19 Ditmars Boulevard (between 43rd and 45th Streets), Astoria, NY, 718-267-1068.
RATING: ⊗ ⊗ ◖

KIMCHI PIZZA

Geraldine Baum

My friend and tennis partner Bob Prince sent me this clipping from the Los Angeles Times *by Geraldine Baum. It took a* Los Angeles Times *reporter to scoop me about the joys of Korean pizza at TJ's in Flushing.*

MOST OF THE BUSINESSES IN FLUSHING, QUEENS, ARE OWNED by Korean Americans. The bakeries, phone stores, groceries and boutiques don't even bother with English on their awnings on Main Street. A few shops in recent years have turned over to Chinese owners, but the Greeks, Germans, Italians, Jews and Irish who once ruled here are all gone. Except for Tony Sala of TJ's Pizzeria & Restaurant.

Tony is still here serving slices and delivering orders to Little League games and high school graduations. Sala has never been a purist about pizza. Personally, he likes it plain, but he'll throw anything on top of a disk of dough. Taco meat. Buffalo wings. Lasagna innards. Then about a decade ago he turned to soul food—better known in this neighborhood as Seoul food. And, thus, "kim-chee pizza" was born at TJ's.

The spicy Korean pickled cabbage, alternately referred to as kimchi or kimchee, served on top of Sala's basic Neapolitan pizza, was an instant big seller. With this invention, TJ's also became something akin to a cultural center, a neutral ground in the most diverse borough in New York City, where opposing ethnic candidates in the last City Council race met after hours to reconcile differences.

This is so New York. Wave after wave of immigrants have come and adapted, bringing their own culture, their own food, their own ethnicity. But those who came before them also have had to adapt. The WASP establishment had to accept the Irish into their politics and into their police force. German bakers had to learn to make bagels for the Jews. And Sala, a child of Italian immigrants, is making pizza with pickled cabbage to please the Koreans all around him.

Something that was strange is now ubiquitous. Sala piles kimchi on top of bowls of spaghetti with red sauce. He's not averse to stuffing it into calzones or rolls because the Korean customers love it.

And now that they're regulars at TJ's, they have branched out. The other day Dennis Yu, who owns a nearby karaoke studio, was digging through a plate of Sala's baked ziti, with a side order of jalapeño peppers. He is not a fan of pizza but he comes to TJ's at least twice a day to watch golf on the restaurant TV and for a meal. Every so often he tries something new, like the ziti dish.

"Most American people eat pizza, but it's too greasy for me," said Yu. "Kimchi makes it better."

Sala has spent his whole adult life in pizza shops. He grew up in Manhattan and began throwing dough in a pizza shop in Jackson Heights, another Queens neighborhood transformed by immigrants. Finally in 1989, Sala had saved enough money to buy his own place.

It is nothing special: a long, narrow restaurant with 20 yellow Formica booths, brick walls and a take-out window onto Roosevelt Avenue. Even though the previous owner had gone bust because Korean immigrants, still new to American foods, were flooding Flushing, Sala thought he could make TJ's a success: "I was young, I was strong, I made a heck of a pizza."

Flushing's commercial district, in fact, had been nearly derelict in the early 1980s before Koreans began moving to Queens after a new government came to Korea and military generals became presidents. The Korean influx gave Flushing new life. But non-Korean merchants couldn't make it on Main Street and despite his confidence Sala was struggling. Then one day his wife's Korean American obstetrician—the Salas have six children—suggested he try putting kimchi on top of his pizza.

"I didn't even know what he was talking about," Sala said. But he went around the corner to the grocery store and bought the already fermented napa cabbage concoction. (Sala knows better than to attempt it from scratch.) To make the pizza look attractive, at first Sala carefully arranged slices of cabbage on top of a regular cheese pie. But the hot cheese would slide off with the big cabbage slices and burn the customers' chins.

So Sala chopped it up before spreading it across a pie. That worked better and in time the older Korean women in the neighborhood advised him how to doctor the kimchi with secret spices to make it blend better with the cheese and tomato sauce. He refuses to give away their secrets.

Before he knew it, TJ's had new customers from the neighborhood. Korean teens came in at first just to gawk at Sala's innovation. Sometimes they'd order a slice; more often they'd go for the pepperoni, still the best seller. But the adults loved the kimchi. And Sala learned that this Korean staple, eaten by many every day with plain rice, appealed as well to non-Koreans, particularly to Central and South Americans who would stop by for a slice at TJ's after they got off the No. 7 train on their way home to the neighborhoods around Flushing.

"The Mexicans and Colombians love the kimchi because they'll eat anything spicy," Sala said. His Indian customers prefer broccoli and spinach toppings; the Russians stick to plain. A slice with a "gourmet" topping such as kimchi costs between $2.45 and $4. (Sala proudly points out that, at $1.75, a plain slice still costs a quarter less than the subway fare.)

Working in the melting pot has been more of an education for Sala than this high school graduate had expected. Naturally, he speaks Italian, but he is now better in Spanish than in his parents' native tongue; he can greet people and make change in Korean, as can most of his kids, ages 16 through 27, who also work in the pizza shop. A few years back, Sala got an offer to build a pizzeria in South Korea. But it seemed too ambitious a project and his health hasn't been too good. It doesn't help that he eats on average three or four pizza slices a day and needs to lose 100 pounds. "I love the stuff, but it's killing me," he said, chuckling.

TJ's close friend Jim Wu, a Chinese-American political consultant who designed the www.tjspizzeria.com website, is helping Sala develop other products for a broader Asian-American market. Koreans are beginning to migrate out of Flushing to more suburban Queens neighborhoods, and a large Chinese population is coming in. A few of the store signs on the colored awnings in Flushing's downtown are now in Chinese.

Sala and Wu are toying with adding a new seafood topping for the TJ's menu. They're also researching where to buy bubble, or *boba*, tea, a milky drink with tapioca pearls in it that is favored by Asian teenagers.

"You got to keep adapting or you die," Sala said, looking at a colorful brochure with different varieties of the tea. But there are limits. He's been experimenting with no-carb pizza dough and no-carb cheese. "People eat it," he said, shaking his head. "But I gotta tell you—it smells and, you know, I'm an old-fashioned pizza guy. I'll only go so far."

TJ's Pizzeria & Restaurant
136-88 Roosevelt Avenue (between Union Turnpike and Main Street), Flushing, NY,
718-321-8571, www.tjspizzeria.com.
RATING: 🍕🍕 (for the regular slices)　🍕🍕🍕 (if you really like kimchi)

🍴 MANETTA'S | You've heard of the Sunni Triangle? Manetta's is in a section of Queens I call the pizza triangle: cornered by Long Island City, Astoria and Forest Hills. It's also a stone's throw from Silvercup Studios, where they shoot "The Sopranos." If Tony and Carmela and Dr. Melfi are in the mood for pizza, they call over to Manetta's. So if your pizza order is backed up at lunch, chances are it's because the cast of "The Sopranos" have placed an order for fifty pies. Don't complain, if you know what's good for you. You may end up like Adriana or Steve Buscemi's Tony B. Manetta's owner, Mario Manetta, built his oven with his own two hands, so when I asked how it worked, the pie man working that day said, "Ask the boss. He built it." The oven is in the back of the room you walk into off the street, past the display case of desserts and antipasti and salads. Mario's pizzas are Roman-style individual pies, ultra crisp and very thin. He uses delectable mozzarella made in the neighborhood at Spatola, and sauce he strains himself from San Marzano tomatoes. Mercifully, he goes fairly light on the cheese, thereby achieving a fine balance on his pies between sauce and cheese and crust. Manetta's is a full-service Italian restaurant, but I couldn't tell you how the rest of the food is. I've never had anything but the pizza (well, okay, I've also had a piece of pretty good cheesecake and a delicious rice pudding studded with macerated Italian cherries from Mario's hometown of Monte Casino in Italy).

Manetta's
10-76 Jackson Avenue (at 49th Avenue), Queens, NY, 718-786-6171.
RATING: 🍋 🍋 🍋

🍴 NEW PARK PIZZERIA | In planning this book, I originally envisioned a chapter on "Beach Pizza," for pizzerias found along the boardwalk in places such as Ocean City and Atlantic City in New Jersey, and Rehobeth, Delaware. I eventually nixed the idea because my research revealed that most beach pizza is pretty awful (there are exceptions along the Jersey Shore that are written about elsewhere in the book). Another exception that I had to include is New Park Pizzeria, located in Howard Beach, Queens, right next to Kennedy Airport.

New Park Pizzeria is the paradigm of a beach pizza joint. You order at the counter and take your slices to the outdoor eating patio in front of the restaurant. There's a small, heated room in the back where people eat their pizza in cold weather. The guys behind the counter are invariably teenagers from the 'hood, and they wear their baseball caps backward, but don't be alarmed; they're reasonably friendly. The pizza comes out of a super-hot gas oven that produces charred-on-the-bottom, crisp-crusted slices topped with just a little too much good commercial mozzarella.

New Park Pizzeria
156-71 Cross Bay Boulevard (at the corner of 157th Street), Queens, NY, 718-641-3082.
RATING: 🍕 🍕 🍕

NOTE: Many people know New Park Pizzeria as the scene of a really ugly racial incident in December 1986, when four black men came to the pizzeria looking for a phone to call a service station because their car had broken down. They were chased out of the pizzeria by a group of white teenagers and beaten with baseball bats and a tree limb. They ran onto the nearby Shore Parkway, where one of them was killed by a passing car. That was eighteen years ago, and though I don't think the NAACP is holding any meetings in Howard Beach, nobody working in the pizzeria was ever accused of any wrongdoing.

NICK'S PIZZA | See page 348.

RIZZO'S | Most Sicilian pizza is just too thick for me, but Rizzo's in Astoria is the home of the wondrous thin-crust Sicilian slice. For forty years, Joe Rizzo has been making thin-crust Sicilian pizza the way his father learned in Sicily. That means he uses homemade sauce (slightly sweet), full-cream mozzarella that lies ever so gently on top of the light—almost demure—crust, and just enough Romano cheese to give his pizza a little zing.

When you walk into Rizzo's, all you'll see on the counter are rectangular trays of fresh-out-of-the-oven Sicilian pizza. After years of maintaining Sicilian-only pizza purity, Rizzo's is now making conventional Neapolitan pizza. I can't tell you how it is, though, because I refuse to order it on general principle—I come here for the Sicilian slice only.

Rizzo's
30-13 Steinway Street (between City Avenue and Dunway Street), Queens, NY, 718-721-9862.
RATING:

ROSE & JOE'S ITALIAN BAKERY | Corona Heights Pork Store coowners Frankie and Mary Lou Cappezza are my culinary EF Huttons. When they talk, I listen. So when they told me I had to check out Rose & Joe Italian Bakery in their old Astoria stomping grounds, I wasted no time getting there. As usual, they were right. R & J's wondrous braided semolina bread has plenty of character and flavor. But as good as the bread is here, R & J's ultimate triumph is their Sicilian pizza. In the back of the bakery a young woman sells slices: plain, broccoli and sausage. The crust is crispy, slightly doughy and surprisingly light. So don't thank me when you bite into your first slice of Rose & Joe's pizza. Thank Frankie and Mary Lou.

Rose & Joe's Italian Bakery
22-40 31st Street (at Ditmars Boulevard), Astoria, NY, 718-721-9422.
RATING:

THIRTY ONE | Ciro Verde, a native of Astoria in Queens, New York, has a fabulous pizza-making pedigree. As a child, he spent every summer in Naples, cooking, eating and learning how to make pizza. At nineteen, he started cooking and making pizzas professionally at such seminal New York wood-burning oven pizza joints as Mezzaluna and Le Madri. At Le Madri he created his now legendary focaccia with *robiola* cheese and truffle oil, one of the great pizzalike foods to come into existence in the last twenty-five years. In 1995 Verde went out on his own—to Da Ciro on Lexington Avenue, just a stone's throw from New York's Grand Central Terminal. He's been making world-class pizza (and of course his aforementioned focaccia) there for nearly ten years now, but he was saving some of his best tricks for later . . .

With the opening of Thirty One in his native Astoria, Verde has now officially entered the pantheon of pizzaioli. Yes, he still makes his celestial focaccia with the creamy, just-tangy-enough, cream cheese–like *robiola* cheese and, as far as I'm concerned, the only judicious and appropriate use of truffle oil (which usually tastes a little too close to a petroleum product for me). Once I sit down with one of those crispy, light babies in front of me, I know that if I'm not careful I could consume three or four of them without even thinking. And at Thirty One that would leave no room for Ciro's pizza by the meter, which is so much better than anyone else's (in this country at least) feeble attempt at replicating that Roman phenomenon. His crust on these oblong-shaped pies is astoundingly good, proof positive that pizza makers who know what they're doing can create great crusts with gas-fired ovens, in this case a state-of-the-art Woodstone oven that easily maintains 600°F heat. (In Manhattan, at Da Ciro, Verde has a conventional wood-burning oven.) The result is crispy and chewy with a lovely, just-charred-enough bottom. And it passes the true test of any pizza crust: Fifteen minutes after it arrives at your table, stripped of sauce and cheese, the crust tastes fantastic when you pop it in your mouth, like a great piece of fresh bread. Verde's house-made mozzarella also contributes mightily to his fabulous pizza, as does the Alpes sausage and salami that he uses for his toppings. There's one more pizza-related item at

Thirty One that you must have, and that is one of the great savory food bargains to be found anywhere. Verde makes crispy pizzettes, deep-fried puffs of dough with fresh tomato, mozzarella and basil in the center. I ate a lot of them in Naples, but had never seen them in the States until now. They're only a dollar each, and I always end up buying a dozen, thinking I'll take them home to my wife, Vicky, and my son, Will. By the time I get home, they're lucky to get one each.

Thirty One
22-48 31st Street (between Ditmars Boulevard and 32nd Avenue), Queens, NY, 718-728-8288.
RATING: 🍊 🍊 🍊 🍊

Da Ciro
229 Lexington Avenue (between 33rd and 34th Streets), New York, NY, 212-532-1636.
RATING: 🍊 🍊 🍊

STATEN ISLAND PIZZA

DENINO'S | See page 266.

JOE & PAT'S | Giuseppe Pappalardo, an owner of Joe & Pat's in Four Corner's, Staten Island, mastered his craft at three legendary Staten Island slice establishments: Nunzio's, Ciro's and Tokie's. His slices are distinguished by a superbly thin, crispy crust. "They're easier to digest," he says, "so you can eat a lot of them." And believe me, I do. Giuseppe's son Angelo has now joined him at the pizzeria. He's a serious chef whose last stop was at Esca in Manhattan. I'm sure he'll do wonders for all the other food at Joe & Pat's. The only way he could improve the pizza is to make it with fresh mozzarella.

Joe & Pat's
1758 Victory Boulevard (at Manor Road), Staten Island, NY, 718-981-0887.
RATING: 🍕🍕🍕🍕

NUNZIO'S | A slice from Nunzio's is a pristine exercise in elegant pizza minimalism. It's not very big, so pizza-by-the-ton Ray's fans should go elsewhere. Yet everything about it is right: the ratio of sauce to cheese, the crisp yet pliant crust and the tangy sauce enlivened by fresh basil. I love the sausage Nunzio's puts on its slices. It's nubby, loaded with flavor, and has plenty of fennel in it. Nunzio's even looks the way a pizzeria should: it is a white stucco shack with a tiny dining room brightened by black-and-white photos of the original Nunzio's in South Beach, Staten Island.

Nunzio's
2155 Hylan Boulevard (at Midland Avenue), Staten Island, NY, 718-667-9647.
RATING: 🍕🍕🍕🍕

Bronx Pizza

Like every other borough of the city of New York, Bronx has a long and proud pizza history. How long? Mario's on Arthur Avenue opened in 1919. How proud? The street that houses Louie and Ernie's is named Ottuso Square after Ernie Ottuso. Many Bronx residents swear by their borough's pizza supremacy, including legendary pie man Louis Palladino (profiled by Alan Feuer on page 132). I do not agree with those claims, but there can be no doubt that the Bronx has a fair amount of pizza to be proud of.

LOUIE AND ERNIE'S | City officials know a good slice of pizza when they see one: the street in front of Louie and Ernie's has been renamed Ernie Ottuso Square, after one of the owners. A Louie and Ernie's slice is a diminutive triangle of pizza pleasure in which grated cheese and full-cream mozzarella sparingly cover a thin-enough crust. Also worth the calories and the trip are the fried calzone and the white pie, both made with ricotta. The white pie, in particular, is Louie and Ernie's pièce de résistance. The overflowing ricotta was so sweet and creamy I could have had it for dessert. The mozzarella on it was clearly full cream, and there wasn't even a hint of tomato sauce on it. This was serious pizza. A word to the wise: Don't arrive too late. The pizzeria ends its day when the dough is gone. "We run out, we run out . . . that's it," says John Tiso, an owner. "We close."

Louie and Ernie's
1300 Crosby Avenue (at Waterbury Avenue), Bronx, NY, 718-829-6230.
RATING: 🍕🍕🍕

MARIO'S | I arrived at Mario's one scorching summer day just before noon, weak from hunger. I looked at the menu, full of classic, red-sauce, Neapolitan-American items. There was no pizza to be found. My waiter came over. "Do you still serve pizza here?" I asked. "Yeah, we got it," he said grudgingly, the way a Cadillac dealer might admit he also sells Hondas. I ordered my usual (large half sausage, half plain) and reflected on my rather curious interaction with the waiter. I remembered that when I ate at Mario's a few years ago, for a story I was working on, the fifth-generation owner, Joseph Migliucci, discouraged people from ordering just pizza at his fine-dining establishment. The pizza arrived ten minutes later. It was a superior pie: crisp, slightly bready crust; terrific fennel-flecked sausage from a local butcher; fresh basil; a sprinkling of Parmigiano-Reggiano; and a simple tomato sauce not overburdened with unnecessary herbs and spices. It would have been a world-class pie if the fresh mozzarella I had asked for (I know they make mozzarella every day at the restaurant for other dishes on the menu) had found its way to the pie. The aged mozzarella was obviously high quality and full fat, but the yellow color gave away its age.

I spotted Migliucci sitting on a chair just in front of the swinging kitchen door. I asked, "Why do you make it so hard to order pizza? You make a great pie here." He smiled and said, "It is good, isn't it? I don't have a problem with people ordering pizza at lunch, but at dinner it's hard to make money if people are occupying tables for four ordering pizza and soft drinks." Migliucci then went on to tell me that his great grandparents had opened Mario's on Arthur Avenue in 1919, serving pizza and other dishes from their native Naples. Before that, they had owned pizzeria/restaurants in East Harlem, Naples and that hotbed of pizza activity, Cairo, Egypt. Migliucci's father once told the *New York Times*' Craig Claiborne, "My grandparents left Naples with my father in the early 1900s and opened the first Italian restaurant ever in Egypt. It was a success, but my father became restless and decided to come to America."

As I was leaving I implored Migliucci to restore pizza to its rightful place on his menu. He laughed. "You know what happened. The chains gave pizza a bad name. They open pizza shops. We're a pizzeria, not a pizza shop." So I'll let you in on one of the worst-kept secrets in pizzadom: They have excellent pizza at Mario's, the reluctant pizzeria.

Mario's

2342 Arthur Avenue (between 184th and 186th Streets), Bronx, NY, 718-584-1188.

RATING: ⊛ ⊛ ⊛ ⊛

PATRICIA'S | It makes my heart sing when I walk into a pizzeria and see the glow of burning wood logs in a brick oven. Patricia's serves pizza made either in the aforementioned wood-burning oven or a gas oven. The pizza is the same price, so why anyone would order a pie made in the gas oven is beyond me. My Margherita had the most tender pizza crust I've had east of Phoenix. It had virtually no crunch, but it had the texture and consistency of fresh-baked bread. The mozzarella was fresh, as was the basil, and the tomato sauce wasn't gummed up by too many spices. The sausage, oblong strips cut lengthwise from what must have been a fat link, had a clean, porky flavor. The menu here proclaims, "The Best Sicilian Pizza in New York City!" Though I appreciated both the fresh mozzarella and the smoky taste the wood-burning oven imparts to the thick Sicilian crust, this claim could not be substantiated by the half pie I had. I thought the crust could have used a bit more olive oil. The menu at Patricia's has a zillion items on it, everything from Rigatoni Pavarotti to T-bone steak, but I've never had anything except the pizza—from the wood-burning brick oven, not the gas oven.

> NOTE: There are three Patricia's, named Patricia's I, II and III. I ate at Patricia's I, and I walked into Patricia's II, where I saw the same wood-burning oven. My friendly waitress at Patricia's I told me that Patricia's III does not have a wood-burning oven.

Patricia's
Patricia's I, 1080 Morris Park Avenue (between Williamsbridge and Lurting Avenues), Bronx, NY, 718-409-9069 or 718-792-1704.
Patricia's II, 3764 East Tremont Avenue (between Randall and Schley Avenues), Bronx, NY, 718-918-1800 or 718-918-1804.
RATING:

PJ BRADY'S | It's not always easy searching for pizza. I had just eaten a fine pie in the outdoor café at Tosca (see next entry) in the Throgs Neck section of the Bronx. It was really hot and muggy, and I was on foot, looking for PJ

Brady's, which a couple of locals had insisted was just a few blocks away. I headed east on East Tremont Avenue. I crossed Interstate 295 on a bridge and walked two hundred yards. I reached Phillip Avenue and made a right. The first house number I saw was 2800, and the numbers were going up, a good sign considering PJ Brady's is at 3201 Phillip Avenue. The houses I was passing were more like bungalows, and many had boats in the driveway. The boats made sense, considering Throgs Neck is surrounded by water. A few of them were guarded by Doberman pinschers that looked ready to defend their masters' possessions with all their fury. When I reached 3100 Phillip Avenue, my shirt was soaked through with sweat, and my heart sank. I was staring at yet another highway, and this time there was no pedestrian bridge to cross. I despaired of ever reaching PJ Brady's, where the legendary pie man Louis Palladino was plying his trade two days a week in semiretirement (see Alan Feuer's profile on page 132). I spotted a pedestrian bridge a few blocks away, crossed it and, ten steamy minutes later, walked into the unprepossessing PJ Brady's. (In keeping with the neighborhood, it's in a one-story stucco building.) It was 3:15 P.M. and I had been told by two different people that Louis starts making pies at 3:00 on Fridays. I ordered a pizza and asked if Louis was in the house. My extremely solicitous waitress informed me that Louis had been delayed, and that he would be in at 4:00. I decided to wait, as I didn't know if I would ever be able to find PJ Brady's again.

At ten minutes to four a man with a full head of gray hair came bounding through the dining room wearing Bermuda shorts and smoking a cigar. A few minutes later he came bounding out of the kitchen. "The dough machine was broken, so I don't know if this pie I'm making for you is going to be any good. It might have too many holes. We'll see. If you don't like it, just come back any other Friday or Sunday, and I'll make you another one." And with that he went back into the kitchen. He was warm and friendly and obviously trying to please, so I didn't have the heart to tell him it was unlikely I would be back before he'd be in full retirement (Louis is, after all, seventy-five).

Louis came out a few minutes later, carrying my pizza in a box. As he put it down, he opened the lid, looked at the pizza and pronounced it fit to eat. He implored me to eat a slice. I was hoping and praying it was good because, if it wasn't, my Throgs Neck trek would have been in vain. Fortunately, it was an excellent crispy pie, as good as a pizza can get when made with solid (not great) commercial ingredients, in a conventional gas oven.

It had been a long time coming, but it was a fine pizza, made with a lot of heart, skill and soul.

PJ Brady's
3201 Phillip Avenue (at the corner of Vincent), Bronx, NY, 718-931-3250.
RATING: ⊛

 TOSCA CAFÉ | At Tosca, the servers wear polo shirts that say "Coal oven pizza since 1922." I was skeptical, because neither my Bronx-born relatives nor my Bronx pizza mavens can recall having a pizza here until a couple of years ago. No matter. I ordered my pizza with fresh mozzarella and sausage on half, and went back to check out the coal oven. Sure enough there it was, a white- and black-tiled beauty that looked as if it had been there for a long time. I wandered back to my outdoor table and waited for my pizza. It arrived in a few minutes, and as soon as I took a look I knew it was a serious pie.

The snow-white mozzarella had little brown blisters and the crust had charred, brown and black spots. I wished the crust had a little more salt in it, and it was a little too crisp for my taste, but this was a fine pie, nonetheless. I'd been living in New York for thirty years as an adult, and somehow Tosca (or whatever it had been called before this) had escaped my attention. My loss.

Tosca Café
4038 East Tremont Avenue (at the corner of Miles Avenue), Bronx, NY, 718-239-3300.
RATING: ⊛ ⊛ ⊛

SECRETS OF THE
DEAN OF THE PIE MEN

Hints From 59 Years in Pizza: Crust Is Thin, and No Avocados

Alan Feuer

New York Times *reporter Alan Feuer wrote this evocative profile of Louis Palladino in 2002, when Palladino was only seventy-three years old. I am happy to report (see page 129) that Palladino has not lost his touch.*

IF YOU ARE READING THIS AND HAVE BEEN MAKING PIZZA PIES SINCE 1943 or before, put down the paper, pick up the phone and dial 718-931-3250. When the voice on the other end says, "PJ Brady's," ask for a man named Louis Palladino. Mr. Palladino wants to talk.

For 59 years now, Mr. Palladino has been cooking pizzas in the Throgs Neck section of the Bronx, which, by his own account, makes him the holder of the longevity record for this particular culinary art. But he is a modest and scrupulously honest man. He would gladly resign his title should a longer-serving pizza cook come forward.

While pizza-making may seem like a minor trade—an occupation no more or less important than pest control or painting traffic lines on city roads—Mr. Palladino has managed to transcend his job. He has gone about this in two ways. Over the years, he has amassed an impressive body of knowledge about the craft of making pizza. More important, he has transformed himself from a mere slinger of sauce and dough into that rare New York phenomenon, a neighborhood institution. Proof of the first: He seasons sausage pies with a little sprinkling of oregano, but puts a dusting of garlic powder on mushroom pies, because that's the way it's done. Proof of the second: Some of his older customers have been eating his pizzas longer than they have been married.

That said, some history.

Mr. Palladino is 73, and got his start making pizzas at 14 at a Throgs Neck restaurant called Amerigo's. He never dreamed that pizza-making would be his calling. He was simply parked in his brother's car outside the restaurant when its founder, Amerigo Coppola, knocked on the window one day and offered him a job.

"My mother said, 'Please, Louie, don't quit school,'" Mr. Palladino said last week, the stub of a Don Sebastian cigar plugged between his lips. "But Amerigo says to my mother: 'Don't you worry, dear. If he learns pizzas, he'll always have a trade.'"

Amerigo's—gone now—was a cavernous, bustling place on East Tremont Avenue. The wood-burning oven fit 18 pizzas and the spatula used to pull them out was six feet long. Mr. Palladino recalls tossing pies as high as 10 feet in the air and the customers watching in awe at the kitchen window, their heads moving up and down in unison as the raw dough rose and fell.

It was there, under Amerigo's tutelage, that Mr. Palladino learned the art of the thin and crispy crust. He is still a thin-and-crispy man today. "These young kids like to fill up on a slice," he says. "They all want dough. But they don't know how to stretch it like it should be stretched."

Something you might not know about a slice of pizza is that it should be cooked to an equal thickness from tip to base. "If it starts out thin and then gets thicker," Mr. Palladino says, "you've got an amateur making the pies."

Mr. Palladino practiced his thin-and-crispy style in the Korean War when the Army sent him to Japan as a cook with an antiaircraft division. The lieutenants and captains loved his pies, he said, even if they did lack mozzarella cheese. "You couldn't get mutz-a-rel in Japan," he said. "The Japanese didn't know what it was."

After the war, he came back to the Bronx and opened Lou Dino's Pizzeria on Bruckner Boulevard, not far from Amerigo's.

In 1970, he opened another pizzeria down the block called Palladino's, which served Throgs Neck until the pizzeria was destroyed by fire in 1980.

Twenty years of itinerant pizza-making followed, in a succession of low-rent bars where the patrons were more interested in drinks and cocktail waitresses than in a decent pepperoni slice. Mr. Palladino has a hard time talking about this period. He waves it off with the same brusque dismissal he reserves for people who order things like pineapple or avocado on their pies.

Then, two years ago, after several months of staying at home to care for his epileptic brother, he got the call that renewed his career. It came from a man called Angelo Angelo, who lives in Throgs Neck and always says things twice. He told Mr. Palladino that PJ Brady's, an Irish bar on Philip Avenue, needed a pizza cook. "You want the job, Lou?" he asked. "You want the job?"

Mr. Palladino is thrilled to be cooking pizzas in the neighborhood again, even though he works only on Friday and Sunday nights. He was born on Pennyfield Avenue in a bungalow directly on Long Island Sound. It was all beach clubs and vegetable farms back then, he says, and he remembers the girls next door, the Lucarelli sisters, out in their blue jeans plowing the fields.

These days, Throgs Neck is still mostly Irish and Italian, although the farms are gone, of course. Every square inch of the waterfront is crammed with condominiums and houses, and the only thing that is plowed is the wet snow that blows in off the sound.

Some things have stayed the same. Peggy Fuerst is still eating Mr. Palladino's sausage and mushroom pies.

The first time she ate a Palladino pizza was 35 years ago. The occasion preceded her wedding.

"Even our children eat his pizza," Mrs. Fuerst said the other day before her husband, Ray, leaned over to proclaim: "Best pizza in the Bronx. Everyone talks about this pizza. And if you've been around, the Bronx has the best pizza in the country."

Mrs. Fuerst just smiled and nibbled at her slice. "And Ray has been around," she said.

Meanwhile, in the kitchen, Mr. Palladino was cooking. He took out his cutting board. He floured his piece of dough. He pressed the dough and flipped it over. He raised it in the air. He laid the dough across his knuckles and spun it like a wheel. "See, I work the edges and only the edges," he said. "The middle takes care of itself."

His sauce is a secret mix of tomato, basil, sugar, oregano and perhaps, he says, a little ash from his cigar. It goes on smoothly. "You can't leave no white spots." Too loose and the pie will be watery. Too thick and it will be dry.

A little salt, a little pepper, a heavy shower of mozzarella cheese. Then the mushrooms and garlic powder are added. Then into the oven and close the door.

There is a science devoted to working the hot and cool zones of the oven, which would require several paragraphs of detailed explanation.

Suffice to say, an average pizza bakes in about nine minutes, at 550°F.

As the mushroom pie began to cook, Mr. Palladino poured himself a drink from the 40-ounce bottle of ale he keeps in the cooler at his knees. He turned reflective as the beer went down. He mused about getting old.

"I must've made over a million pies," he said, "and I put my heart in every one. I like to make my pies. I'm a pie man. That's what I am. I might be 90 years old, and if I can still make 'em, I'll make 'em."

The kitchen smelled good now. The savory smells of baking dough and melting cheese.

"I was born in Throgs Neck," he said. "I'll die here, too. And you know? It's not such a bad place to do it either."

WESTCHESTER PIZZA

SAL'S PIZZERIA | America would be a lot better off if every town had a Sal's Pizzeria instead of a Pizza Hut or a Domino's or some other awful chain monstrosity. Sal DeRose opened his eponymous pizzeria on Mamaroneck's main thoroughfare in 1964, and there have been lines out the door ever since. A Sal's Neapolitan slice has a yeasty crisp crust that holds up well to the whole-milk Grande mozzarella and the thankfully not-too-sweet sauce on top of it. Even better is Sal's Sicilian slice. It's just oily enough, and though it's not exactly a light snack, it's not so heavy that it would hurt if two slices landed on your big toe. A slice of Sal's pizza won't change your life, but it will lift your spirits, at least temporarily.

Sal's Pizzeria
316 Mamaroneck Avenue (at Palmer Avenue), Mamaroneck, NY, 914-381-2022.
RATING: 🍕 🍕 🍕

TOTONNO'S | See page 353.

CHAPTER
5

*Long Island
Pizza*

Long Island Pizza

LONG ISLAND PIZZA IS MY HOMETOWN PIE. I GREW UP IN Cedarhurst, just over the Queens border next to Kennedy Airport. I ate my slices at Cedarhurst Pizza on Central Avenue. They cost twenty cents in the late fifties and early sixties, and my standard lunch was two slices and a meatball hero. Perhaps that explains why I was not a thin child. Occasionally we would go to Far Rockaway, Queens, in order to save a nickel on the slices. When my family went out for Italian food, it was Ricci's (or maybe it was Ricky's) on Washington Avenue. Our main course was inevitably spaghetti and meatballs or veal parmigiana, but we would always start with one of Ricci's thin-crusted pizzas.

The family's most bizarre pizza-eating ritual took place on Sundays in the summer. My dad would grill steak, but always it was accompanied by a pizza from Cairo's Restaurant in the neighboring town of Inwood, home to many American families from southern Italy. My Mom and I would drive to pick it up. I don't really remember the specifics about Cairo's pie, other than that it had a thickish crust and browned cheese bubbles on top. I do remember loving those dinners—the steak and the pizza. It is a surprisingly felicitous combination, though not exactly light.

Long Island has a rich pizza tradition. Starting in the thirties, Italian-American families moving up the socioeconomic ladder in the New York metropolitan area often bought their first houses on Long Island after leaving the Italian enclaves in Brooklyn, Queens and Manhattan. Italian restaurants with pizza on the menu and pizzerias serving pizza by the slice opened in virtually every town in Nassau and Suffolk Counties, starting in the fifties. Eddie's in New Hyde Park opened in 1931, Umberto's in the same town opened in 1965.

On Long Island in the sixties, thirteen-year-olds celebrated their passage to teendom by going to eat pizza by themselves, riding like a motorcycle gang on their Schwinns and Raleighs down tree-lined suburban streets to their favorite slice places. Bowling-league nights were capped off by eating pizza and drinking beer, and big nights such as graduation and communions and confirmations were often spent in pizzerias.

Even now in the twenty-first century, Long Island's pizza culture is still healthy and thriving. Places like Umberto's, King Umberto's and Gino's in Long Beach are now being joined by relative newcomers such as Salvatore's in Port Washington, where Fred Lacagnina is turning out coal-fired, brick-oven pizzas trying to emulate the success of his great uncle Patsy Lancieri, who started Patsy's in East Harlem in 1933.

One piece of Long Island pizza culture, grandma pizza, is emblematic of the story of Long Island pizza as a whole. Pride and passion are the driving forces of Long Island pie men today, just as they were seventy years ago. Pride mixed in with a stubborn, independent streak keeps the Long Island pizza culture thriving, and the pizza chains at bay.

After reading Erica Marcus's story, which you'll find in the upcoming pages, I had to try a half-dozen grandma-slice joints all over Long Island. I was mightily impressed with all of them, and my only regret is that I didn't get to try all twenty-one joints on Erica's list.

Pizza a la Grandma

How this Long Island Specialty Came to Be

 *Erica Marcus*

Erica Marcus, a pizza-loving colleague and first-rate food reporter for the paper of record on Long Island, Newsday, *tried to uncover the mystery surrounding the origins of another piece of Long Island pizza lore, the grandma slice.*

AMERICAN PIZZA FALLS INTO TWO BASIC CATEGORIES: THIN AND round, thick and square. But in many Long Island pizzerias, regular and Sicilian pies are joined by a third: Grandma. A starting player in the local pizza lineup for the past decade, grandma pie is virtually unknown west of Queens. "I've never heard of it," said Jeremy White, executive editor of *Pizza Monthly,* the nation's leading pizza industry magazine.

Pizza Monthly, it should be noted, is headquartered in Louisville, KY. But even closer to home, grandma pie flies well below the radar. Michele Scicolone, Manhattan resident, Italian food expert and co-author of *Pizza: Any Way You Slice It* (Broadway Books) hadn't heard of it, either. "What is grandma pizza?" she asked.

Variations abound, but the basic outlines are as follows: a thin layer of dough is stretched into an oiled, square "Sicilian" pan, topped sparingly with shredded mozzarella, crushed uncooked canned tomatoes, chopped garlic and olive oil, and baked until the top bubbles and the bottom is crisp.

Scicolone observed that grandma pie sounded a lot like "*pizza a la casalinga*" (housewife-style pizza), "the kind of pizzas you'd get in Italy if you were invited to someone's home."

And indeed, among the men who left Southern Italy to find their fortunes making pizza on Long Island, many cherished childhood memories of a pizza made at home by mama or grandma. This pizza was modest, thin-crusted, strewn sparingly with chopped tomatoes from the garden and just a little cheese (it was expensive), then baked in a pan (mama had no pizza oven).

For such a recent culinary phenomenon, grandma pie's origin is curiously cloudy. Interviews with many area pizza makers yielded only a vague sense that it started popping up during the '90s. A break came from Emilio Branchanelli, owner of Emilio's in Commack and Pasta-eria in Hicksville. "It started at Umberto's in New Hyde Park," he said. "A guy who worked for Umberto made it."

After a few phone calls, Branchanelli came up with a name: Angelo Giangrande, now of Da Angelo in Albertson. With the help of Giangrande and the principals at Umberto's and King Umberto's in Elmont, we pieced together the history of this Long Island specialty:

In the early 1970s, a home-style pan pizza surfaced at Umberto's of New Hyde Park. Founded in 1965 by Umberto Corteo, who came from Monte di Procida near Naples, Umberto's now is a vast operation encompassing a pizzeria, restaurant and catering hall. But when Carlo Corteo arrived in 1970 to work with his older brother, it was a simple 60-seat pizza parlor. "Back then," Carlo said, "we used to make the grandma pizza for ourselves. Umberto would say to me, 'Make me that pizza that Mama used to make.'"

Umberto served the pizza to friends who urged him to put it on the menu, but he resisted. "In the old days," Carlo said, "there weren't so many pizza places and there were lines out the door at night. Umberto said, 'How are we going to put another pizza on the menu? It will slow us down.'"

Here the story moves about two miles south, to Elmont. The Corteos had opened a satellite pizzeria, King Umberto's, that was the domain of another Corteo brother, Joe. In 1976, after Joe moved to Florida, the restaurant was sold to two Umberto's employees, brothers Rosario and Sal Fuschetto. During the '80s, they in turn hired two other pizza makers—first Ciro Cesarano, then Angelo Giangrande—who also got their start at Umberto's.

"Umberto still wasn't selling [grandma pie] to customers," Rosario said, "but Ciro and Angelo saw its potential." So when they arrived in Elmont, they put the still-nameless pizza on the menu.

Some time between 1986 and 1989, a conversation occurred at King Umberto's that would change the course of this very narrow slice of pizza history. Cesarano and Giangrande were chatting with a customer, Anthony "Tippy" Nocella, about what to call the pie. Cesarano recalled that the word "grandpa" came up, "but Tippy said 'No, it's really more grandma. You want to call it grandma.'"

Another milestone in the spread of grandma pie: In 1989, Nocella (who died in 1999) accompanied Giangrande and Sal Fuschetto to a pizza-making contest in Farmingdale, Long Island, sponsored by Delicato Foods, a pizza-supply wholesaler. Giangrande recalled that, over Fuschetto's objections (like Umberto, he was a bit of a traditionalist), he took the grandma pie. It was a hit. "All the pizza guys loved it; everybody ate it," Giangrande said. "My pizza was gone before the competition even started."

By this time, other pizzerias, including Umberto's, had put grandma pizza on the menu. But it really took off in about 1993, a chronology that dovetails with the evolution of grandma pie sales at King Umberto's. From the beginning, pizzas destined to be sold by the slice sat on high counters above the eye level of many customers, but in 1994, King Umberto's undertook a renovation: the installation of a glass-enclosed showcase, much like a jeweler's display, that displaced the posted menu as the focal point of customers' deliberations.

"When we put in the showcase," said King Umberto's co-owner, Rosario Fuschetto, "people saw the grandma pie and asked 'What's that thin one? Let me have one of those.'"

(Fuschetto regrets never having trademarked the name "grandma pizza," but was determined not to make the same mistake twice. One of the most popular items at his restaurant is a fritter-like morsel fried to a golden brown and filled, improbably, with a creamy amalgam of capellini and white sauce. In 1995, Fuschetto secured a trademark for "fried capellini balls," which now appear on the menu bearing a government-certified "TM.")

As with books and knock-knock jokes, pizza popularity is transmitted by word of mouth. Unaware of the origins of grandma pizza, local pizza makers put it on their menus in response to customer demand. Natale Tartamella first

WHERE TO BUY
GRANDMA PIZZA

An admittedly incomplete list of places that serve grandma pie.

NASSAU COUNTY
Carlino's, 204 Jericho Turnpike, Mineola, NY, 516-747-6616.
Cinelli's, 1195 Hempstead Turnpike, Franklin Square, NY, 516-352-2204;
        346 Hillside Avenue, Williston Park, NY, 516-742-8989.
Cugini's, 432 Jericho Turnpike, Mineola, NY, 516-248-7770.
Da Angelo, 815 Willis Avenue, Albertson, NY, 516-741-8694.
Gino's of Long Beach, 16 West Park Avenue, Long Beach, NY, 516-432-8193.
King Umberto's, 1343 Hempstead Turnpike, Elmont, NY, 516-352-8391.
Pasta-eria, 440 South Oyster Bay Road, Hicksville, NY, 516-938-1555.
Umbertino's, 2054 Lakeville Road, New Hyde Park, NY, 516-326-2953;
        633 Jericho Turnpike, New Hyde Park, 516-437-7698;
        361 Nassau Boulevard, Garden City South, NY, 516-481-1279;
        420 Newbridge Road, Hicksville, NY, 516-433-7575.
Village Pizzeria, 169 Tulip Avenue, Floral Park, NY, 516-775-0612.
Vinnie's of Mulberry Street, 287 North Broadway, Jericho, NY, 516-933-7974.

SUFFOLK COUNTY
Emilio's, 2201 Jericho Turnpike, Commack, NY, 631-462-6267.
Mamma Lombardi's, 400 Furrows Road, Holbrook, NY, 631-737-0774.
Our Little Italy, 636 Union Boulevard, West Islip, NY, 631-737-0774.
Villa Michelangelo, Eastport-Manorville Road, Manorville, NY, 631-878-1555.

QUEENS COUNTY
Carlo's Pizza, 74-02 Metropolitan Avenue, Middle Village, NY, 718-894-7915.
Gino's, 158-46 Cross Bay Boulevard, Howard Beach, NY, 718-738-4113.

BROOKLYN
Papa's Pizza, Fifth Avenue, Bay Ridge, NY, 718-630-5593.

heard of grandma pie during the '90s at a pizzeria he owned in Valley Stream, adjacent to Elmont. "People used to say 'Why don't you make grandma pizza?' I didn't know what the heck it was." But he's a quick study. Since he took over Vinnie's of Mulberry Street in Hicksville two years ago, Tartamella has been making a grandma pie that was voted Long Island's best in a 2002 longisland.com contest.

Another mechanism for the dissemination of pizza varieties is the migration of pizza makers. Just as Cesarano and Giangrande moved from Umberto's to King Umberto's, so dozens of pizza makers moved from the grandma-nexus of central-western Nassau County, west to Queens, south to the Five Towns (Lawrence, Cedarhurst, Hewlitt, Inwood and Woodmere), and even east into Suffolk County. And these pizza-pollinators took grandma with them.

In 1991, Angelo Giangrande and his cousin Antonio Franzella opened Cugini's in Mineola and, in 2000, Cugini Due in Albertson. (The Albertson location was renamed Da Angelo in 2004.) Giangrande developed a grandma pie that was thicker than the one he had left at King Umberto's, but still thinner than Umberto's. It was this pie, he said, that his brother Mario took with him when he got a job at Gino's in Long Beach, now a prime purveyor of grandma pie.

Branchanelli said grandma pie arrived at Emilio's in Commack via his partner's father-in-law, who was friends with Umberto Corteo. At Emilio's, Branchanelli took the heretical step of substituting a smooth tomato sauce for the uncooked chopped tomatoes that are grandma's hallmark. "I defied their recipe, yes," he said, "but sales have quadrupled."

Peter Cinelli, scion of the family that owns Cinelli's pizzerias in Franklin Square and Williston Park, said, "We started making it 10, 12 years ago in the Franklin Square store." Three years ago, Cinelli, who refers to Umberto Corteo as "the pope of pizza," moved south of the Mason-Dixon Line and opened up a Cinelli's pizzeria in Cary, NC, where grandma pie now outsells regular.

And remember the Corteo brother Joe, who moved to Florida? He presides over Umberto's of Long Island, a restaurant in Pompano Beach that serves grandma pie to former Long Islanders and native Floridians. Corteo also is part-owner of Pizzeria da Enzo in Las Vegas' Venetian Hotel. Now that's taking grandma pizza to the big time.

Even in Brooklyn, grandma pie is making inroads. Tommy Napoli, at 25, a pizza-making tenderfoot, opened Papa's Pizza on Fifth Avenue in Bay Ridge a year ago. "We put this menu together with stuff from all over," he said. "And where I come from—Franklin Square—they make grandma pie."

Initially, Brooklynites were wary of the alien pizza. "But every week we sell more and more," Napoli said. "The people, they love it."

AUTHOR'S NOTE: Sadly, grandma pizza has not hit Manhattan full force. But when I want my grandma pizza fix in Gotham, I head to Maffei Pizza, on the southeast corner of 22nd Street and Sixth Avenue (212-929-0949). The dough is light, they go easy on the mozzarella and the canned tomatoes are just sweet enough.

🍴 GINO'S OF LONG BEACH | Dave Pasternack, chef/coowner of

the Italian seafood restaurant Esca in Times Square, has been living in and around Long Beach his whole life. Dave knows his food, so when he talks about pizza, I listen. This is what he says about Gino's, located on the main street of Long Beach, a three-block walk to a stunning Atlantic Ocean beach. "I tell everyone in New York. Buy a round-trip train ticket to Long Beach. The ticket includes a beach pass, so it's a really good deal. Get off the train, and walk across the street to Gino's for a slice. Nice, crisp crust, not too thick and not too much cheese. That's what kills most pizza these days, an overdose of cheese." Dave was, as usual, right about Gino's regular slice. Even better was the grandma slice, which had even less cheese to go with a sweet tomato sauce. With its delicate, slightly oily crust and fresh mozzarella, the Crostino slice would have been the best of the bunch, if they hadn't ruined it with slivers of raw garlic. Raw garlic should never go on a pizza. That's one of the ten commandments of pizza-making.

Gino's of Long Beach
16 West Park Avenue, Long Beach, NY, 516-432-8193.
RATING: 🍕 🍕 🍕

KING UMBERTO'S | King Umberto's, a sprawling pizzeria restaurant right next to Belmont Racetrack, snakes through several dining rooms with names like Toscannini and Giannani, and just might be the best conventional gas-oven pizzeria on Long Island. Nicola Cesarano makes the mother of all grandma pizzas. It's a thin, light, crisp masterpiece, with a crust that's just oily enough. The grandma pie here is addictive. It lingers in your taste memory long after the last slice disappears. Cesarano makes the grandma pizza in a special Marsal & Son Oven, which burns 100°F hotter than regular gas pizza ovens. King Umberto's regular Neapolitan slice is first-rate, as is the Sicilian pizza here. The Sicilian pizza has a much thicker crust than the grandma pie, but it is still surprisingly light.

One other unique touch at King Umberto's: There are many red rugs throughout the restaurant with gray lettering that reads, "King Umberto's Real Italian Real Good." In fact, given its proximity to Belmont, I would bet anyone even money that King Umberto's leads the nation in pizza rugs and grandma slices.

King Umberto's
1343 Hempstead Turnpike (at the corner of Mitchan Avenue), Elmont, NY, 516-352-3232.
RATING: 🍕 🍕 🍕 🍕 (grandma pizza)   🍕 🍕 🍕 (Neapolitan pizza)

LA VERA | New York pizza aficionados speak in reverential tones about the crispy, fresh slices at the legendary slice joint, Gloria, in what is now Flushing Queens Chinatown. Gloria closed a few years ago after thirty years of giving serious pizza mouth burns to pizza-loving New Yorkers. The patriarchal figure at Gloria was Lucio Mosco, affectionately known as El Presidente. His son Joe now owns Agata & Valentina, the gourmet grocery on the Upper East Side. So when Joe told me I could get a slice of Gloria-ous pizza at La Vera, his brother-in-law's place in New Hyde Park, I called up my 85-year-old cousin Terry, who lives there, and told her I would pick her up in an hour (Terry's up for a food adventure anytime).

We drove to La Vera, located in a strip mall across the street from Eddie's, a seminal Long Island bar/pizzeria. I ordered a regular slice and a grandma slice. The regular slice had a nice crispy edge and not too much slightly brown and bubbly Grande mozzarella. I felt like I had channeled a Gloria slice. The grandma slice had a slightly bready and oily crust, a modest cheese covering and some fresh seasoned tomatoes. I loved it, and asked Terry, who grew up in the Bronx in a kosher household, what she thought of the grandma slice. "Ed, dear. It's very good," she said, "But I hope they didn't call it grandma pizza just for me."

La Vera
2085 Hillside Avenue (at Denton Avenue), New Hyde Park, NY, 516-355-2278.
RATING: 🍕🍕

NICK'S PIZZA | See page 348.

SALVATORE'S | Salvatore's coowner, Fred Lacagnina, was born into one of the first families of American pizza. His great uncle Patsy Lancieri opened the original Patsy's Pizzeria in New York's East Harlem in 1933. Seventy-five years later Lacagnina is turning out gorgeous pies baked in a coal-fired brick oven for about three and a half minutes at 800°F. Lacagnina takes no shortcuts. He makes his own mozzarella every day, roasts his own peppers and uses fresh Israeli basil on his Margherita pies. Here's how he describes his perfect crust: "It has to be well done, with black spots on bottom, thin but not paper thin, hard on outside, softer on the inside, with nice air holes throughout the crust." Lacagnina proofs his dough in wood boxes in the fridge for twenty-four hours. "I learned the hard way. If you don't use wooden boxes, the dough doesn't come out right." His regular pies are sensational, and his white pies, made with the fresh mozzarella, garlic and grated Romano, are very fine as well. Just don't make the mistake I did the last time I was there, when I listened to our warm and

friendly waitperson, who recommended we add ricotta cheese to our white pie. The result was a white, blobby mess of a pie, with enough ricotta cheese to top ten pizzas. But if you manage to avoid that pitfall, you will surely have a peak pizza-eating experience at Salvatore's. Somewhere up above, Patsy Lancieri is smiling down on Fred Lacagnina, admiring his great-nephew's handiwork.

Salvatore's
124 Shore Road, Port Washington, NY, 516-883-8457.
RATING:

 SAM'S | Out in the Hamptons, the far southeastern edge of Long Island, it can be hard to wade through the BMWs and Jaguars to find some real food. That's why Sam's is so important. For more than fifty years, Sam's has given locals and interlopers alike a place to go in East Hampton for pizza and Italian-American staples like spaghetti and meatballs and chicken parmigiana. When you walk into Sam's you feel like you're leaving the pretentious Hamptons far behind. It's kind of dark, even though the menu says, "The lights are always on at Sam's." You sit at wooden booths surrounded by paneling on the walls. The pizza at Sam's comes out of a conventional gas-fired oven. It has a thin, browned crust that is uniquely flaky, and flaky is not a word that immediately comes to mind when I'm thinking about pizza crusts. The cheeses on a standard pie here are aged mozzarella and Romano, which lends the pie a little salty tang. I don't know who Rose is, but if it was her idea to put sausage, fresh tomatoes and bacon on the pizza called Rose's Midnight Special, she has a fine palate. At Sam's they have lots of specialty pizzas with toppings like shrimp, clams and andouille sausage. I've just never had occasion to order one.

Sam's
36 Newtown Lane (just north of Montauk Highway), East Hampton, NY, 631-324-5900, www.samsrestaurant.com.
RATING:

🍴 **UMBERTO'S** | The original Umberto's, on Jericho Turnpike in New Hyde Park, Long Island, is the friendly local slice place we would all be lucky to have in our neighborhood. The countermen seem to know everyone who comes in and, even if they don't, they still treat you like a regular. The last time I was there every customer was ordering Sicilian slices, which are good enough, certainly, but not the best that Umberto's has to offer. My favorite Umberto's slice is the grandma slice, a thin-crusted rectangular slice topped with whole-milk mozzarella and a blend of canned crushed tomatoes and chopped fresh plum tomatoes (see Erica Marcus's piece on page 140). But not far behind is the grandma slice topped with fresh mozzarella and diced tomatoes, which many of the locals eat at room temperature. I like it heated in one of Umberto Corteo's gas ovens for a minute and a half or so, so that the mozzarella just starts to melt. Umberto's Neapolitan-style slices are excellent, too.

Umberto's
633 Jericho Turnpike, New Hyde Park, NY, 516-437-7698.
RATING: 🍕🍕🍕🍕 (grandma pizza)   🍕🍕🍕 (Neapolitan and Sicilian pizza)

NOTE: I can't vouch for the other Umberto's that have cropped up all over Long Island.

CHAPTER
6

*New Jersey
Pizza*

NEW JERSEY PIZZA

A STATE EITHER HAS THE PIZZA MAGIC OR IT DOESN'T. NEW JERSEY has it. In fact, if you were a pizza history doctoral candidate, you would be spending a lot of time in the Garden State. Sciortino's opened in Perth Amboy with a coal-fired brick oven in 1934, and when urban renewal forced it to close in 2003, there was a major town uproar. Before that, there was Trenton pizza, called tomato pies. Papa's, which is still going strong, opened in 1912. Joe's Tomato Pies opened before that, in 1910. It just closed two years ago. DeLorenzo's Tomato Pies opened in 1936 and moved to its current location in 1947.

New Jersey is home to many pizza taverns and bars and grills, where families, bowlers and softball players all gather to eat pizza and recount the day or the evening's exploits. Every town seems to have its favorite local tavern pizza. There's Kinchley's and Nelly's in Ramsey, the Reservoir Tavern in Boonton, the Star Tavern in West Orange and the Top Road Tavern in West Trenton. I haven't tried them all, but I have listened to devotees wax poetic about the pizza found in all of them.

There are other pizza traditions in Jersey as well. There are the Jersey Shore mainstays such as Vic's in Bradley Beach and Pete and Elda's/Carmen's in Neptune, where the crust is thin, the patrons are tan and the hair-dos are high. Every Jersey Shore town seems to have a local favorite.

Though Sciortino's is now closed, coal-fired, brick-oven pizza is alive and well in New Jersey at Grimaldi's in Hoboken. DeLorenzo's and Papa's are still going strong, though each of them has replaced its coal oven with the conventional gas-fired variety.

And until very recently, as the *Asbury Park Press* restaurant critic Andrea Clurfeld laments, there was even purist Neapolitan pizza at Anthony Mangieri's Una Pizza Napoletana in Point Pleasant Beach, which Clurfeld once described to me as the single best bite of food she's had in New Jersey. That's high praise from someone who has spent the last twenty years eating out in the Garden State. Mangieri has moved his particular brand of pizza fanaticism to New York's East Village, and Clurfeld is still in mourning as we go to press.

Long live Jersey pizza, or tomato pies, or pizza Napoletana, or whatever the Garden State pie men want to call it. Long live Papa's, DeLorenzo's and the Reservoir Tavern. May your crust always be puffy, chewy and pliant, and may you live to fight off the chains for another fifty years.

Frank Sinatra and Pizza

Judging by the number of pizzerias displaying photos and really bad watercolor portraits of Frank Sinatra, Ol' Blue Eyes must have been on a bizarre all-pizza diet for the first fifty years of his life. Sinatra was born in Hoboken, New Jersey, so it's easy to imagine that in his youth he developed a taste for good pizza in both neighboring New York City and his home state. Once he moved to southern California (first Los Angeles, then Palm Springs) he, like many before and after him, discovered that there was not a decent slice of pizza to be had in the Southland, as the local newscasters call the Los Angeles basin. So according to pizza lore (and whom you choose to believe), Sinatra was forced to take one of three actions: Send his plane and a couple of lesser members of the Rat Pack to pick up pizza at places like Sally's in New Haven and Patsy's in East Harlem; have pizza shipped from the East Coast whenever he had a craving; or show up unannounced after a concert somewhere on the east coast and eat pizza 'til the wee small hours of the morning. If all of the above were true, and if Sinatra really ate in every pizzeria that has his photo or likeness on a wall, he would have looked like Pavarotti, and he wouldn't have looked so good in his trademark pullover sweater.

TRENTON PIZZA

MAURIZIO DeRosa, ONE OF MY PIZZA ORACLES, WAS DRIVING LIKE A
Neapolitan (he was, in fact, born and raised in Naples), which is to say we made
great time driving to Trenton. DeRosa, a former restaurateur and Italian wine
salesman, and the proud recipient of a doctorate in accounting, was accompany-
ing me to one of the oldest notches on the Pizza Belt, Trenton, the capital of New
Jersey and a sad example of Northeastern urban blight. It used to be said that,
"Trenton makes, and the world takes," because of all the manufacturing that went
on there. Not any more. The loss of hundreds of thousands of manufacturing jobs
and the resulting diminished tax base and white flight have left Trenton in rather
dire economic shape. But in spite of it all, Trenton's pizza culture, almost as old as
New York's, has remained intact, serving state office workers, teachers and expats
who come back for the pizza much the same way people come back for the food
shopping on Arthur Avenue in the Bronx.

DeRosa, a Neapolitan pizza purist (see page 39) and a keen and extremely
astute student of culinary cultures, had invited along his friend Giancarlo
Quadalti, one of New York City's best Italian chefs and coowner of three successful and very fine Italian restaurants in New York, including one, Celeste, that
serves better-than-creditable Neapolitan pizza. Quadalti has strong opinions
about Italian food, and though he's from Emilia Romagna, a region not known for
its pizza, he's been making and eating pizza for twenty years.

We arrived in the heart of Trenton's Little Italy, called Chambersburg,
shortly after 11:00 A.M. I had called DeLorenzo's at 8:30 that morning and made
a reservation for 11:15. DeLorenzo's is an idiosyncratic place. It takes reservations
only for Friday lunch, has no bathroom and let's just say it's never been known for
customer service.

When we arrived at DeLorenzo's shortly after eleven, the door was locked.
We parked the car, and I could see that Giancarlo and Maurizio were fascinated to

experience an utterly Italian neighborhood in a decaying city. "This place is so pure, so isolated," noted Maurizio as we passed old signs for long-defunct Italian restaurants and shops. "I feel like I'm hurtling back in time." Since it was clear that DeLorenzo's was not open yet, I decided to try to get a new flash card for my digital camera. Right next door to DeLorenzo's was a camera shop, Jimmy's. I was in luck.

We walked into the shop and found ourselves staring at a signed copy of an oversized poster of the old pop lounge singer Vic Damone. "Good morning, gentlemen," said the dapper man who was clearly the proprietor. Jimmy's was filled with bric-a-brac and piles of slightly dusty disposable cameras, next to a neat stack of videocassettes of movies old enough to indicate that a certain premodern sensibility ruled the day at Jimmy's Camera. "My name's Jimmy DeLorenzo. What can I do for you today?" I replied, "We're just waiting for the pizzeria to open, and I need a new flash card for this camera." Mr. DeLorenzo responded, "I don't sell any of that digital stuff. I never got into it; it's just too expensive. But you've come to the right spot for pizza. That's my family's joint, my brother's place," he said, pointing next door. "We've been making pizza in Trenton since 1936. Made my share of pies before I opened the camera shop. I used to go to the market every day. We'd buy fresh tomatoes for the sauce. Walk around the neighborhood. Hardly any Italians here any more. We got everybody here now, Latinos, blacks. It's all right with me, though. Hey, they're just like my family was when we first got here. I'm sure my brother will open up in a few minutes. Then I want you to come back and tell me how you liked it."

We walked into an Italian bakery, the last one standing in Chambersburg. I ordered a cannoli. The counterwoman filled the cannoli to order, always a good sign, though most of the baked goods looked pretty generic. We wandered into what must have been the last Italian produce market. But instead of escarole and broccoli rabe there were plaintains, mangoes and huge bags of rice. There was also frozen squid and *baccala* (salt cod) for sale. I asked a young T-shirt-clad man behind the counter when the market opened. "This market has been here since 1928. First it was an Italian market, now it's a Hispanic market, and if this becomes a Polish neighborhood, this will be a Polish market. We adapt as the neighborhood changes. It's the only way we survive."

We wandered back to the pizzeria, which was now open, and ordered a couple of pies. There are three DeLorenzo's working there these days, Gary and Eileen Amico (born DeLorenzo) and their son Sam. Eileen took our order: two tomato pies, one plain and one with mozzarella and sausage, and I wandered over to the small counter to watch Sam and Gary make the pizza. They stretched the fresh dough and then, unlike almost every other pizzeria I have been to, they put the hand-sliced cheese on the pizza first, then added the sauce with a spoon. When I asked why they did it that way, Sam replied, "It keeps the crust crisper." The pizza was eminently satisfying and delicious in a homey sort of way. The crust was thoroughly baked and very crisp, though not ultrathin, and the cheese formed a second, molten crust below the tomato sauce. The fennel sausage tasted homemade. I looked over to Maurizio and Giancarlo for their reactions to this decidedly not-Neapolitan pie. They were smiling and eating contentedly. "I like it," Giancarlo spoke up. "It's honest food. It tastes like it was made by someone who cares about what they do."

After pizza we went back to Jimmy's. It was now one o'clock. I bought a disposable camera. Jimmy DeLorenzo smiled and said, "It's my first sale of the day. That's okay. It's Good Friday, and not too many people buy cameras or film on Good Friday."

We drove to the other DeLorenzo's, operated by another branch of the DeLorenzo family. I once asked Sam Amico if the two pizza-making branches of the family got along. "We get along okay. I mean we only see each other at funerals, weddings, things like that. We say hello and good-bye." The other DeLorenzo's is a modern, generic-looking restaurant. The crust there was slightly thinner, but none of us liked the pizza as much, or the feel of the place, for that matter. I wandered back into the kitchen. There was a machine stamping out dough—not a good sign. In my experience, good pizza is entirely a handmade food. When I returned to the table, Giancarlo whispered to me, "This pizza, this place, it's not for me. I like the other place much better."

Our last stop was Papa's, which opened in 1912. We ordered a pizza and asked our teenaged waiter if the owner was around. Ten minutes later Abie, a man who looked to be in his seventies, wandered out of the kitchen with our pizza. As we started to eat, Giancarlo said, "This is real food, honest food, it smells real, feels real, looks real. I see a lot of heart in this place." The pizza is similar to DeLorenzo's, with a little less cheese and a little thinner crust. I asked Abie to tell me about the pizza. He said, "It's not pizza. It's tomato pie."

He told me that he took over the place from his father-in-law. "Has the pizza changed over the years?" I asked. Abie replied, "You did it again. It's not pizza, it's tomato pie." He explained that the ovens used to be coal-fired, and that they changed over in the fifties to gas. Other than that, the pizza—I mean, tomato pie—is the same.

I asked Abie if he ever thought about getting out of the pizza-making business. He said, "You know about thirty years ago a nice fellow came in and offered to buy this place. He said that he had a few pizzerias in the Midwest called Domino's. He seemed like a nice fella, but we didn't want to sell. Making this 'pizza,' in this way, is what we do. This is what we're all about. I don't know if it makes us special or not. I just know it makes us feel good to make it this way."

DeLorenzo's Tomato Pies
530 Hudson Street, Trenton, NJ, 609-695-9534
RATING: ❀ ❀ ❀
1007 Hamilton Avenue, Trenton, NJ, 609-393-2952.
RATING: ❀ ❀

Papa's Championship Tomato Pies
931 Chambers Street, Trenton, NJ, 609-394-7437.
RATING: ❀ ❀ ❀

Pizza Love Affair

~ *Andrea Clurfeld* ~

*Andrea Clurfeld (Andy to her friends) is the restaurant critic for the Asbury
Park Press. I will forever be in her debt for turning me on to Anthony
Mangieri. Andy knows a good pie when she tastes one.*

I FIRST LEARNED OF PIZZA IN THE BACK OF A '58 VW BUS. THAT'S
what it was called—a bus, not a van. It was red and black. The pizza was red and
white, take-out from a joint in Rockland County, NY. Circa 1959, it probably tasted
like red and white, too, but it sure thrilled the 5-year-old tomboy who heretofore
had hungered for nothing but Mickey Mantle and a Yankees World Series.

Change scene to Jersey, where pizza is religion. Folks worship at DeLorenzo's
Tomato Pies in Trenton, Federici's in Freehold, Kinchley's in Ramsey, Vic's in
Bradley Beach, or one of a dozen other sources for destination pies. (Definition: Pies
not picked up on the way home from work—that's what a strip-mall, soggy-crust
pizzeria is for—but eaten during a dedicated pilgrimage.) Jersey's pie of choice has a
super-thin crust, cracker-like, yet it oozes marinara and mozzarella.

I leaned toward DeLorenzo's, occasionally Vic's, but I'd cheat on the locals
at John's, on Bleecker Street in New York City. Until, that is, Anthony Mangieri
opened Una Pizza Napoletana in Point Pleasant Beach.

Anthony makes pizza like the best make it in Naples. His oven is wood-
fired. He makes his own dough, natural rise; his only other ingredients are buffalo
mozzarella, San Marzano tomatoes, garlic, oregano, basil, olive oil and Sicilian

sea salt. It's his crust that gets to me: earthy, gutsy, blackened and blistered in spots. I now live in a one-pie world.

Mangieri is moving Una Pizza Napoletana to the East Village in New York. At least it's not Seattle.

DeLorenzo's Tomato Pies, See page 155. Vintage tomato pie, with hidden cheese and ultra-thin crust.

Una Pizza Napoletana, 349 East 12th Street (between First and Second Avenues), New York, NY, 212-477-9950. The purist's pie—wood-fired, with a blistered, blackened crust and minimalist toppings. The undisputed champ.

Vic's, 60 Main Street, Bradley Beach, NJ, 732-774-8225. Very 1950s, with eau de garlic in the air, a scent thicker, really, than the pie's crust.

A Jersey Boy's Paper Route Pizza Picnic

Willie Reale

> *Television writer and playwright Willie Reale is the only contributor to A Slice of Heaven who has won a MacArthur Genius Grant. Although he would like to think otherwise, it was not for his considerable culinary talents (he won it for his work with theater and adolescents at the 52nd Street Project).*

IN NEW JERSEY, THE GARDEN STATE, I DELIVERED THE *BERGEN Record* through the winter of 1968. I was ten. It was a lousy route, hilly and exposed. On Fridays I would collect for the week's service, keeping track of the accounts with cards on a metal ring. The ring was cold against my wrist that Friday. I'd gotten a late start, it was dark and cold and I was hungry. I'd finished my collections and the change in my pocket pulsed the dull metallic jangle of a slinky as I began the mile walk home. As I passed the green-and-orange neon heralding Park Pizza, I saw the hand-painted card in the steamed-up window promising: Slice 15 Cents. It hit me: I am a working man on the road. I have money, not burning, but certainly wearing a hole in my pocket. I can take myself to dinner on my own dime (and nickel). And so I did. Except for the fact that I will remember it until the day I die, the slice was unexceptional.

CHAPTER
7

*Connecticut
Pizza*

New Haven Pizza

I'VE BEEN EATING NEW HAVEN PIZZA SINCE I WAS ELEVEN, WHEN my parents and I went to visit my brother at law school. Since then, I have used any excuse to eat at Pepe's or Sally's or Modern or Paul's, which is now, sadly enough, closed (more about that later). All summer vacations on Cape Cod occasion a trip to a New Haven pizzeria, and blessed be the highway planner who put in a Longwharf Theatre exit on I-95, mere minutes away from Wooster Street, home to three of the best pizzerias in America: Frank Pepe Pizzeria Napoletana, The Spot (now owned by the Pepe family) and Sally's Apizza, where Sal Consiglio's widow, Flo, and her three children are carrying on brilliantly. How serious are New Havenites about pizza? So serious, reports Nicholas Dawidoff on page 173, that high school newspapers in the area have pizza columnists.

An immigrant Neapolitan bread baker named Frank Pepe opened his first pizzeria in 1925 at what is now The Spot. Seven years later the Spadacenta family opened Paul's Apizza in East Haven. "Apizza," by the way, was just a bit of bastardized Neapolitan dialect that made its way to the New World via New Haven. Two years later, in 1934, State Street Apizza opened (it's now called Modern Apizza). Frank Pepe moved to Pepe's current location in 1936. Two years later, in 1938, Frank's nephew Sal Consiglio opened Sally's down the block from his uncle. In 1981, more than a decade after Frank's death, his family bought The Spot from the family that owned it, so now Pepe's has two adjoining locations. Wooster Street had its own version of Murderer's Row, three of the greatest pizzerias in the world, within a couple of blocks. As time went by, other coal-fired, brick-oven pizzerias, such as Paul's and Tolli's and Westville Apizza, opened on (and off) Wooster Street, in New Haven.

Thirteen years ago the Brü Rm. at Bar, the first New Haven microbrewery pizzeria, opened, serving the characteristic oblong pies cut into irregularly shaped pieces and served on metal trays. Purists complained that Bar used a gas-fired brick oven, and wondered aloud if mashed potatoes was a suitable topping for a pizza. But the Yalie community totally embraced the idea of drinking "ALTernative Blonde" ale and eating mashed potato and bacon pizza surrounded by exposed brick walls and copper beer vats.

The New Haven pizza culture, featuring stunningly good pizza topped with just tomato sauce and a sprinkling of Romano cheese, or freshly shucked clams, or just mozzarella and fresh fennel sausage, made in coal- or oil-fired brick ovens, is under attack. Sally's is still going strong, but Frank Pepe's legacy is being threatened by internal family warfare. Nine grandsons, grandnieces and grandnephews now run the two Pepe's locations. Though the pizza is still very fine at Pepe's (and at The Spot next door) what will happen in the future is anyone's guess. Nick Nuzzo sold Modern Apizza to Bill Pustari sixteen years ago, and he and his wife, Maria Teresa, continue to turn out excellent pizzas from their oil-fueled oven. Paul's in East Haven, run by Sue and Paul Spadacenta, the son of the founder, has recently been sold to people who—gasp!—threw out the coal-fired brick oven and opened up a conventional by-the-slice place with a regular gas-burning pizza oven. Paul's pizza was every bit as good as the pizza on Wooster Street, and Paul Spadacenta was the only one-armed pie man I've ever seen.

Other places like Tolli's, Westville Apizza and Palm Beach Apizza have gone out of business or switched to conventional gas-fired pizza ovens. It may be time to break out the Save New Haven Pizza bumper stickers.

THE BEST PIZZA
IN THE WORLD

Ruth Reichl

Gourmet *editor-in-chief and former* New York Times *restaurant critic Ruth Reichl is the author of the memoirs* Tender at the Bone *and* Comfort Me with Apples. *After repeatedly telling me she didn't know if she had anything to say about pizza, Ruth came up with this lovely pizza memory.*

THE BEST PIZZA IN THE WORLD, AS EVERYBODY KNOWS, NO LONGER exists. It is the pizza of your childhood. That first magical bite sets the flavor, which you spend the rest of your life attempting to recapture.

In my case the pizza literally no longer exists. It was served at Phil Baker's, which was attached to a bowling alley in Norwalk, Connecticut. The fragrance, as it neared your table, was intoxicating—the sweetness of the tomato set off by the slight sharpness of the cheese and then, something else. Yeast perhaps . . . or a bit of basil? I'm not sure. The crust was thin, yet so crisp that the wedge did not crumple when you picked it up, and you could put the point right into your mouth. It was wonderful stuff and when they tore Phil Baker's down to make room for the new Route 7 (which went right through the dining room), my brother and I were despondent.

My family moved on to the next great Norwalk pizza place, The Blue Moon. It was a tavern near the railroad station, on the wrong side of the tracks, and part of the fun of being there was the soupçon of danger. Inside it smelled like beer, and one of those signs with the waterfall flowed endlessly on. Big waitresses with big hair and crepe soles on their shoes served pizza that was almost as good

as the one at Phil Baker's. But the last time I was there the waitress—she still had big hair and crepe soles—looked at me silently for a minute or two. "Oh, Hon," she said at last, "we haven't made pizza here for twenty years."

You can get similar pizzas at that famous place in New Haven—you know the one I mean. I'm always happy to snaggle a slice, but it never makes me completely happy. It tastes good, but it's lacking a certain something: It's just not seasoned with nostalgia.

FRANK PEPE PIZZERIA NAPOLETANA | Among pizza

cognoscenti, the whispers were getting louder. "Pepe's is going downhill fast," said my brother's friend Alan. "The last time I went to Pepe's, the pizza was just not that good," my brother Mike said with an all-knowing tone informed by more than forty years of eating white-clam, sausage-and-mozzarella and plain tomato pies. "Ed, you gotta find out what's going on there."

So I forced myself to drive up to Pepe's one gorgeous early summer day in 2004 and ordered a medium clam pie, a medium sausage and mozzarella and a medium tomato pie, my three litmus-test pies for New Haven pizzerias. I wanted to order a medium bacon-and-clam pie without mozzarella, but decided four pizzas was a little excessive. My waitress was the effervescent Nancy Purificato, who knows just a little bit about New Haven pizza. She worked as a waitress at Modern Apizza for ten years before moving to Pepe's some sixteen years ago. I asked her about the downhill reports. "Come on, the pizza's still great here," she said with a knowing half smile. Do all the owners get along? "I have no idea. You'll have to ask them."

She was right about the pizza. The pies were all exemplary. The clam pie was perfect in its simplicity: fresh topneck clams, garlic, Romano cheese and a little olive oil. The sausage-and-mozzarella pie had a gloriously pliant crust and chunks of locally sourced fennel sausage.

Even the tomato pie, which I usually order only at Sally's unless I'm engaged in serious pizza research, was pretty darn fine. Maybe the dough wasn't as soft as usual, or maybe the oven was too hot, because the crust wasn't quite as good as it normally is.

But these pies were still worthy of the Pizza Hall of Fame.

I spotted Gary Bimonte, one of the owners and the managing partner of Pepe's. Bimonte, bespectacled and in his forties, has the gut of a man who enjoys the product of his work. He sat down with me over a pitcher of birch beer, made by the local soda maker Foxon Park. It's not the greatest birch beer, but when you come to New Haven and have a pizza at Pepe's, you simply must have Foxon Park.

Gary had been working on and off at Pepe's for a long time. Before Frank Pepe died, in 1969, he told Gary, "Don't use your hands. Use your brain." Gary was nine at the time, and though he gave college a shot, it was clear that Gary was more comfortable working with his hands. "I like punching a clock," he told me. Gary has worked every position at Pepe's over the years, from pie man to clamshucker to waiter to manager.

The young Frank Pepe was called "Old Reliable" because if he was sleeping in his family's apartment above the shop and someone called to him to come down and make a pizza at two in the morning, he would do it. Gary Bimonte is not so young and not so accommodating. "This place is very demanding. I'm tired. I've been doing this for a long time, maybe too long."

It was not clear whether Bimonte was tired from the work involved in the day-to-day running of Pepe's, or tired from something else, namely the stress he came under from being one of nine relatives (seven siblings and two aunts) who were partners in a family business. He had just come from an owners' meeting. I asked him what happened, and he just shook his head. "It's like any other family business. Everyone has their own agenda, and their own ideas about how we should run things here, and how we should grow the business. The trouble is everyone is afraid that they're going to be the one that kills the goose that lays the golden egg." I asked him about his grandfather, about the past and future of Pepe's. "You gotta talk to my cousin Francis about that stuff. He's the historian and dreamer in the family."

Francis Rosselli, unlike his cousin, was thin, angular, wiry and intense. We met one morning as he and Gary were fixing the wheels on one of the double-decker carts that transport the dough back and forth from the ovens to the kitchen. He seemed to relish every particular of his grandfather's life story. "Frank Pepe came to New Haven from Maiori, which is just south of Naples, when he was sixteen. He had learned how to bake bread in a local bakery there. When he came over, he didn't know how to read or write. He married a tenacious, willful woman, Filamena, who did read and write. My grandfather did some factory work when he first got to New Haven, which he hated.

"He went back to Italy to fight in World War I for his native country. When he came back he worked for some bread bakers—Apicella, who had two bakeries, one on Hamilton, the other on Chapel and Grand. He opened a bread bakery in what is now The Spot, on Wooster Street. He didn't use the store-front. He had a horse cart and went through the neighborhood selling bread. Because of his illiteracy, he couldn't notate who bought what, so he decided to make and sell pizza, something he had learned to do back in Maiori. So he piled the pizzas on his head and went around selling them. He also put tables in the bakery and started selling pizzas right there. At the time he made only one pizza, with grated cheese, tomato and anchovy—what the Neapolitans call a marinara. The official opening date of the pizzeria/bakery was June 16, 1925. The Boccamiello family owned the lot where Frank's bakery was, and they kicked him out to start up their pizzeria, which they called The Spot. Frank then opened in our current location in 1936, right next door to The Spot. In the alleyway between the two pizzerias, Boccamiello's nephew Bear would open clams and sell them on the half shell to passersby. Frank decided to sell freshly shucked clams from local waters on the half shell at the pizzeria. Eventually, he decided to experiment with putting the clams on the pizza. In the old days we would use one dozen for a small clam pie, two dozen for a medium clam pie, and three dozen for a large clam pie. After a while we started chopping up the clams. It was the only way Frank could afford to put clams on pizza."

It's been thirty-five years since Old Reliable, Frank Pepe, passed on to that great pizzeria in the sky, and from the way both Francis Rosselli and Gary Bimonte tell it, there's been very little filial harmony in that time. Frank Pepe was both a craftsman and a canny businessperson. Gary seems to have inherited the business genes, while Francis is the artistic dreamer. Francis says, "What I'm passionate about when it comes to pizza is the creative element. I'm a Renaissance musician by training, and maybe as a result I have a different vision of our pizza. I believe there should be a complete adherence to freshness. I don't want to say there's been a cutting of corners, but eventually something has to give here. I want my passion to drive this business instead of drudgery and the cashing of checks every week. We still make a great pizza here. I just want to make sure we'll still be making the best pie at Pepe's ten years from now. My grandfather did everything by hand. He was a true artisan. I want to make sure his spirit is alive in every pie."

POSTSCRIPT: A month after my talks with Francis and Gary, I went to Pepe's to look at some photos. I cleared my visit with Francis, the designated keeper of the family lore. I arrived one perfect summer evening and asked for Gary. When I told him that I had spoken to Francis the week before about the photos, he said, "That's interesting, because Francis resigned from the business last week. Nobody has heard from him in a week."

I don't know what this all means for Pepe's future, but I had a superb white-clam pie as I pondered the question.

Frank Pepe's Pizzeria Napoletana
157 Wooster Street, New Haven, CT, 203-865-5762.
RATING: ⊛

MODERN APIZZA | Many veteran New Haven pizza eaters (those who have eaten one thousand or more pies in their lives) say that Modern is where they go most often when they need their New Haven pizza fix. Why? Not because it's better than the Wooster Street joints. No, they go to Modern because it's open for lunch six days a week. In fact, Modern opens at 11:00 A.M. six days a week (3:00 P.M. on Sunday), so if you're a late riser, you can have freshly baked pizza for breakfast or brunch, which to me is sheer heaven. Folks also choose Modern because the line, if there is one, moves a lot faster than at other pizzerias. Now of course these two factors would not be compelling reasons to go to Modern if the pizza wasn't up to snuff. But Modern, which opened in 1934 as State Street Apizza, makes a very, very fine pizza. Its beautiful pies play in the same league as Pepe's, Sally's and The Spot's. Bill Pustari, who bought Modern in 1988, has been making pizza since he was thirteen, when he walked into his local pizzeria in Norwalk, Connecticut, and was told to make his own pie because the pizzaiolo was on break. Pustari fires his oil-fueled brick oven up to a thousand degrees, which produces a lovely crust with little char spots. My favorite pies at Modern are the simple tomato pie; the Margherita, made with fresh mozzarella from Liuzzi's in North Haven; the white pie; and a mozzarella-and-sausage pie made with sausage from Lamberti's butcher shop. The tomato pie is pristine, dotted with pecorino Romano. Sometimes Modern's pie men put too much cheese on the regular pies made with aged Grande mozzarella from Wisconsin, so ask your waitperson for a pie made with fresh mozzarella, light on the cheese. If Pustari only used fresh clams on his clam pie, Modern would be the perfect New Haven pizzeria.

Modern Apizza
874 State Street, New Haven, CT, 203-776-5306, www.modernapizza.com.
RATING:

SALLY'S APIZZA | See page 350.

New Haven Pizza

Nicholas Dawidoff

I asked New Haven resident, writer and "This American Life" contributor Jack Hitt to weigh in on the pizza in his fair city. Selfless gent that he is, he demurred, telling me that New Haven born-and-bred writer Nicholas Dawidoff, author of The Catcher was a Spy: The Mysterious Life of Moe Berg *and* The Fly Swatter, *a Pulitzer Prize finalist, was the most passionate and eloquent person he knew on the subject. Dawidoff went back to New Haven and looked in on his childhood tomato-pie haunts.*

I WAS ONCE THE EDITOR OF A HIGH SCHOOL NEWSPAPER IN NEW Haven, Connecticut, that counted among its most valued contributors a pizza columnist. His name was Steven Palluotto, and around the time he was pressed into this particular branch of journalistic service, it came to my attention that when American newspaper editors plan their coverage, they generally forgo the pizza beat. I could understand why they all backed off. New Haven pizza is like Maine lobster, Gulf shrimp, Gilroy garlic or Florida sunshine: you can get something like it elsewhere, but none compares with the original. And in Steven Palluotto, we had someone whose ecstatic appreciation of his subject was as singular as the pizzas themselves.

When I think back on my youthful interactions with Palluotto, early Monday mornings come to mind. That was the time when he'd return to school fresh off a weekend of festive meals with his large extended Italian family, and regale us into submission with accounts of the many delectables prepared by his mother, a sensational cook with particular gifts in the realms of pasta and shellfish. Steven ate, in his own words, "like an anaconda," and was an ample teenager—beginning in eighth grade he wrestled the unlimited class for the high school varsity—a fellow whose early physical proportion reflected his broader existence as a person of precocious gusto and appetites. He had a heavy, affable face with a dimpled chin, and a great affection for the works of Machiavelli—which perhaps explains his ritual fondness for Monday morning victual assaults: "The first is to devastate them," counseled the prince-maker.

Now I wouldn't trade my own mother for anybody's, but as an impoverished, working single parent she was more concerned with getting supper on the table every night than the fact that it might taste like Chunky Soup poured over rice—which is what it often was. I used to sit there salivating as Palluotto held forth on "the liberation of flavors" in a spaghetti with homemade crab sauce, and "the succulent juices" that had "emerged" from a plate of "delicately blanched greens." Unlike the Dawidoffs, who never went out to dinner, the Palluottos were also frequent customers at Leon's, DelMonico's and New Haven's many other fine Italian restaurants, and these meals, too, Steven described with punishing elan. Yet he was most adept at liberating the juices of my mouth on those Mondays following a family pizza outing. Pepe's, Sally's, Modern—the Palluottos went to all the storied pizza joints located in and around Wooster Square, the old Neapolitan neighborhood that is the cradle of American pizza. They were also habitués of more obscure tomato-pie emporiums, most notably Tolli's in East Haven—pronounced Eas-Stave-en by the cognoscenti—about whose product Palluotto once raved "It's like heaven! Angelic! A pizza Tchaikovsky would have composed!"

I was never sure if what Palluotto intended to serve me was vicarious pleasure or utter misery, but either way it was thrilling, and so when eventually I became the school newspaper editor, an ongoing investigation by Palluotto to determine the best pizza in New Haven seemed like the kindest gesture that could be extended to our readership. In a report touched with much gravitas, and even more adverbs, he eventually went with Tolli's.

By then I had a driver's license and was able to sample his recommendations myself. Which New Haven pizzeria you prefer is a matter both personal and subjective. Frank Sinatra, for instance, used to send from New York for a Sally's pie. (This is nothing; long before Federal Express, the Wooster Square pizzerias were receiving telephone orders from former Yale students and relocated natives whose cravings led them to make arrangements with an airline to have fresh pizzas shipped as far as the West Coast.) A Sally's apiz', in the New Haven parlance, is a thin and noble creation, but I myself became a Pepe's man, done in by the tangy tomato and cheese atop the signature burn-marked and flour-dusted savory/sweet crust that Frank Pepe and his descendants have been baking in the same coal-fired white brick oven on Wooster Street since 1925.

I left New Haven after high school, and my mother no longer lives in the state, but I have several friends in New Haven who accuse me of keeping up with them only because I need an excuse to go to Pepe's. This is, of course, nonsense. Pepe's is reason enough on its own for a trip to New Haven, though I do admit that the hour-long waits in line outside in frigid winter temperatures pass more quickly when you have a little company.

After high school, in the way of the world, I lost touch with Palluotto, though I thought of him gratefully on my periodic visits back to Pepe's. Recently, however, more than twenty years since our high school graduation, we met up again for a little pizza. Palluotto, it turns out, is now in the aiding and abetting business—he has a dental practice. Other than the acquisition of a profession, a lovely wife and son, and a case of chronic heartburn, he seemed to me unchanged. That's to say that he still ate, as he said, "like an art historian," and remained much engaged with that formidable gustatory conundrum: Why should New Haven, of all places, produce such astonishingly good pizza?

Theories abound, and in the course of an eight-pizzeria tour, we reviewed the major oral literature. Most of the current thinking tends to accredit some combination of family pedigree, rigorous standards and unmatched equipment. Early in this century, a New Haven baker named Frank Pepe, lately returned to New Haven from the battlefields of Europe, flattened out a piece of bread dough, covered it with leftovers and pronounced it "the poor man's dinner." The reviews were sufficiently transporting that soon he was flogging his creations by food cart around the old neighborhood. The restaurant opened in 1925, and met with such success that in 1938, the Consiglio family down the street began using their own coal-fed, red-and-white brick oven to produce the thinner apiz'. More pizza shops soon followed. The concentration of transplanted Neapolitans around Wooster Square might not be wealthy, Palluotto explained, "but they were always very demanding about their food. The old world demanding of quality from food preserves this pizza. It's insulting if it's not good. Their pride was at stake, especially because they were in New Haven, which had Yale, where world leaders are made." In other words, it might only be *a la rustica*—rustic, peasant-style cookery—but it had better be so cunningly constructed that when you take a bite you can imagine no other food on this earth tasting so good.

From the first, the great New Haven pizzerias used only premium ingredients, as they do today. Pepe's, for instance, still relies on lush and costly San Marzano tomatoes imported from Italy, hand-made sausage and cheeses, Spanish olive oil, and fresh-shucked locally dug clams for the breathtaking "white" pie.

Techniques such as "easying" the dough are rigorously followed by the family, which disdains "boom-booming it" as they do in the less gentle New York shops. Other mysteries of preparation remain between the family and the family: "If I told you, I'd have to kill you," explains the current co-proprietor, Gary Bimonte, Frank Pepe's grandson. And then there are what no competitor can match—the original ovens. Palluotto refers to the bricks on which Pepe's and Sally's pizzas bake as "the Rosetta Stones, the sacred tiles," and even he is at a bit of a loss trying to explain the subtleties of flavor imparted by such venerable masonry.

Traveling around the city, Steven and I found that while both of us had seen a good part of the world and tasted a surfeit of pizzas while doing so, we agreed that no pizza compared to what we'd grown up with. Pepe's, Sally's, The Spot, and Modern, we determined, were still what we remembered, though the decline of Tolli's made us both sad. Reason for optimism, however, was found in a couple of more recent additions to the scene. Steven is enamored of the gauzy creations that come out of the massive brick beehive of an oven that has been installed down at Bar on Crown Street, while I discovered myself much-taken with the sausage and broccoli rabe white pie served at Amato's, hard by the Modern on State Street. Steven likes it too, and when we confronted the shop owner, Amato Bernardo, about the audacity of opening a relatively new business in what Steven and I were now affectionately calling "Pizza City," Amato explained that it was really no decision at all. He'd grown up in New Haven and then gone to live in Italy, he said, "but I come back from Italy because there's no pizza in Italy like New Haven pizza. You have to make it good to be in New Haven."

Amato's Apizza and Restaurant
858 State Street, New Haven, CT, 203-562-2760.
RATING: ⊛ ⊛ ⊛ (my rating, not Nicholas Dawidoff's)

BEYOND NEW HAVEN

ALFORNO | Baseball fans love to talk about players so gifted that they are members of the 30/30 club; that is, they hit thirty home runs and steal thirty bases in a season. Bob Zemmel thinks he might be the charter member of pizza's 30/30 club, estimating that he ate 30,000 slices of pizza before he turned thirty. After eating pizza all over the world under the guise of operating an import/export business, Zemmel opened Alforno in a nondescript shopping center. He installed a gas-fired, 600,000-BTU Brickstone oven that gives Alforno's pies the charred crust Zemmel is looking for. He uses Grande whole-milk mozzarella on his pizza, his sauce is simply crushed plum tomatoes, and he finishes his pies with a sprinkle of Sardinian pecorino Romano cheese and a squirt of olive oil. Perfectly located, it's less than two minutes off Exit 66 of Interstate 95. Alforno is extremely receptive to desperate families making urgent cell-phone orders from their cars.

Alforno
1654 Boston Post Road, Old Saybrook, CT, 860-399-4166.
RATING: ◉ ◉ ◖

MYSTIC PIZZA® | Although pizza had a strong supporting role in movies like *Do the Right Thing* and *Saturday Night Fever*, it has been the star of only one, 1987's *Mystic Pizza*, which introduced the world to Julia Roberts. Eighteen years later Roberts is a huge star, and Mystic Pizza is still turning out solid Greek-American-style pan pies. John and Chris Zelepos have taken the place over from their late father, and they still make the dough fresh every morning. I wish the Zelepos used fresh mozzarella, but maybe they are saving something for the sequel.

Mystic Pizza
56 West Main Street, Mystic, CT, 860-536-3700, www.mysticpizza.com.
RATING: ◉ ◉ ◖

CHAPTER
8

*Philadelphia,
Boston,
D.C. and
Baltimore
Pizza*

Philadelphia Pizza

WHEN I THINK OF GREAT PHILADELPHIA FOODS, I THINK OF CHEESE-steaks, pretzels, roast pork and broccoli rabe sandwiches, hoagies and butter-cakes. I don't think of pizza, which is odd, considering how Italian the city is. (Think of Rocky and Adrian in *Rocky* . . . or the city's best-known former mayor, Frank Rizzo . . . or the Italian market in South Philly.) Yet I've never heard a native Philadelphian wax rhapsodic about his hometown pizza.

This lack of pizza image has nothing to do with a shortage of pizza places in the City of Brotherly Love. There's Tacconelli's, in Port Richmond, where you have to order your pizza a day in advance. It opened in the 1920s, as a bread bak-ery, but didn't start serving pizza until 1946. And then there's Marra's in South Philly, and Alex's in Mannyunk, not to mention Joe's, Lorenzo & Son, Mama Palma's, Sam's and even Santucci's Square Pizza. Each has its fans, but none does the job of lifting Philly's status as a Pizza Belt City.

Even Philly food critics are lukewarm on the slices to be found there. *Philadelphia Daily News* restaurant critic, Craig LaBan, weighs in on page 184 and basically says Philly is not much of a pizza town. On page 185, Philadelphia born-and-raised food critic Alan Richman extols the virtues of Rizzo's, his childhood pizzeria in suburban Glenside. It seems to me there's a heck of a lot of nonchain pizza in Philly, and surely some of it must be good. It is interesting to note that LaBan lauds the virtues of Lombardi's, a New York institution that opened a branch in Philadelphia ten years ago. Another New York pizza invader, Pietro's, opened a few years ago. Pietro's tries to hide its New York roots, which are in the Angelo's/Patsy's minichain. Can you get a slice of heaven, imported or otherwise, in the City of Brotherly Love? I had to find out for myself.

LOMBARDI'S ORIGINAL PIZZA | The Philadelphia branch of Lombardi's was the first stop on our pizza tour of this city. I was with my friend Ron Stanford, who, having raised four children in Philadelphia, has eaten a lot of Philly pizza in his life. We ordered a half white and half mozzarella-tomato-and-sausage pie. We had a tough, smart and funny waitress who made up in moxie what she didn't know about Lombardi's pizza. The white half had a base of mozzarella topped by swirls of fresh ricotta, with a healthy dose of roasted garlic. On the red half the mozzarella was fresh, the tasty sausage was from a Philadelphia purveyor named Maglio's and the tomatoes were freshly strained San Marzanos. What made both halves of the pizza swing really hard was the crust. It had just the right balance of crunch and tenderness. Unused to my five-pizza-a-day regimen, Ron proceeded to eat five slices. "You'll be sorry," I told him. "I couldn't help it," he replied. "This is great pizza." And so it was.

Lombardi's Original Pizza
132 South 18th Street (off Rittenhouse Square), Philadelphia, PA, 215-564-5500, www.LombardisOriginalPizza.com.
RATING:

MARRA'S | I had a good feeling about Marra's as soon as Ron and I came upon its ancient vertical sign. Maybe it was the autographed John Travolta photo in the window. Maybe it was the moosehead that stared at us as we sat down in the back room next to the bar. It could have been our waitress, who was as warm and gracious and solicitous as a South Philly waitress could be. Or perhaps it was the picture of Salvatore and Chiarina Marra, the pizzeria's founders, that was next to the moosehead. In the end, our good feelings were justified by the fine pizza made in the gas-fired pizza oven (our waitress told us the oven was originally fueled by wood, then coal). We asked for fresh mozzarella on half, and it was very creamy mozzarella, indeed. The crust was that brown, crunchy crust I first had at Cairo's more than forty years ago on Long Island. It's the crust I will never forget.

Marra's
1734 Passyunk Avenue, Philadelphia, PA, 215-463-9249.
RATING: ⊛

 PIETRO'S | The mozzarella and sausage on Pietro's pies used to come from Frankie Cappezza of the Corona Heights Pork Store in Queens, New York, who is merely one of the greatest mozzarella and sausage makers in America. Ultimately Pietro's owner decided 180 miles round-trip was just a little too far to go for pizza fixins'. So he started buying locally and, based on the pizza I had, he's found pretty good replacements. The pizza here had a crispy, fragile crust, with plenty of height on the lip. The mozzarella could have been creamier, and the sausage was chopped into strange little chunks. I know the drive from Philadelphia to Queens can be brutal, but for Frankie's mozzarella and sausage, it's worth it.

Pietro's
1714 Walnut Street, Philadelphia, PA, 215-733-0675.
RATING: ⊛ ⊛ ⊛

Additional Locations:
121-123 South Street, Philadelphia, PA, 215-733-0675.
140 West Route 70, Evesham, NJ, 856-596-5500.

▥ TACCONELLI'S | For many pizza aficionados across the country, Tacconelli's is *the* pizzeria in Philadelphia. As I noted earlier, the Tacconelli family started baking bread in their Port Richmond location in the 1920s, and began serving pizza in 1946. Because the oil-heated oven they have there is so small, you must reserve your pizzas a day in advance. Reserving the dough is a fabulous marketing tool. It probably even makes the pizza taste better. I had a solid if unspectacular pie at the Port Richmond location a couple of years ago, so this time I opted to try the Tacconelli's recently opened in suburban south Jersey by the next generation of Tacconelli's, son Vincent and his wife, Doris. The new Tacconelli's is located in a nondescript strip mall. It has none of the shabby, chic charm of the original location. It does, however, have one distinct advantage over the original. You don't have to reserve the dough. Vincent Tacconelli installed a gas-fired Woodstone oven that can turn out 120 pies an hour. We ordered a white pie and a red pie with sausage. Both pizzas came out with a brown, crispy crust with lots of air bubbles. According to the menu, the white pizza had a refreshingly modest amount of aged mozzarella, salt, black pepper, a little soybean oil and plenty of granulated garlic. I could have done without the granulated garlic and I wish the mozzarella was fresh, but it was a fine pizza, nonetheless. The red pie had the ubiquitous (in Philadelphia, at least) Maglio sausage and a sauce Vincent claims is made from Frumani-brand canned Pennsylvania tomatoes.

Tacconelli's
450 South Lenola Road (across from the Moorestown Mall), Maple Shade, NJ, 856-638-0338.
RATING: ✹ ✹ ✹ ◖

Additional Locations:
2604 East Somerset Street, Philadelphia, PA, 215-425-4983.

A Philadelphia Restaurant Critic's Take on Pizza in Philly

Craig LaBan

Craig LaBan is the restaurant critic for the Philadelphia Daily News. He responded quickly to my request for a Philadelphia pizza correspondent. Guess he likes pizza.

WEIRD AS IT SEEMS FOR A CITY WITH SUCH A STRONG ITALIAN tradition, pizza is not Philly's strong point. In fact, one of my local favorites, Lombardi's near Rittenhouse Square, is a branch of the New York original. To my mind, they have the best combination of heat-charred, flour-dusted crust, good ingredients and fresh basil. That said, there are some other very good local pizzerias, the best most certainly being Tacconelli's in Port Richmond, where the massive 16-foot-deep brick oven occupies half the kitchen and fresh sausage (not precooked) and garlic oil give their pies an amazing zest. The distinctive crushed-tomato, no-cheese pies of nearby Trenton, most notably at DeLorenzo's, are also wonderful, but these almost constitute another food group altogether.

I grew up near Detroit, the nexus of corporate pizza. My first job was at Little Caesar's. Ann Arbor, where I went to school, is also home to the great deep-dish pies of the Cottage Inn. Imagine my wonder then to discover the pleasures of the minimalist pie in Naples, where the pizza I confronted was little more than a paper-thin round, a smear of crimson sauce and a bloom of basil. How could so much flavor exist in just two dimensions? It's an ideal I've been unable to rediscover ever since.

Pizza Bar Mitzvah

Alan Richman

Alan Richman is the author of Fork It Over, a collection of his GQ food pieces. Alan loves to skewer sacred cows, but he couldn't find anything bad to say about his beloved Rizzo's pizza.

EVERY JEWISH BOY EXPERIENCES A DAY WHEN HE BECOMES A MAN. Maybe in Brooklyn, home of the Hassidim, that blessed occasion is his Bar Mitzvah, but for me it was being given the car keys, a dollar bill and permission to drive to Rizzo's and pick up a pizza for myself at age 16.

I understand that Jewish boys of today would not understand or appreciate such an innocent act. By the time they're 16, they've all stayed out all night and eaten bruschetta in Soho with Israeli models. In my day, we knew nothing like that. When I got in my parent's car—a four-door, two-toned Oldsmobile sedan—and headed for Rizzo's Restaurant & Pizzeria in Glenside, PA, I was so flush with excitement I might well have been running away to sea.

I almost never got to eat restaurant food. My mother cooked dinner religiously, except on the infrequent occasions when she and my father went out with friends, leaving my sister and me at home. On the night I first bought my own pizza, my sister was already away at college (a good thing, or I would have had to share it with her), and my parents were thoughtful enough to ask their friends to drive the group to dinner, leaving the car for me. I dressed carefully for the ride, for I was going out, even if it was only to pick up something to take home. In the fifties, nobody walked into a restaurant in sweat pants and running shoes. For that matter, nobody had ever heard of running shoes.

I took the dollar my parents had left for me, exactly enough to pay for a cheese pizza, and added a dime out of my own savings so I could have pepperoni on it. So vital was the pepperoni that I didn't mind contributing to the cost, astounding for a fellow of my frugality. A barren tomato-and-cheese pizza can be all right, providing the sauce is very fresh, and I have to admit I've had some unusual toppings, like clams in New Haven, Connecticut, that were appealing, but back then I always had pepperoni on my pie. Anything else was an emergency ration, acceptable only when a neglectful pizzeria ran out of pepperoni.

I knew there was no reason to purchase beverages at Rizzo's because my mother kept the house well stocked with Pepsi-Colas. Whenever all of us were on a family car trip (yet another quaint fifties custom, like dressing up to get take-out) and my sister and I would complain of being thirsty, she would tell us, "You can have a Pepsi when we get home." It didn't matter where we were, although generally we were stuck in shore traffic in our un-airconditioned car, returning home from a day in Atlantic City. Not only did we never get drinks on the road, but also our stash of Pepsis wasn't kept in the refrigerator, so we had to wait, panting, while my mother poured the contents of one medium-sized bottle into two small glasses.

She measured carefully so neither of us felt cheated, added exactly two ice cubes to each drink and admonished us to wait until the ice did its work and the Pepsi was cold. I waited. I was as well trained as one of those dogs that will sit for endless minutes with a biscuit perched on its nose before it gets the command from its master allowing it to eat.

My pizza from Rizzo's required plenty of Pepsi, because the pepperoni was the real thing: thinly sliced, spicy from hot-pepper flakes, baked until its edges were a perfect reddish-black. I don't think this particular russet shade is found anywhere else in nature except in pork products cooked crisp. I don't believe, for that matter, that there is much in the world more beautiful than a pepperoni pizza with a slightly charred, irregularly shaped, hand-formed crust. Add tomato sauce, which possesses yet another welcome shade of red, and mozzarella cheese, white with golden hues, and you have a product more lovely than a reddish-gold sunset, and, for that matter, much the same shape and color. Yet it was the pepperoni that mostly drew me to Rizzo's pizza. Never again have I been able to duplicate the meaty pleasure it provided.

For years afterward, wherever I lived, I would attempt to relive that experience by taking Hebrew National salami, slicing it thin, and pan-broiling it at high heat. While this is a fine gastronomic experience that I can heartily recommend, it never was a substitute for the incomparability of the pepperoni on the Rizzo's pie.

I don't know what it was about that pepperoni. Perhaps it was shipped here from Italy, which would account for me never finding its equal again. There is nothing that Americans like less than authentic *salumi;* we prefer anemic substitutes produced in meat-packing plants in the United States and Canada. The intense love affair that Americans have with the pepperoni pizza, I believe, is somewhat of a sham, inasmuch as the pepperoni we commonly consume is not the real thing. It reminds me of the *omelettes du fromage* we carelessly eat at Sunday brunches, so unlike the authentic French article. Yet to this day I must have pepperoni on my pizza, even if it is not genuine. For me, a pizza without pepperoni is a sirloin without creamed spinach, a baked potato without butter, a television cowboy without a six-gun strapped to his waist.

When I got home I immediately put the entire pizza in the oven, set to 300°F (perhaps too high for maintenance-level warmth, but my mother always served hot meals and I never allowed my food to get cold), placed a lot of ice in a glass of hot Pepsi, took out the TV section, and formulated a plan for eating while watching "adult westerns." These had just come into existence, and they magnificently fulfilled every young man's entertainment needs. I had already graduated from the somewhat adolescent adventures of *The Lone Ranger* (although I never will tire of the opening sequences, with the Lone Ranger on Silver, rearing high to the thundering sounds of the *William Tell Overture*). For me, first among westerns was Hugh O'Brien in *The Life and Legend of Wyatt Earp*, followed by Richard Boone in *Have Gun Will Travel*. It probably says something about my lack of ambition that one of my early role models was Wyatt's long-forgotten deputy, Shotgun Gibbs.

The gunfights were great, but what I most recall about those evenings was unlimited pizza, hour after hour of pizza, pizza whenever and wherever I wanted it, although I always ended up eating every slice in front of the television. (Like most families we had just one, and it was in the recreation room.) I don't recall much about the crust; in those unenlightened days, people didn't endlessly discuss crust the way we do today and, anyway, we had other thing to worry about, such as whether the Russians were going to drop an atomic bomb and fry our butts. I have no idea how the crust was made, although I don't believe Rizzo's had a coal-fired or wood-burning anything and I wouldn't have thought a thing about it if they had. Crust was crust. The cheese was gooey and the sauce was there.

I do know this: On the way out of Rizzo's, I opened the cardboard box and shook a lot of grated Romano cheese on the pizza. This, of course, would have obliterated any fine points. I clearly recall the smell of Rizzo's, the aroma of coarsely grated Romano, a bouquet evocative of life in Philadelphia. I don't believe wheels of genuine Parmesan ever made their way through the great ports of my home town. We were Romano cheese territory, appreciating the lusty tang that sheep's milk cheese added to our southern-style Italian specialties.

Like all pepperoni epicures, I always ate my slices carefully. I folded them along the long axis and leaned far over the coffee table, keeping the dripping oils well in front of me. The oil that oozes out of heated pepperoni is like nuclear waste material; if it touches a piece of your clothing, you are doomed. In those days, such a stain could not be removed by any known product, and my mother would immediately inform me of the cost of any item that I had thoughtlessly and selfishly ruined. (Actually, it didn't cost so much, because we got a discount at Gimbel's, where my father worked.) Not caring for your clothes was a major sin in our house. I could have run into a burning building to save a trapped baby and my mother would have admonished me for coming home with clothes that smelled of smoke.

By the time the evening was over, the pizza was gone. I never left a slice. I remember that seldom were there sufficient westerns to occupy the entire dining portion of the evening, which ran about two-and-a-half hours, and I usually had to switch to situation comedies, but I didn't mind. I have to tell you something else about the fifties: Not only was the pepperoni better back then, so were the jokes.

Rizzo's Restaurant & Pizzeria, 21 East Glenside Avenue, Glenside, PA, 215-887-2909.

A Boston Pizza Hunt

ON THE FACE OF IT, BOSTON HAS ALL THE INGREDIENTS TO BE A
first-rate pizza town: an old, thriving southern Italian-American community; hundreds of thousands of college kids who need a daily pizza fix; and a sophisticated, well-educated population that likes to eat. After all, Boston is part of the Pizza Belt. Pizzeria Regina opened in the heavily Italian North End section of Boston in 1926. A bread bakery, Santarpio's, started selling pizza in 1933 in its equally Italian East Boston neighborhood. So why does every food person I know in Boston pooh-pooh the city's pizza? Boston chefs Todd English (of Olives and Figs) and Michael Schlow (of Radius and Via Matte) both just shook their heads when I asked them about the state of pizza in Boston.

But I had to find out for myself, so one hot summer's day in August I embarked on a whirlwind pizza tour of Boston. It was to be my last whirlwind pizza tour for the book, as my editor had threatened me with a chain pizza life sentence if I didn't turn in the manuscript two days after my proposed trip to Beantown. I e-mailed Corby Kummer the morning of my arrival, asking if he might like to join me, and he immediately signed on for pizza duty, even though he had already written a piece for *A Slice of Heaven* (see page 292). Corby, a senior editor at *Atlantic Monthly* and the restaurant critic at *Boston Magazine,* knows an awful lot about Italian food.

Armed with the annual "Best of Boston" issue of *Boston Magazine*, I arrived at Logan Airport shortly before 1:00 P.M. The only reservation I could get going back to Cape Cod was at 5:00 P.M., so I didn't have a moment to lose. I called Corby on my cellphone, and he had already come up with a plan: He was going to get a pie at Pizza Oggi in Jamaica Plain. It had just been named Best Traditional Pizza in the aforementioned "Best of Boston" issue. It should be noted that Kummer does not contribute to the "Best of Boston" issue. Why? He says it's because "I value my life, and it's already threatened regularly by furious Boston restaurateurs who consider me killably demanding, though I consider myself the model of generosity and good will."

I was to take a cab to Emma's in Cambridge, which had been designated Best Designer Pizza in said magazine, and order a couple of pizzas. He would meet me there with the Oggi pizza in tow. I ordered a number two at Emma's: cherry tomatoes, basil, garlic, traditional sauce and mozzarella, and a number five: sausage, caramelized onion, traditional sauce and mozzarella. While I waited for my pizzas and Corby, I looked at the wall full of awards Emma's has won over the years. Basically, they had won every food award one could win in Boston. I started thinking that Todd English and Michael Schlow might be wrong. To whet my appetite I returned to my table and reread the entry from *Boston Magazine*: "The super-thin crust that flies out of Emma's Kitchen is addictive in its own right. Add to that such innovative combinations as Canadian bacon, caramelized onions, and rosemary sauce, or a scallion, garlic and gorgonzola mix. The restaurant may have changed hands, but nearly everything else has stayed the same—right down to the à la carte toppings (three kinds of tomatoes, sweet and gold potatoes, capers, even dried cranberries)." Dried cranberries on pizza? Yuck! My pies arrived a few minutes later. The crust was super-thin. In fact, it was basically a homemade lavash cracker. I like thin-crust pizza with a simultaneously crisp and tender crust, a crust with some breadlike characteristics. The cheese was standard-issue aged mozzarella that blanketed the whole pie in overwhelming fashion. I loved the sweet caramelized onions, and the sausage had a pleasant, porky flavor. This couldn't be the best pizza Boston has to offer, I thought to myself. Just then Corby arrived, looked at the two pizzas and immediately asked for them to be boxed and for the check. He said the Oggi's pizza awaited us on a counter at his garage, con-veniently located just around the corner from Emma's, so we brought the two pizzas there. Corby had promised the guys at the garage our leftovers. On our way over I had read the Pizza Oggi Traditional Pizza entry in "Best of Boston": "Let the gourmets pile on their trendy precious toppings: the best serious classic pizza is the kind that gets the basics right. This barely decorated brick storefront in Jamaica Plain has its thin, simple pizzas down to a science: They're doused with herbed olive oil and scattered with cornmeal, then slathered in a tomato sauce that's slightly smoky. The crowning mozzarella starts out blistering hot, then cools to a smooth, gooey sweetness. If you really want it, you can get a version decked out with spicy sausage and such, but with flavor as pure as this, why bother?"

Unfortunately the pizza we ate in Corby's garage was so substandard that we found ourselves asking the same question: Why bother? The crust had a quarter-inch layer of spongy, gooey, unbaked dough. The sauce tasted as if it had been cooked, a pizza no-no. If this was the best traditional pizza to be found in Boston, I found myself asking just what tradition it was trying to adhere to.

We needed a pick-me-up, a pizza palate cleanser, so Corby drove us to nearby Toscanini's Ice Cream. There Gus Toscanini makes some of the best ice cream on the planet. His ice cream is ethereally light, satiny smooth and intensely flavored. I tried the spiced peach and fresh mint ice cream (both were transcendent) before settling on a coffee ice cream sandwich. Corby had two chocolate egg creams, skip the milk. We discussed Boston pizza with Gus, who professed a fondness for the pizza at Emma's and for a place called Campo De Fiori in Harvard Square. Corby's face lit up. He informed me that that's where I was going to go next. On the way over Corby told me that Campo De Fiori was opened by a not very friendly Italian five years ago. He thought the pizza bianca there was just about as good as he'd found at Il Forno di Campo de' Fiori in Rome and at Sullivan Street Bakery in New York. I ordered four pizzas: a Margherita, a sausage, an Allesandro (made with potatoes, fresh tomatoes, pesto and prosciutto de Parma) and a plain. They were all delicious: fresh-tasting, yeasty, obviously made with good ingredients. The crust was thicker than what I found in Rome or New York, but it had terrific hole structure. Gus Toscanini turned out to know pizza as well as he does ice cream.

Our last stop was the 78-year-old Pizzeria Regina. With its weathered signs and old wooden booths, it looked and felt like a traditional pizzeria. It was now the flagship store of a multiunit chain. I asked our waitress if I could get my pizza with fresh mozzarella. This flummoxed her. "We got one kind of mozzarella here. I think it's fresh. I don't know. Just when you think you've heard everything, someone comes along and asks you something like this." She sent out the manager, who calmly informed me that they used aged mozzarella. I asked him about the oven, which was ancient-looking. He told me that it was a gas oven lined with bricks that had been converted from coal sometime ago. I ordered a large Margherita with sausage on half. We then walked around the corner to Corby's favorite Italian bakery, Marie's. I had a very fine *sfogliatelle*.

When we got back to Regina's, our pizza was ready. We brought it back to the *Atlantic Monthly* offices, where Corby knew it would be appreciated and inhaled by the hard-working staff. I sat at the conference table eating a slice of the Regina pizza. The crust had bubbled up beautifully. It was indeed crisp on the outside and tender on the inside. It was, as I like, both puffy and chewy. The mozzarella was, as advertised, decent-quality aged mozzarella, but what made the pie in my estimation besides the crust was the Romano cheese generously sprinkled on the top. It lent the pizza a much-needed salty tang. The sausage, made according to the menu in-house, was those gray pellets with no discernible fennel flavor.

I had wanted to go to Figs, Todd English's pizzeria, but my plane was leaving in forty-five minutes, and I had tasted Figs' fine designer pies many times over the years. So what could I say about my Boston pizza sojourn? I would say with two exceptions its place in the Pizza Belt was in jeopardy. The college kids are out of luck, and so are the foodies. One more thing: I learned not to trust what has been designated the Best of Boston.

Campo De Fiori
1350 Massachusetts Avenue (Holyoke Center Arcade), Cambridge, MA, 617-354-3805, www.campodefiori.org.
37 Center Street, Weston, MA, 781-893-6135.
RATING: 🍕 🍕 🍕

Emma's
40 Hampshire Street, Kendall Square, Cambridge, MA, 617-864-8534.
RATING: ✸ ✸

Pizza Oggi
8 Perkins Street, Jamaica Plain, MA, 617-971-9797.
RATING: Zero Pies

Pizzeria Regina
11½ Thatcher Street, Boston, MA, 617-227-0765, www.pizzeriaregina.com.
RATING: ✸ ✸ ✸

Pizza in Our Nation's Capital

It was at Ella's Woodfired Pizza, the first stop on my Washington, D.C., pizza tour, that I developed my owner-occupied pizza theory (see page 19). I sat down at a table across from the beautiful, fire-engine red, wood-fired brick oven and ordered a Margherita and a marinara pizza. I asked my waiter where Ella's got its mozzarella and sausage. He said he didn't know, but that he would ask the chef, who was sitting at the bar. The chef then walked past my table on the way to the kitchen. I repeated the questions directly to him. He said, "I don't really know. I think the mozzarella comes from California, and the sausage, well, I don't have any idea. A lot of sausage comes from Pennsylvania, so maybe it's from there." This exchange did not fill my stomach with confidence; at the very least a chef should know where his ingredients come from. Maybe he's new, I consoled myself, and his name couldn't be Ella. But there was no Ella in sight, and nobody else in charge.

Unsurprisingly, the pizzas were thoroughly mediocre. Much better than your run-of-the-mill slice place or chain, but nothing you'd travel even ten blocks for. Our next stop was Matchbox, which makes a big deal on its menu about its coal-fired oven and all the trips made to the great pizza emporia in New York. I ordered a medium half-plain, half-sausage pie, and asked our waitress where they got their mozzarella and sausage. She came back and said the guys making the pizza didn't know. Our pie arrived, and it was yellow, which meant they were using aged, not fresh, mozzarella. The sausage had a nice fennelly taste, but the sauce was overpoweringly herbaceous. It tasted of dry, old oregano. The waitress came over and said they get their sausage from Cisco, a megasized food distributor. I appreciated her candor, but not the pizza. Once again I felt there was a pizza leadership vacuum at Matchbox. I was beginning to get discouraged about pizza in the District of Columbia. How could our nation's capital, full of college students, twenty-somethings working on Capitol Hill, not to mention a hundred senators, 532 members of the House of Representatives, nine Supreme Court justices and the president and vice president not have at least a few solid slices? This state of affairs is unpatriotic, not to mention unregulated.

My next stop was Pizzeria Paradiso, located upstairs in a townhouse and touted as the gold standard of Washington pizzerias. It had a gorgeous wood-burning pizza oven. Once again, however, there appeared to be no one in charge. My waiter, a genial sort, took my order, a Margherita made with half regular cow's-milk mozzarella and half water-buffalo mozzarella. It was a good sign that they had *mozzarella di bufala,* and a few minutes later the pizza arrived at my table. It had a high lip, a puffy and chewy crust and very good hole structure. It was the first good pizza on the tour. Still there was clearly no owner present.

When I asked my waiter about the mozzarella and the sausage, he went back to the kitchen and returned with, "We get the mozzarella the same place we get our goat cheese. The sausage we make ourselves, we fry it up every morning." Only in Washington, D.C., would they consider sausage taken out of a package and fried to be house-made.

I spent the night with our friends Merrill and Tim Carrington. I had called Merrill the night before I took the train to Washington, hoping she could pick up a pizza at 2 Amys, the highest-rated pizzeria in Tom Sietsema's *Washington Post Dining Guide*, because the place wasn't open on Monday, the day of my journey. Merrill, a wonderfully spiritual sort, was appalled by my plan. "We love 2 Amys, and it's five minutes from our house, but if you eat a day-old pizza from there, you can't possibly judge the quality of it. It won't be fair, and it's not right." I find it's hard to argue with really smart spiritual types, because they're invariably right. I asked if I could spend Monday at their house and pick up a pizza from 2 Amys at 11:00 A.M. on my way out of town.

We called in our order at 10:30, and I arrived at 11:00 to pick up my Margherita. It's a very pretty place, 2 Amys, with mustard-colored walls and high ceilings. It felt like a church of pizza. Most important, there was someone in charge, a dark-haired person barking out orders. "Will someone pick up that phone, please?" It turned out to be Tim Giamette, one of the owners. He wasn't very friendly but he clearly had the fever, and he was there, right when it opened, on a Tuesday morning at 11:00 A.M., when there was no one except me in there, and he didn't have to be. I asked him about the pizza, made in a white, dome-shaped, wood-burning oven. "We run a bakery. Everything is in the dough. All it is is flour, salt and water. We make it fresh every day, roll it out by hand, stretch it and proof it twice. A great pizza starts and finishes with the dough. Everything else is secondary. If you do that right, everything falls into place. We use a combination of La Parisienne low-gluten flour, made by Gusto's in San Francisco, and regular King Arthur flour, fresh cake yeast, canned San Marzano tomatoes, which we drain and puree in a Mouli grater. We save the water and add it if we need to. We get our mozzarella, both the *fior di latte* and the *mozzarella di bufala*, three times a week. The pizza makers top the pie with a little sauce, some mozzarella. Our pies are minimally topped. They bake at 600°F for a couple of minutes. We are constantly adding wood because we need the flame to produce a convection effect in the oven. We get a little bit of char on the bottom and top of every pie. We got this pizza maker, Edan McQuaid, he's the best pizza guy on the East Coast. He's only thirty, but he probably came out of his mother's womb making pizza."

I was glad to hear a pizza rant in Washington, D.C., by an on-the-premises owner of a pizzeria. Someone who cared and watched over the whole process. Just then my pie came out of the oven. They sprinkled some extra virgin olive oil on it and placed it gently in the box. It looked perfect. It tasted even better. It was perhaps the best traditionally Neapolitan-style pizza I've had in the States. But unlike Neapolitan pizza it had a crisp crust, beautiful hole structure and just the right amount of char. It was a perfectly balanced pizza. I ate half and dragged the other half with me onto the subway to Union Station to catch the train back to New York. I opened the box and took a bite of one of the remaining slices. It still tasted great, a full hour after it was made. Another mark of a great pizza is that even an hour after it comes out of the oven, it still tastes like great bread with melted cheese and tomatoes and basil.

Maybe there is hope for the pizza in Washington, D.C. It has at least one owner-occupied pizzeria. All we need is a few more, so that I won't write to my congressman asking for federal pizza standards.

Pizzeria Paradiso
3282 M Street NW, Washington, D.C., 202-337-1245.
2029 P Street NW, Washington, D.C., 202-223-1245.
RATING:

2 Amys
3715 Macomb Street NW, Washington, D.C., 202-885-5700, www.2amyspizza.com.
RATING:

Baltimore Pizza

Baltimore is not on anyone's list of great pizza towns. Or so I thought, before I talked to the wonderfully talented mystery writer and life-long Baltimorean Laura Lippman. She asked if I had tried Matthew's, Baltimore's oldest pizzeria (it opened in 1949). I said I had, and that I loved the feel of the place—the wood-paneled walls filled with maps of Italy, the linoleum floors and the old-fashioned Coke-bottle case. Befitting Baltimore's status as the crab capital of America, Matthew's serves a backfin crab pizza with onions, mozzarella and Old Bay seasoning. It's served on Matthew's thick, slightly crispy crust, on a paper plate. I reported to Laura what I had found at Matthew's.

Laura said she wasn't all that impressed with the breadth and depth of my Baltimore research so, with that opening, I pounced like a beagle that's just discovered a piece of steak on the floor. "Would you consider writing a piece about Baltimore pizza for the book?" I asked. She said yes, and what follows is her smart take on Baltimore pizza, reported with love and compassion for the city in which she lives.

Pizza: A Love Story

Laura Lippman

Laura Lippman sets her mysteries in her native Baltimore. You can tell from her books that she loves to eat. When I asked her to contribute to A Slice of Heaven, *she knew immediately that she wanted to find out more about her beloved Al Pacino's Egyptian Pizza.*

BEFORE I CAN EXPLAIN HOW EGYPTIAN PIZZA ESTABLISHED A beachhead in one Baltimore neighborhood in the late 1980s, I need to provide some context about my hometown's nicknames and mottos. Long promoted as Charm City, Baltimore declared itself *The City that Reads* under Mayor Kurt Schmoke (1992–2000), who was apparently undeterred by the 20-percent illiteracy rate. Given that the city also has a per-capita homicide rate persistently in the top five nationwide and a rather remarkable number of teenage pregnancies, *The City that Reads* was twisted, inevitably and respectively, into *The City that Bleeds* and *The City that Breeds*. Schmoke was succeeded by Mayor Martin O'Malley, who promised that homicides would drop to historic lows. They did—briefly. The pesky fact that they bounced back the next year, and the year after that, did not prevent O'Malley from changing the city's official slogan to *The Greatest City in America*.

An advertising campaign for National Bohemian Beer, known locally as Natty Boh, dubbed the region *The Land of Pleasant Living*, but the brewery pulled up stakes a few years ago, so we're mad at them. History buffs know the city as *Mobtown*, a tribute to the city's, um, feisty partisanship in antebellum times, shenanigans that may have contributed to the death of Edgar Allan Poe. Film director John Waters inspired the Chamber of Commerce to print up pink-on-yellow bumper stickers reading: "Come to Baltimore and Be Shocked." The *City Paper*, an alternative news weekly, tried *Tiny Town*. (The Census Bureau says there are more than 600,000 of us, but it feels like 600 because you can't go anywhere without seeing someone you know. Don't try to get away with anything in Baltimore. Except, perhaps, murder.)

I prefer, not surprisingly, the motto that *I* modestly floated back in 1997—*Baltimore: Where Trends Come to Die.* The Chamber of Commerce has yet to recognize my contribution with a bumper sticker, but I meant it as the greatest compliment I could bestow. Baltimore's indifference to what is hip is what makes it so delightful. Because we're not in a hurry to do things first, we sometimes do them quite well. Pizza falls into that category. Also coffeehouses and crack cocaine, but that's another story.

Matthew's, reputed to be Baltimore's first pizzeria, did not open until 1943, a relatively late date for a Northeastern city with a thriving Italian population. Four years later, Matthew's, named for baker Matthew Ciociolo, moved around the corner and it's been on Eastern Avenue, in the heart of Highlandtown, ever since. True Baltimoreans, who give directions according to landmarks that no longer exist, might tell you to go out Eastern Avenue to where the Patterson Park Theater used to be. (It's still there, marquee and all, but reborn as the home of the Creative Artists Alliance.) Matthew's is directly across the street.

Matthew's makes a justifiably celebrated crab pie, a surprising rarity in this crustacean-crazy town, but my personal favorite is the aptly named "Everything." You will be asked if you want the anchovies. You do. The crust recipe is said to be secret, according to local journalist Jacques Kelly, from whom I cribbed several of the facts above. (However, I did all the eating required for this piece.) True to its founder's baker roots, take-out pizzas are not placed in boxes, but sandwiched between two cardboard plates and wrapped in white paper.

While I take out-of-towners to Matthew's for its authentic atmosphere and excellent food, my own pizza needs—and my pizza needs occur with alarming frequency—are usually met by what Baltimoreans call Egyptian pizza. Or, given the local tendency to use names that aren't strictly correct, Al Pacino's Egyptian Pizza, a name that a lawyer advised restaurateur Mohamed Mahoud to drop if he hoped to pursue franchise opportunities.

And Mahoud, who came to Baltimore in 1987 after two years of working in various Manhattan restaurants, was thinking about franchises from the day he opened his restaurant in a former shoe store. The narrow storefront, then known simply as Al Pacino's, was a plain, no-frills place, whose only real décor was, of course, a poster of Cher.

So what's with the name? "True story," Mahoud said. "I was sitting around with my cousin and we both liked Al Pacino, so I said, 'Why not call it Al Pacino's?'" This was four years after *Scarface* came out, although I'm sorry to say that Al Pacino's never found a way to capitalize on the catch phrase "Say hello to my leetle friend." (I'd have used it as a heading for the appetizers, for example.) Today, there are three local restaurants that still use "Al Pacino" as part of their names, but Mahoud no longer owns them and the original is shuttered. Mahoud's sole remaining restaurant is in the Belvedere Square area, a Phoenix-like development in North Baltimore that has reinvented itself at least twice in the last decade. Egyptian Pizza, as this site has always been known, is one of the constants in the area, thriving even when surrounded by empty shops.

Mahoud said the ancient Egyptians made the first pizzas. "The Egyptians and the Chinese invented everything," he insisted, but I'm not foolhardy enough to get drawn into a subject as fraught as pizza's origins. (I had a calendar when I was a kid that said the first pizzas were invented by Roman soldiers, who put tomatoes on matzos, which strikes me as even less likely, but much funnier.) He said he once made pizza for his Italian-born sisters-in-law and they pronounced it the best pizza they had ever eaten. Again, who am I to doubt him?

I should note, however, that my own pizza bona fides are not unimpressive. I have eaten at Ray's in New York, one of the authentic ones. During my four years at Northwestern University outside Chicago, I may have been enrolled in the Medill School of Journalism, but my true major was deep-dish, stuffed pizza, and the pizza turnover, a kind of calzone, but infinitely better. On a three-month sabbatical in Cuernavaca, I ate a terrific Mexican version of pizza at least once a week at Marco Polo's. Given this promiscuous history, I am willing to say only that Mahoud's restaurants, past and present, produce the best *Egyptian* pizza I've ever had. For me, it's all about the crust, which is soft and chewy, seemingly whisked out of the oven at the exact moment that it would no longer be called undercooked. Mahoud, who claims "Egyptian pizza" as his original concept—not to be confused with the pizza that ancient Egypt invented—credits his use of flour and semolina for its distinctive texture.

My favorite is the Monzese, a traditional pepperoni pie. "Very American," Mahoud said to me, and I felt so sheepish about my provincial palate that I was compelled to list the others I have tried over the years—the Manhattan (a so-called white pizza), the Margherita, the Di Funghi, the Mexico, the California. I once ordered the whole-wheat/soya-cheese vegetarian when I had a brief flirtation with abstemiousness. (It was *very* brief, about a month back in 1991.)

Even as I was attempting to impress Mahoud with my broad-mindedness, I realized I've never eaten the pies influenced by the owner's Middle Eastern roots—such as the Giza, basically lamb *schwarma* on pizza, and the Maser, which has falafel and feta mingled with traditional pizza toppings. I also decided I should order the actor's namesake pizza, which—my apologies, Mr. Pacino—features shrimp as its primary topping.

One day later—it would have been that same night, but I had plans—I picked up a Giza, an Al Pacino, a Monzese and a Manhattan and took them to the home of old friends, who happen to have three reliably hungry daughters. We liked them all, but mom, Carol Frigo—a native Chicagoan who also knows a thing or two about pizza—agreed with me. The Monzese is exceptional. Simple, straightforward, crowded with quality pepperoni.

Nostalgic in the company of a couple who know—and keep—the secrets of my youth, I found myself compiling a list of pizzas, past and present, a list much longer than the roll call of men I've dated. In the Baltimore metro area, there was the Robin's Nest, Marino's, the Grotto, Columbo's, Mama Illardo's and Fortunato's. Mike's in Plymouth, Wisconsin, where they let kids from my summer camp make our own Tombstone pizzas. My college hangouts: Dave's Italian Kitchen, Michelini's East, Giordano's, Uno's, Due's. The Pizza Inn in Waco, Texas, where a friend was once banned for life from the all-you-can-eat buffet, on the grounds that he was driving the restaurant into bankruptcy. Maria's in San Antonio, which didn't bill itself as Egyptian, but it had a belly dancer and a shrimp pizza similar to the Al Pacino. There were more, their names forgotten. And there were the pizzas that got away—primarily, LAPD Pizza, a brand glimpsed at a highway rest stop in England. ("Do you think they pummel the dough with batons every time it tries to rise?" my companion wondered.)

Given all those possibilities and my own fickle nature, can I really proclaim one pizza the love of my life? I will say yes, conditionally. If I had to be monogamous with a single pizza, it would be the Monzese. But I don't, so I reserve the right to visit Matthew's for the Everything, whenever the mood strikes. My hometown is The Land of Pleasant Living, after all, although I'll never drink a Natty Boh again. Trends may die in Baltimore, but grudges are forever.

Egyptian Pizza, 542 East Belvedere Square, Towson, MD, 410-323-7060.
Matthew's Pizzeria, 3131 Eastern Avenue, Baltimore, MD, 410-276-8755.

CHAPTER
9

*Pizza in
the South and
Southwest*

That Magic "Pizza Moment"

 Christine Lauterbach

I never made it to many Southern and Southwestern cities in my quest for great pizza, so I asked my friend and colleague Christine Lauterbach, restaurant critic for Atlanta Magazine/Knife & Fork to write about Atlanta pizza. Christine is French, but she is equally passionate and curious about non-French food.

I AM FRENCH, AND UNTIL I MOVED TO THE U.S., I HAD NEVER HEARD of pineapple or smoked salmon on a pizza. On the other hand, I had eaten marvelous thin pies topped with paper-thin zucchini, eggplant and even potato in the streets of Rome, and decided that vegetables were okay on a freshly stretched crust that was an extension of the bread we the French so love.

In America, New York has the best pizzas by far. My most magical "pizza moment" has been sitting in a room the Smithsonian should think about preserving—the original Totonno's on Coney Island—and eating their amazingly simple pie. I wouldn't have dreamed of ordering a topping and spoil the intensity of the cheese (homemade) and the tomato sauce (reduced almost to a paste) baked like enamel on a charred disk of dough.

I can't stand wet/goopy pizza and I don't like wrestling with my slice. The best slice in Atlanta is available at Fellini's Pizza: basic New York–style, thin bottom, light crust, very tender, with a sweet taste of fresh bread. This excellent dough tends to be overwhelmed when too many ingredients are requested. The whole pies are never as good unless you take them home, let them get cold, and then rebake the heck out of them. Everybody's Pizza is just the opposite, a formidable heavy pie of the kitchen-sink variety beloved by famished students and young families on a budget. It is perhaps more typical of Atlanta and is a bit of a cult.

Fritti, despite its name, is a gourmet Italian pizzeria (fancy brick oven, lots of basil and prosciutto) and its thin pies bake in minutes without damaging the delicate toppings. It is pretty ideal if you don't mind dropping real money on pizza or having chi-chi neighbors. It gets my vote for being just like in Italy: fresh and effortless. 🍕

Everybody's Pizza, 1040 North Highland Avenue NE, Atlanta, GA, 404-873-4545. 1593 North Decatur Road NE, Atlanta, GA, 404-377-7766.

Fellini's, 2809 Peachtree Road NE, Atlanta, GA, 404-266-0082.

Fritti, 309 North Highland Avenue, Atlanta, GA, 404-880-9559.

WELCOME-WAGON PIZZA

 Peter Reinhart

Peter Reinhart is the author of American Pie: My Search for the Perfect Pizza. *He recently moved to Charlotte, North Carolina, to teach baking at the new Johnson & Wales University. He filed the following report shortly after moving there.*

WHEN YOU MOVE TO A NEW CITY THERE ARE CERTAIN SUPPORT-network priorities that must be met, which include finding a new doctor, dentist, banker, barber, chiropractor, optometrist, long-distance and cable carrier and, of course, a decent barbecue shack, taqueria, Chinese restaurant, and, most important, a pizzeria.

Moving to the South—Charlotte, North Carolina, to be specific—I figured barbecue would be a lock but I had my doubts about a pizzeria. As I always do after a move, I asked every new person I met where to get the best pizza in town. I sifted through the data, considered the sources, and then my wife, Susan, and I systematically began checking them out.

After a few months of almost-but-not-quite-successful pizza hunts, Tizz Benson, a local pastry chef, the owner of the fabulous Tizzerts Cakery (well, I figured, at least we found our special-occasion-cake support system), came unexpectedly to the rescue. She and her husband, Ben, insisted we go with them to Luisa's Brick Oven. I've been long dubious of any place that feels it necessary to bill itself as "brick-oven pizza" because having a brick oven doesn't

mean you actually know how to properly use it. It is about as useful as saying DOC or VPN, the Italian "certification" of authenticity, which almost always disappoints me as a pale imitation of real Napolitano pizza. But the moment I saw the Luisa, the house special, with small dots of bright pesto nestled between thin slices of fresh tomato on a properly and lightly applied cheese-and-sauce foundation, all sitting atop a dynamically bubbling crust with its slightly charred *cornicione*, I exhaled fully for what seemed like the first time since we left Providence and said to Susan (and to Tizz and Ben who wore the proud smile that I recognized as the look of the vindicated and validated pizza hunter), "Well, we can cross 'finding a pizzeria' off the list. Now, if we could just find a decent doctor and dentist."

Luisa's Brick Oven, 1730 Abbey Place, Charlotte, NC, 704-522-8782.

WE'VE COME A LONG WAY

Dotty Griffith

Dotty Griffith, food writer for the Dallas Morning News, *is the author of seven books, including her most recent,* Celebrating Barbecue. *She apparently has strong feelings about pizza as well.*

MY FIRST PIZZA WASN'T COVERED WITH TACO MEAT, ALTHOUGH considering I'm from Texas, that might surprise some. No, my first pizza was at now-defunct Shakey's, sometime in the early 1960s, and I mostly remember lots of stringy cheese, orange grease and what I suppose were canned mushrooms, because I'd never had a fresh one. Pizza in Dallas has come a long way since then. Campisi's remains the first great Dallas pizza joint although its thicker crust dates it somewhat. My top places are Arcodoro & Pomodoro, where wood-burning ovens turn out thin, crisp crusts with fresh and sometimes very fancy and unusual ingredients at this Sardinian restaurant. Antonio also makes a marvelous thin-crust pizza with more traditional, but always top-quality, ingredients. Newcomers Fireside Pies and Taverna are tied in my book, again both because of the crust. The former is almost buttery, but not too thick, with locally made Italian sausage and heirloom tomatoes. Taverna again is more traditional but tops for me is the crackling focaccia-style crust with fresh arugula, pancetta and pine nuts.

Antonio Ristorante, 4985 Addison Circle, Addison, TX, 972-458-1010.
Arcodoro & Pomodoro, 2708 Routh Street, Dallas, TX, 214-871-1924.
Campisi's, 1522 Main Street, Dallas, TX, 214-752-0141; 5610 Mockingbird Lane, 214-827-0355.
Fireside Pies, 2820 North Henderson Avenue, Dallas, TX, 214-370-3916.
Taverna, 3210 Armstrong Avenue, Dallas, TX, 214-520-9933.

PIZZA MEMORIES

Robb Walsh

Robb Walsh, restaurant critic for the Houston Press *and author of* The Tex-Mex Cookbook, *is a native of the Pizza Belt, namely southern Connecticut. Now that he lives in Texas, where he indulges his passion for Tex-Mex food, barbecue and fried chicken, he feels he's in pizza purgatory.*

WE HUNG OUT IN LITTLE PIZZERIAS AROUND BRIDGEPORT AND Trumbull, Connecticut, when I was in high school. A floppy cheese slice and a root beer was my regular. On special occasions, Dad would drive the whole family up the Connecticut Turnpike to New Haven, where we'd stand in line at Frank Pepe's for a coal-oven pie.

I have been writing about pizza ever since I became a food writer, but in Houston, where I've been a restaurant critic for the last five years, there isn't much to write about. I drove around the entire city when I first got here, trying to find one good pie. Nothing. So I called Roma Foods in Dallas, a Texas purveyor that sells premium Italian ingredients. The sales guy was Geno from Naples. "They put too much stuff on the pizza," he told me. Seems Houstonians judge a pizza by how much lunchmeat they can pile on top of it.

To get a good pizza in Texas, you have to go to a fancy Italian restaurant with a wood-burning oven like Da Marco in Houston or Vespaio in Austin. But it's not the same. It's like going to a steakhouse for a hamburger. It isn't street food anymore. Your kids don't grow up knowing pizza.

They sure know their barbecue though. 🍕

Da Marco, 1520 Westheimer Road, Houston, TX, 713-807-8857.
Vespaio, 1620 South Congress Avenue, Austin, TX, 512-441-6100.

MIAMI SLICE

Victoria Pesce Elliott

I asked food and travel writer Victoria Pesce Elliot to report on pizza in Miami.

THE YOUNGEST DAUGHTER OF SECOND-GENERATION ITALIAN immigrants, I grew up in Miami, cooking alongside my Mom, who made her own sauce from tomatoes we grew in the yard next to the basil. For birthdays she always made rectangular pizzas with snappy and chewy crusts. This, of course, made an invite to one of the Pesce parties especially coveted in a neighborhood dominated by Cohens and Schwartzes.

Well, after a dozen years in New York City and as many trips to Italy, I am back home where there are now a surprising number of excellent pizza places. I've tried Argentine, Brazilian and even Cuban style, but my favorite is from a place called Pizza Rustica. It looks like any of the dozens of by-the-slice spots on South Beach. But here they load the chewy squares with prime ingredients. The best is the Florentine with hunks of juicy roasted chicken, baby spinach tossed in olive oil, cubes of tomatoes, slivers of red onion and lots of roasted garlic. When the slabs come out of the oven they are painted with an emulsion of extra-virgin olive oil, fresh garlic, thyme, oregano and basil, giving them a phenomenally aromatic sheen. Also craving-inducing is Spris on Lincoln Road. At outdoor tables they serve round, Roman-style pies that are crispy and thin and coated with the thinnest veil of tangy but not sweet sauce then topped with creamy mozzarella or any of dozens of other quality toppings. 🍕

Pizza Rustica, 863 Washington Avenue, Miami Beach, FL, 305-674-8244.
Spris Pizzeria, 731 Lincoln Road, Miami Beach, FL, 305-673-2020.

CROSS-CULTURAL CREATIVITY

Barbecue Pizza and the
Creolization of Southern Foodways

❧ *John T. Edge* ❧

I have traversed the entire state of Tennessee with John T. Edge, director of the Southern Foodways Alliance at the University of Mississippi in Oxford, and author of Apple Pie: An American Story, *in search of the best week-ends-only, whole-hog barbecue joints. We have also visited ten Memphis barbecue joints in one day, including Coletta's, home of the barbecue pizza.*

"CROSS-CULTURAL CREATIVITY: BARBECUE PIZZA AND THE Creolization of Southern Foodways" was the title of a paper I wrote while in graduate school. I thought I was blazing a new trail. I thought I was pondering big ideas. And just in case the reader was not inclined to agree with me, I sprinkled the text with sufficient polysyllabic blather to bring Bill Safire to his knees. An excerpt from my early opus:

> *Though a 1980s Pizza Hut marketing campaign brought barbecue pizza to the fore, Coletta's Restaurant in Memphis, Tennessee, has proffered the product since the 1950s. It is a culinary hybrid born of cultural cross-pollination. Deceptive in its simplicity, barbecue pizza, when ethnographically analyzed, provides a prime example of the creolization of Twentieth Century culture.*
>
> *How does a meat, traditionally associated with African-American pitmasters, come to be combined with an Italian staple to create a distinctively Southern delicacy, distinguished as regional, not ethnic, food? Such are the questions a student of foodways should ponder.*

Rather than an aberrant combining of Italian and African-American foodways, this dish represents a melding of cultures that mirrors the societal changes of the twentieth century. Herein, I will explore the multifarious cultures and individuals that merged to create this distinctly original Southern dish.

Reading back over that paper is painful. Was I really that obtuse? And yet, two things about barbecue pizza still ring true for me:

One, it really is a simpatico dish. Smoked pork shoulder, awash in a puddle of molasses-kissed barbecue sauce, topped with a confetti of mozzarella. What's not to like? (Well, the crust could be a bit crisper and I wish the barbecue was a bit smokier, but . . .)

Two, I stand by my concept of creolization. The interplay of black and white, African and European, is the defining story of the South. And barbecue pizza, as served at Horest Coletta's Memphis joint, might just be the best way to ponder that legacy.

Coletta's Restaurant
1063 South Parkway East, Memphis, TN, 901-948-7652.
RATING: ⊛ ⊛ ⊛ (my rating, not John T.'s)

I'M A THIN-CRUST MAN

Brett Anderson

Brett Anderson, *restaurant critic of the* New Orleans Times-Picayune, *grew up in Minnesota where he ate lutefisk, hot dish and underrated Sicilian pizza.*

I GREW UP IN MINNESOTA, WHERE I CUT MY TEETH ON THE fantastically over-cheesed and rather underrated square-cut pies indigenous to the region. Tacconelli's in Philly serves my pizza ideal, which is to say that I'm a thin-crust man. New Orleans is not a great pizza town, but when the craving hits I go to one of these three places: R & O in Bucktown, for the meatball and onion pizza; Ciro's Côté Sud, a (yes) French bistro that happens to serve thin, generally wonderful pies blistered in a brick oven; or Reginelli's, a local minichain where the pizzas have a crackly, crackerlike crust.

Ciro's Côté Sud, 7918 Maple Street, New Orleans, LA, 504-866-9551.

R & O, 216 Metairie Hammond Highway, Metairie, LA, 504-831-1248.

Reginelli's Pizzeria, 741 State Street, New Orleans, LA, 504-899-1414.
3244 Magazine Street, New Orleans, LA, 504-895-7272.
874 Harrison Avenue, New Orleans, LA, 504-488-0133.
5608 Citrus Boulevard, New Orleans, LA, 504-818-0111.

GREEN-CHILE PIES?
HEY, IT'S NEW MEXICO!

Cheryl Alters Jamison

I have sent Cheryl Alters Jamison, coauthor of Chicken on the Grill: 100 Surefire Ways to Grill Perfect Chicken Every Time, *all over New York to eat pizza and Chinese food. She lives in the great eating town of Santa Fe, where she has found green chile pizza.*

I GREW UP IN CENTRAL ILLINOIS. PIZZAS THERE WERE OFTEN influenced by the Chicago deep-dish, cast-iron-cooked style to the north, made with enough soft crust to resemble a Pillsbury Doughboy family reunion. It was just too much bread. I prefer sizzling thin-crust, brick-oven pizza like that found in superlative style at Pizzeria Bianco in Phoenix. At home in Santa Fe, I favor the pizzas from a joint called Vinny's El Primo. The pies are thin and crisp-crusted, well balanced with sauce (tasting of tomatoes rather than tomato paste) and mozzarella. I always top them with the local favorite, green chile. Hey, it's New Mexico! My second choice is the more stylish Il Vicino, which has a place in Albuquerque too.

El Primo, 234 North Guadelupe Street, Santa Fe, NM, 505-988-2007.
Il Vicino, 321 West San Francisco Street, Santa Fe, NM, 505-986-8700.

CHAPTER 10

Pizza in the Midwest

Chicago and Midwestern Pizza

My peak Midwest pizza-eating years were 1969–73, when I attended Grinnell College in Grinnell, Iowa. Grinnell was where I came up with the idea that pizza needed a meat chaser—usually a hot dog, a fried pork tenderloin or a sausage sandwich from the Longhorn, the local bar where the college students hung out. Or maybe it was a vestige of all those pizza-and-steak dinners I had growing up.

Grinnell had two pizzerias, Ahrvano's and Pagliai's. Ahrvano's pizzas were top-heavy, fairly soggy and very dense. For students studying and partying till the wee hours, Ahrvano's pizza was merely fuel. Even when extremely inebriated, my friends and I could never convince ourselves Ahrvano's was any good. But Pagliai's was another matter. Pagliai's pizza was cut into little squares, perhaps twenty-five to a large pie. Its crust was thin and crisp, and its toppings were certainly sparser than Ahrvano's, so it was easy to convince ourselves that Pag's made a mean pizza. I was already a jaded New Yorker, and I would always say, "Pag's is pretty good, but it's certainly not New York."

We would make periodic forays into Chicago to go to blues clubs, and blues clubbing almost always included a visit to one of the seminal deep-dish, Chi-town pizzerias—Uno's or Due's. Uno's and Due's were both founded by Ike Sewell, who came back from serving his country in Italy during World War II with a desire to open a thin-crusted pizza emporium. His business partner convinced him that Chicagoans would want their pizza to be something more substantial and, according to my friend John Ayers, they ended up opening the first Uno's in 1943, serving a pizza devised by two African-American cooks in the kitchen.

I fondly remember Uno's sausage and sauce-heavy pies, mostly because they were a cheap fill-up. In fact, an Uno's pizza was and is so heavy and substantial that, according to rumor, one of John Ayers's friends broke his toe when someone dropped a large Uno's sausage pie on it. One night, out with friends born and raised in Chicago, I blurted out, "I like Chicago pizza, but you know what? It's not really pizza. It's a casserole." I might as well have said the Grateful Dead sucked. They pounced on me with a ferocity I didn't know existed in the pizza-discussion realm. That's when I realized how deeply Chicagoans feel about their pizza.

I feel that my four years of living in the Midwest don't really qualify me to write the Midwestern pizza chapter in *A Slice of Heaven*, though I must point out that I had pizza in every Midwestern city the Grateful Dead played in those years. That would include Iowa City, Chicago, Kansas City, St. Louis, Minneapolis and Detroit. So I enlisted the aid of Don McLeese, a former jazz critic who moved to Des Moines to work for *Midwest Living* and teach journalism at the University of Iowa. Don had lived in the Midwest almost all his life (he had worked in Austin, Texas, for a few years, where he reported the barbecue was great and the pizza was not), and had family in Chicago and Omaha.

We met in Chicago in early June 2004 for some pizza explorations. Our first stop was the Wells Street location of Gino's East, which I was predisposed to like because it was started by a guy named Levine. We ordered a Gino's East sausage pizza, and when it arrived at the table it was topped by a shelf of sausage. It was actually very tasty, though I didn't care much for the sauce. We ate a slice each, and I warned McLeese to pace himself. We had at least three more pizzerias on the itinerary.

We stopped for an Al's Italian beef-and-sausage sandwich, because you have to have one of those when you're in Chicago, and for a Chicago hot dog with the works at Portillo's. Both were mighty fine, and functioned as a palate cleanser for the pizza.

Our next stop was Vito & Nick's, on the far South Side of Chicago. V & N's turned out to be a tavern in a working-class, Italian-American neighborhood. It had a sign on the door, "No one under 21 allowed without an adult." Inside there were a couple of middle-aged couples at the tables and what looked like a half-dozen regulars at the bar. Everyone was having pizza. We were joined a few minutes later by John Ayers, a lifelong Chicagoan who couldn't figure out why he had never heard of, and never been to, Vito & Nick's. We ordered a large pizza, half sausage, half plain. It arrived twenty minutes later, with an ultracrispy thin crust and loaded with chunks of fine Italian sausage. This was the other side of the Chicago pizza culture, the thin-crusted bar pizza that families and large gatherings of men eat after bowling or some other bonding endeavor.

Our next stop was Barcello's, anointed by an obscure Chicago pizza web site as "Chicago's Best Pizza" in 1999. Barcello's turned out to be a neighborhood Italian restaurant in a hip section called Bucktown, and its pizza was almost identical to Vito & Nick's. I didn't like it as much, because the sauce was overpowering, with way too many dried herbs.

McLeese cried uncle and begged off at this point. I had just given him another version of the "pace yourself" lecture, but he insisted he had to return to his wife and two daughters in their hotel room, and that he had room for a lot more pizza if he could have stayed.

Our last pizza stop for the night was Lou Malnati's Pizzeria, the most highly regarded of the newer deep-dish Chicago pizza palaces. We picked up two pies, one with spinach and one with sausage, and brought them home to John's wife and two spectacular daughters, Dede and Maya, who made short work of them. I liked Malnati's buttery crust more than the crust at Gino's East, and I thought in general the pie had a certain textural balance and sharper flavors that the other pizzas hadn't achieved. I convinced John to take me to a nearby Italian beef sandwich emporium, Johnny's, for another palate-cleansing snack. We ordered a beef sandwich wet (dipped in a delicious gravy made up mostly of pan drippings), an order of fries, a sausage sandwich dry (for research purposes) and two Italian ices for John's daughters. The ices supplied us with cover in case John's wife, Judy, accused us of overeating.

My plan was to hit Uno's or Due's in the morning on the way to the airport, but I woke up the next morning with a serious pizza hangover. The great ones learn to eat with pain, so when Judy drove me to the airport, we stopped for a Home Run Inn pizza, a local brand of frozen pizzas based loosely on the recipe used at, yes, the Home Run Inn. The pizza was closer to a single or a double than it was to a home run. Then we passed a hot-dog place, Gene and Jude's, that Chicago restaurateur and hot-dog maven Jerry Kleiner had taken me to a couple of years ago. We kept going about a half-mile past Gene and Jude's. I sheepishly asked Judy if she would consider going back for a hot dog. "They put fries right on top of the hot dog. You're going to love it." Judy, one of the great good sports of our time, turned around. I ordered two hot dogs. They were great. The fries were salty and golden brown, and cascaded off the hot dogs as we munched contentedly. The hot dog and fries were the perfect pizza chaser. I closed my eyes, and I was transported back to the Longhorn in Grinnell, snarfing a tenderloin chaser after my Pagliai's pizza.

Barcello's
1647 N. Milwaukee Avenue, Chicago, IL, 773-486-8444, www.barcellosrestaurant.com.

RATING:

Gino's East
633 North Wells Street (at the corner of Ontario), Chicago, IL, 312-943-9589, www.ginoseast.com (with 12 additional locations in Illinois).

RATING:

Lou Malnati's Pizzeria
439 North Wells Street, Chicago, IL, 312-828-9800, www.loumalnatis.com (with 20 additional locations in Illinois).

RATING:

Vito & Nick's
8433 South Pulaski Road, Chicago, IL, 773-735-2050, www.vitoandnick.com.

RATING:

NOTE: Vito & Nick's is not affiliated with Vito & Nick's II, which has locations in Mokena and Hickory Hills, Illinois.

THE PLATONICALLY
PERFECT PIZZA

Don McLeese

*Don McLeese loves jazz, rock and roll and pizza, which makes him my
kind of guy. His day job, though, is teaching journalism at the University
of Iowa. I first met him over a plate of barbecued shrimp at Pascal Manale's
in New Orleans. There was no pizza on the menu.*

THOUGH SOME CULINARY HISTORIANS TRACE THE ORIGINS OF PIZZA
to the flatbreads of ancient Greece, I have no evidence that Plato ever developed
a passion for pepperoni, or a preference for thick crust over thin. For all I know,
he might have been as likely to favor a nouvelle Thai chicken pizza as a classic
quattro formaggi. I'm almost certain he couldn't find decent home delivery.

So I hardly anticipated that Plato would emerge as my go-to guy when I
embarked on a quest to find the best pizza in the Midwest. I was working for
Midwest Living, a magazine that never has heard a discouraging word about the
twelve-state region it celebrates (where the skies are not cloudy all day). My
assignment was to write one of those subjective survey features—"The Top This,"
"The Best That"—that are a staple of service publications.

I was happy to play along. We Midwesterners are justifiably proud of our
pizza, eager to debate and defend our favorites. As a native of Chicago, where
pizza places are as prevalent as fire hydrants, I've eaten more and developed
stronger opinions about it than just about anyone I know. Soliciting tips from
readers and coworkers would give me a golden (i.e., expense-account) opportunity to expand my pizza horizons across the region. While chomping my way from
Ohio to the Dakotas, I figured I'd discover a bunch of great new pizzerias, and if

all I had to do was anoint one of them the best—or maybe compile a top ten—what was the harm?

I couldn't do it. A few weeks into my pizza pilgrimage, I recognized the futility of trying to pass even provisional judgment on a topic where feelings run as strong as traditions. Midwesterners love pizza, but the pizza we love varies so significantly from city to city that ranking types of pies—let alone individual places—would be arbitrary at best. It would be like trying to proclaim which is superior: Catholic or Protestant? Tiramisu or crème brûlée? A walk-off, grand-slam home run or a "Hail, Mary" game-winning touchdown pass?

I experienced my flash of epiphany (or perhaps it was incipient heartburn) as I inhaled another slice of sausage and pepperoni at Imo's in St. Louis, a representative chain in a city where the crust of choice is thinner than a cracker, while the favored cheese is a tangy provel rather than the sweeter, creamier mozzarella. Nobody (at least nobody outside St. Louis) seems to talk much about St. Louis–style pizza the way they do Chicago-style or New York–style, but it's as unique to that city as the Gateway Arch.

If you're a native, this is the pizza you love, the one you crave, the standard by which you measure all others. Yet a friend of mine, transplanted there from Chicago, dismisses it as "that cardboard with a little tomato sauce that passes for pizza around here." For someone raised on Chicago deep dish, St. Louis pizza doesn't even speak the same language.

Anybody who thinks that pizza is pizza just hasn't eaten enough pizza. Where the St. Louis crust suggests a cross between a communion wafer and a crispy tostada, the hand-tossed pizza in a family Cleveland parlor such as Mama Santa's or Geraci's is more like a doughy bakery good, an artisan bread. Topped with gobs of cheese and barely a hint of tomato (a few small slices rather than a paste), it's a pizza best eaten with a knife and fork.

Where pizza preferences are concerned, geography is destiny. Pizza lovers in the cattle state of Nebraska prefer hamburger over sausage at the Valentino's chain so popular in Lincoln and Omaha. Along the Lake Superior shore of Minnesota, the ubiquitous wild rice highlights the list of toppings at Sven and

Ole's pizzeria in Grand Marais. You'd think that a juicy bratwurst pizza might flourish in Milwaukee, though I was unable to find one.

No matter. The point, as Plato postulated, is that perfection is an abstract ideal that takes different physical forms. In this case, pizza perfection manifests itself very differently as you travel across the American heartland, a region that is second to none in its love for this all-American food. (Italy copied us, dammit.) Yet the Platonic ideal remains the same—the harmony of contrasts in taste and texture, the yin-yang of crisp crust and chewy cheese, the soulful satisfaction of a meal complete in itself, one that renders appetizers, side dishes and even dessert superfluous. If you're still hungry, have another slice.

Try to think of a dish that can better encompass meat, seafood, fruit, vegetable and dairy, and that goes equally well with wine, beer, pop, milk or water. To my mind, pizza is perfect, and perfection is a quality that doesn't permit gradations, qualifications or subjective value judgments. Just as a pizza can't be "somewhat unique" (it's either unique or it isn't), my favorite pizza can't be "more perfect" or "less perfect" than yours. Yet that perfection tastes different in Chicago than it does in Cleveland or St. Louis.

From my Windy City perspective, I might have some trouble stomaching a pizza as bland as Nebraska's hamburger (there's also a cheeseburger variation with pickles) or as weird as Minnesota's wild rice. Yet it's a sign of pizza's permeability—another indication of its Platonic perfection—that a culture as different from mine as Sven and Ole's can produce a pizza that its patrons love as much as I love my favorite Chicago pizza.

Such diversity offends the tender sensibilities of pizza purveyors in Italy, who have successfully lobbied to have the Neapolitan pizza recognized as that nation's legal standard for authentic pizza. In a country where there is one true church, perhaps there can be only one true pizza. Yet in America, land of the free and home of the stuffed, pizza is far more ecumenical.

Throughout my native region, where devotion to pizza is almost religious, the thousands of kitchen cathedrals each attract a loyal congregation. Though I worship with the old-school pizza carnivores, I've occasionally indulged in a so-called "white pizza," topped with cheese and likely vegetables but no tomato paste, or ordered whole-wheat crust. I'll even accept that anchovies and pineapple have their place (though not at my place).

Thus, I won't absolutely insist on what I secretly believe: that the thin-crust, sausage, pepperoni and bacon pizza at Chicago's venerable, relatively unheralded Father & Son is the best in the Midwest, and thus the best in the world. As my Platonic ideal asserts, it may be possible to get a pizza this delicious at dozens of other places in the Chicago area, perhaps hundreds across the country. But I can't imagine tasting a better one anywhere.

In classic Chicago fashion, the sweet, succulent sausage has some spark to it and comes clumped like tiny pillows rather than the arid slices or rabbit pellets prevalent elsewhere. The crisped edges of the bacon and pepperoni provide the necessary crunch against the softer sausage and cheese. The tomato sauce is in perfect balance with the cheese, always underneath but never soaking through. (In Chicago, a pizza can suffer from too much tomato sauce, but no pizza could ever have too much cheese.) And the crispy thin crust—"the kind that made us famous," crows the menu—soaks up just the right amount of grease, which is as integral to a great pizza as juice is to a great steak.

The menu additionally lists three other crusts of increasing thickness and a range of "gourmet" toppings, from "south of the border" to chicken alfredo to crispy eggplant parmigiana. Such something-for-everyone options don't tempt me. Part of being a pizza partisan is knowing what each place does best. What Father & Son has been doing best since 1947—before thicker pizzas became the local rage (or gimmick), before Thai and Southwestern entered the pizza lexicon—is serving the crispiest thin-crust pizza with the best toppings to a working-class, ethnically-diverse neighborhood on the city's near northwest side. If you go to a classic Chicago pizzeria you order a classic Chicago pizza.

At such a pizzeria, service can be brusque. You'll never hear, "Hi, I'm Lance, and I'll be your waiter this evening." (The waiter is there to take your order, not be your buddy.) The wine list might not extend much further than house red, white and white zinfandel, with most of the patrons preferring beer.

The pizza might take some time; I could have had a chain pizza delivered to my house in less than the half hour or so it might take Father & Son to deliver it from the kitchen.

The décor will likely evoke the 1950s—the tiled mural of Italian street vignettes, the hanging baskets of vines—while the surrounding neighborhood remains defiantly unfashionable. The best pizza is blue-collar food; it never originates in posh surroundings, though it may move or expand into pricier zip codes once it develops a following. (As neighborhood patrons move to the suburbs, so might their pizzeria.)

A classic Chicago pizzeria can serve both thin crust and deep dish, but it invariably specializes in one over the other. Though pan pizza is more than a tourist gimmick, it is less than the overwhelming preference of the locals. I'd estimate that the percentage of deep-dish consumed by Chicagoans is comparable to the percentage of "blackened" entrees ordered by New Orleans natives. And pizza in Chicago isn't nearly as divisive as baseball, where local fans must restrict their allegiance to either the Cubs or White Sox. Pizza lovers needn't choose one or the other; we'll go through thick or thin.

Though I've eaten some scrumptious deep-dish pizza—from the layer of sausage at Uno's to the buttery crust at Lou Malnati's—thin crust remains my default order, mainly because it's tougher to screw up. Even in those places that specialize in it, an undercooked pan pizza or one delivered lukewarm to your table tastes like gooey, soggy sludge, or might have too much stuff for the crust to support. A perfect pan pizza is a miracle of precision, but the deeper the dish, the more that can go wrong with the pizza.

As a corollary, the farther a deep-dish pizzeria extends its brand from home base, the greater the risk to quality control. A Chicago favorite might expand across the metropolitan area without spreading itself too thin, as Lou Malnati's, Gino's East and Giordano's have, but once it goes national—like the franchising of Uno's—the product in the outlying provinces is never the same. The best that can be said about the Uno's minipizzas found at airports across the country is that they're better than the rubbery hotdogs at the next stand.

Despite my occasional allusions to thick and thin, there's a profound distinction between deep dish and thick crust. As waiters at Lou Malnati's insist, their deep-dish pizza does not have a thick crust, and it's not nearly as doughy as the crust at some of their competitors. Instead, the thin, flaky crust is pulled high on the sides of the pan to enclose the ingredients, with cheese directly on that dough, then the sausage and pepperoni or whatever on top of the crust and tomato sauce on top of it all.

Though this relatively light concoction is my deep-dish favorite, Malnati's recent response to the low-carb craze challenges the very definition of pizza. To appease dieting disciples of Dr. Atkins, the restaurant has introduced a "deep-dish, crustless pizza," dispensing with that buttery crust entirely. It may be delicious, but it ain't pizza. It's a casserole. No matter how far we stretch the possibilities, in order to have a pizza you have to have a crust.

Even Plato knew that.

Father & Son, 2475 North Milwaukee, Chicago, IL, 773-252-2620.

Geraci's, 2266 Warrensville Road, University Heights, OH, 216-371-5643.

Imo's, 4479 Forest Park, St. Louis, MO, 314-535-4667.

Lou Malnati's, 6649 N. Lincoln, Lincolnwood, IL, 847-673-0800.

Mama Santa's, 12305 Mayfield Road, Cleveland, OH, 216-231-9567.

Sven and Ole's, 9 West Wisconsin, Grand Marais, MN, 218-387-1713.

Uno's (Pizzeria Uno), 29 East Ohio, Chicago, IL, 312-321-1000.

Valentino's, 3457 Holdrege, Lincoln, NE, 402-467-3611.

CALVIN TRILLIN AND FATS GOLDBERG

CALVIN TRILLIN LIKES TO EAT. HE LOVES THE BARBECUE OF HIS native Kansas City, he loves the greens sandwiches he gets on a street corner in Manhattan's Chinatown and he loves to eat the boudin (a kind of pork and rice pudding in casing) he gets from his friend James Edmunds of New Iberia, Louisiana. Shockingly, he doesn't love pizza. I found this out when I asked him to contribute to *A Slice of Heaven*. "I don't think I have much to say about pizza, Ed. I've never been truly devout about it." But what about those wonderful pieces you wrote about Fats Goldberg, who opened New York's first Chicago-style pizzeria, the eponymous Goldberg's? "Fats was my friend. My whole family was crazy about Fats. We liked his pizza. We loved Fats."

I decided to include one of Trillin's classic Fats Goldberg pieces anyway, because no book about the pleasures of eating could be complete without something from Trillin, who has shown all of us how to write about unpretentious food with wit, style and grace. But I wanted to probe Trillin's indifference to pizza, so he graciously agreed to be interviewed over—what else—a pizza lunch.

"Pizza is just not something I yearn for or even dream about," Trillin told me as we sat down at a very small table at Moustache, a Middle Eastern restaurant near his house in Greenwich Village. "There are exceptions, of course. I was at one of those fancy benefits the other night, and afterwards I was so hungry that I had a slice at Joe's. It was pretty good." We ordered three Middle Eastern–style pizzas on pita bread: a green pizza, a chicken pizza and a Moustache special with mozzarella and red peppers.

Trillin described a series of lost pizza-eating opportunities in his past. "When I grew up in Kansas City in the late forties, there wasn't any pizza. I remember seeing a pizza place in New York when my Dad took us there in high school. But I don't think we ate any. When my dad took me to New Haven to look at Yale, we could have had great pizza, of course, but I refused to look at anything there because I really wanted to go to the University of Missouri."

His father won out, and Trillin did end up going to Yale, but even there he didn't become a passionate devotee of Pepe's, Sally's or The Spot. "At Yale, everyone always represented the one they went to as the best." According to Trillin, arguments often ensued, but he just never got involved.

For Trillin, pizza was an excuse to spend time with the people he truly loved; his friend Fats Goldberg, who owned the semilegendary Chicago-style Goldberg's Pizzeria in New York; his daughters Abigail and Sarah; and his late wife, Alice. Every Sunday he and Alice would take the girls to Goldberg's, where Fats himself would escort them to the kitchen to make their own pizzas while Alice and Calvin would drink a glass of wine and catch up. The girls adored Goldberg, a lovable eccentric who was more kid than adult anyway. "Abigail and Sarah thought he was a tall child." On their birthdays, Fats would bring the girls a heart-shaped pizza with "Happy Birthday" and their initials spelled out in green pepper.

Fats was in the same Sunday school class in Kansas City as Trillin's sister Suky, which is how Trillin met him. Fats developed a mad crush on Suky, which went unrequited. As Trillin notes, "Fats would tell you that everything is unrequited love when you're that fat. Fats must have tipped the scales at three hundred pounds at that time, and there aren't a whole lot of scales that go up that high."

Fats Goldberg graduated from the University of Missouri and was working in ad sales in Chicago when he decided to open a Chicago-style pizzeria in New York. "Fats claimed he tried to steal the Uno and Due's recipe by hanging out in the alley in back of the restaurants kissing his then-girlfriend. He hadn't figured on the wind coming off the lake. The girl was willing to smooch, but she wasn't willing to freeze."

Trillin didn't love pizza, but it didn't stop his whole family from adopting Fats. "When he was here, he was part of the family. Alice adored him from the start. The girls thought he was much cooler than me. They loved musicals, so one year he bought them the *Singin' in the Rain* album and two parasols.

Another time he brought them a metal detector so they could search for coins on the beach in Nova Scotia."

I kept probing further into Trillin's relationship with pizza. He admitted that when he and Alice became volunteer counselors at a camp for kids with cancer, they would go to Willimantic Pizza in Connecticut on their day off. "That was really good pizza, Ed. You should go up and try it for the book." He then recalled, "On a beautiful spring evening Alice and I would walk to Lombardi's on Spring Street and have a clam pie. The clam pie was good, but really the best part of the evening was the walk with Alice."

I realized that for Trillin, pizza was an okay food; it just never rose to the level of barbecue or Chinese food. Yet he did offer, "I'm not opposed to pizza, Ed. I'm pizza-neutral. If God would come down and say I could never eat in a three-star French restaurant again, I would say, 'So. No. I don't really care. That's all right with me.' If he did the same thing with pizza, I'd ask God if we could make a deal. I would ask that justice be tempered with mercy."

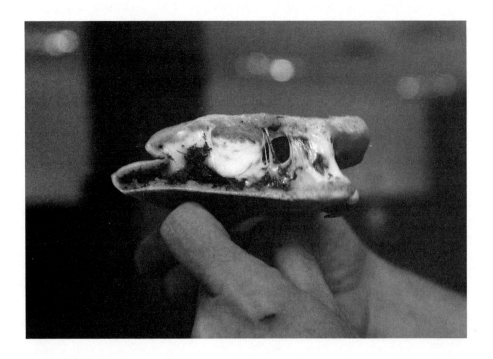

THE ORDEAL OF FATS GOLDBERG

❧ *Calvin Trillin* ❧

MY FRIEND FATS GOLDBERG, THE PIZZA BARON, HAS BEEN SLIM enough to be called Larry for years, of course, but I still think of him as Fats Goldberg. So does he. Although he has "been down," as he puts it, for fourteen years, after twenty-five years of exceptional fatness, he sees himself not as a man who weighs 160 pounds but as a man who is constantly in danger of weighing 320 pounds. "Inside, I'm still a fat man," he sometimes says. When Fats and I were boys in Kansas City, he was already renowned for his corpulence—though I can't say I was ever approached about posing for Refugee Relief ads in those days myself. During college, at the University of Missouri, he reached three hundred pounds and became known as both Fats Goldberg and Three Cases Goldberg— Columbia, Missouri, having been, through a derivation process that must still puzzle students of the language, the only place in the country where anybody rec- ognized a one-hundred-pound unit of measurement called the case. I occasionally saw him when I visited Columbia, where he was one of a number of storied eaters. According to one tale, when a restaurant near the campus instituted a policy of giving customers all they wanted to eat on Sunday nights for $1.35, a fraternity brother of Fats's called Hog Silverman, who weighed less than two and a half cases, went over one Sunday and put it out of business. Fats was known not only for that kind of single-sitting tour de force but for the fact that he never stopped eating. When he talks about those days, a lot of his sentences begin with phrases like "Then on the way to lunch I'd stop off at the Tastee-Freez . . ."

    Although Fats has never cared much for salad, he used to eat just about anything else within reach. He had a catholicity of taste comparable to that of a

Southern eater I once heard mentioned as being happy to eat "just about everything except Coke bottles." His specialty, though, was always junk food. "I did not get fat on coq au vin," he once told me. Candy bars. Lunch-meat sandwiches on white bread. Sweet rolls. Hamburgers. Chili dogs. Cake. Fats loves cake, and I suspect he likes it even better when it comes in a package. When he was visiting our house one day, long after he had forbidden himself to eat cake in New York, we wondered why he kept wandering in and out of the kitchen; then Alice remembered that there was a cake on the kitchen counter. Fats had been prowling back and forth in front of it, like a tiger circling a tethered goat. At Missouri, Fats often brightened up the late afternoon with something called a Boston sundae, which is, more or less, a milkshake with a floating sundae on top—a floating chocolate sundae with bananas if Fats happened to be the customer. I don't mean to imply that Fats was completely undiscriminating. There are good chili dogs and bad chili dogs. The only food that Fats still finds almost literally irresistible is, of course, a double cheeseburger with everything but onions at Winstead's, and our afflictions differ only in that I prefer the double hamburger with everything and grilled onions. For a number of years, Fats was in the habit of reading the latest diet book at Winstead's—holding the book in one hand and a double cheeseburger with everything but onions in the other.

I didn't see Fats for ten years after college, and when I did see him I didn't recognize him. It was a Sunday morning in New York, and I was at Ratner's on Second Avenue. I was having eggs scrambled with lox and onions, trying to ignore the scoop of mashed potatoes that Ratner's, for some reason, always includes on the plate—perhaps as a way of reminding the customer what less fortunate people may be eating in London, or wherever it's late enough for gentiles to be having dinner. I was glancing around constantly, as I tend to do at Ratner's, to see if some other table was being given a roll basket with more of my favorite kind of onion rolls than our roll basket had. Fats didn't even look familiar. In fact, if we hadn't had some intimate discussions since then about Winstead's hamburgers and Arthur Bryant's barbecued spareribs, I might even suspect him of being an imposter. Fats later told me that on the morning of May 1, 1959, while employed as a 320-pound salesman of newspaper advertising space in Chicago, he had decided to lose weight. Naturally, he had made similar decisions several dozen times in the past, and he still doesn't know why he was finally able to stop eating. He can't remember any single incident having set him on his course—no humiliation by some secretary who called him fat stuff, no particularly embarrassing experience buying trousers or trying to tie his shoelace. He is certain that it was not fear for his health that stiffened his willpower; several years before, his reaction to a serious warning by a doctor in Kansas City was to think about it over three Winstead's cheeseburgers, a fresh-lime Coke, and a Frosty Malt. On May 1, 1959, Fats started losing weight. He didn't use pills or gimmick diets. "It was cold turkey," he says now, referring to the method rather than the food. "I suffered." In a year, Fats weighed 190. Then, gradually, he went down to 160. In other words, by the time I saw him at Ratner's, the Fats Goldberg I had known was half gone.

Fats was still selling advertising space then, but he wasn't happy in his work. He believed that his true calling was stand-up comedy. After he moved to New York, he and a young woman he knew formed a nightclub comedy act called Berkowitz and Goldberg. Their first public performance was at the Bitter End, in the Village, which has what amounts to an amateur night on Tuesdays, but they got on so late that the audience consisted of only four people, all of them grim-faced. Berkowitz later discovered that none of them spoke English. As it turned out, a knowledge of the language did not vary the audience response. I never saw the act, but I think I have a pretty good idea of what it was like from a chance remark Fats once made while we were reminiscing about our show-business careers. (At Southwest High School, I had a comedy act with a partner who specialized in foreign dialects and took great advantage, I realized some years later, of the fact that none of the people we performed for had ever met any foreigners.) "We were called Berkowitz and Goldberg but we didn't do Jewish humor," Fats told me during that talk of lost opportunities. "That was one of the jokes."

After having inspired audiences all over town to puzzled silence, Berkowitz and Goldberg finally folded. Fortunately, Fats had one joke left; he opened a restaurant called Goldberg's Pizzeria. He was armed with not only the gimmick of having a Jewish pizza parlor but with the recipe for an excellent version of what the connoisseurs call a Chicago pizza—characterized by a thick, crisp and particularly fattening crust. I have only an occasional craving for pizza—a craving that I used to nurture carefully, like a small trust fund, at The Spot in New Haven, Connecticut—but I have eaten enough of it to know that Fats serves superior Chicago pizza. Almost as soon as Goldberg's Pizzeria had opened, Fats had what every comic dreams of—a lot of free publicity, critical acclaim, and "exposure" on *The Tonight Show*. (Actually, it was the pizza that was exposed rather than Goldberg; one was given away to a member of the audience who named a tune the band couldn't play.) Fats himself became so celebrated that he was able to publish a pizza cookbook—a volume that may add little to the literature of food but seems at least to have provided a resting place for some old jokes from the Berkowitz and Goldberg days. (One chapter is called "The Goldberg Variations, or How to Make Johann Sebastian Roll Over on His Bach.") Within a few years, there were three Goldberg's Pizzerias, and Fats was getting feelers from conglomerates.

Although Fats enjoys the trappings of a pizza barony, he realizes that his most notable accomplishment is not having created a successful business but having stayed thin. Among his pizza customers are some experts in obesity, and they have informed him that any fat man who remains slim for fourteen years can safely consider himself a medical phenomenon. (Since all Goldberg's Pizzerias display poster-size pictures of Fats when he weighed three cases, the subject of fatness often comes up, particularly on Sunday night, a traditional time for eating pizza and making diet resolutions.) Fats has been told that specialists can always make fat people thin through a variety of hospital treatments—treatments that a layman would probably summarize as solitary confinement. But once released, the patients almost invariably become fat again—meaning that, according to any reasonable assessment of the odds, Fats really is someone constantly in danger of weighing 320 pounds.

Someone who has gone without a relapse since 1959 is so rare that one researcher from Rockefeller University asked Fats if he would mind donating some of his fat cells for analysis. Researchers at Rockefeller and at Mt. Sinai Hospital have found that fat people who were fat as children have not only larger fat cells but more of them. When a chronically fat person loses weight, all his fat cells just shrink temporarily, remaining available for reexpansion—or, as someone who apparently enjoys taunting the fatties once put it, "screaming to be refilled." Fat-cell research has led to the depressing speculation that a person who was fat as a child faces horrifying pressure to become fat again and again, no matter how many times he sits in Goldberg's Pizzeria on a Sunday evening and vows that the diet he is going on the following morning will be different. Fats is unenthusiastic about the Rockefeller people's method of studying his fat cells, which would amount to withdrawing a section of tissue from the part of the body in which it is most accessible (or, as Fats sees it, "having three nurses stick an eight-inch needle in my *tushe*"), but he sometimes hints that he might be willing to cooperate. The more he thinks about the effort required for a fat man to stay thin, the more he thinks that he is extraordinary enough to be a boon to medical research.

A thin psychologist I know, Stanley Schachter, has done a lot of research at Columbia on obesity, and I once asked him it if was scientifically sound to consider Fats Goldberg truly amazing. After I had described Fats's accomplishments, Schachter seemed filled with admiration. According to Schachter's research, staying thin would be even more difficult for a pizza baron than for a run-of-the-mill fatty. The research indicates that what causes fat people to eat is not the physical sensations that go along with an empty stomach but what Schachter calls "external clues"—the sight of candy in the candy dish or the smell of hamburgers frying or the information that it is dinnertime, or in the case of poor Fats, the constant presence of delicious, aromatic pizza. One of Fats's doctor friends told him that a remarkably high percentage of the few former fatties who have managed to stay thin had fetched up in businesses having to do with food in one way or the other—tightrope walkers who want to defy the odds a bit more by working in unsnapped galoshes.

Schachter believes that fat people are unable to recognize the physical sensation of hunger—so that they actually eat less than thin people if external cues are missing. When two Columbia doctors, Theodore Van Itallie and Sami Hashim, removed virtually all external cues—they allowed people to eat all they wanted of an almost tasteless liquid, but nothing else—the thin people ate about the same number of calories per day that they had eaten of normal food but the fat people ate so little that one of them lost more than two hundred pounds in eight months. Schachter has found that among Jewish college students with roughly the same habits of synagogue attendance, the fat ones are more likely to fast on Yom Kippur than the normal-sized ones—and that their fasting is more likely to be helped by staying in the synagogue, where there are few food cues. The normal-sized ones get hungry. Normal people given food in a laboratory will eat less if their stomachs are full or if they're frightened, but if a plate of crackers is put in front of a fat person who has just eaten or who has been led to believe he is about to receive some electric shocks, he is likely to clean the plate anyway—or, in Shachter's terms, to eat until he is out of cues. The crackers have to be decent crackers, of course; fat people tend not to be interested in food that doesn't taste good.

After listening to Schachter explain the peculiar eating habits of fat people for a while, it occurred to me that what he had really discovered was that fat people are smarter than other people. For instance, in an experiment to test the hypothesis that fat people are less willing to work for their food than ordinary people, he found that the appeal of a bowl of almonds to normal-sized people who were filling out some meaningless forms he had concocted (Schachter is a very devious researcher) was unaffected by whether or not the almonds had shells on them. But when fat people were given the same test, only one out of twenty ate almonds that had to be shelled and nineteen out of twenty ate almonds that were already shelled. That seems to me a simple matter of intelligence. Who wants to spend his time shelling almonds? Testing the same hypothesis, Schachter and some of his students loitered around Chinese restaurants and found that fat Occidentals are much less likely to try chopsticks than thin Occidentals—the difference being, Schachter assured me, too great to be accounted for by the problem of manipulation inherent in chubby little fingers.

"But the fat people behave the way any normal intelligent person would behave, Stanley," I said when I heard about the discovery.

Schachter didn't say anything. Then I began to realize that a lot of the fat-people habits he had talked about applied to me. I have always thought that anyone who sacrifices stuffing power by using chopsticks in a Chinese restaurant must be demented. I would use a tablespoon if I thought I could get away with it, but I know that the people I tend to share my Chinatown meals with, terrified that I would polish off the twice-fried pork before they had a chance to say "Pass the bean curd," would start using tablespoons themselves, and sooner or later we would be off on an escalating instruments race that might end with soup ladles or dory bailers. Although I may have talked about being hungry from the moment I learned to talk, I am still not sure precisely what physical feeling people have in mind when they describe hunger. The last piece of food I left on my plate—that was in the fall of 1958, as I remember—had a bug on it. I suppose I might be persuaded not to finish a normal helping of Grand Marnier soufflé if a reputable and eloquent person I had every reason to trust insisted that my host had poisoned it, but I really couldn't say for certain until the situation actually came up. Schachter's theories, I decided, must be incorrect.

I tried to prove it to myself the next time I saw Fats by asking him a question in what I knew was a somewhat misleading way.

"Do you ever get hungry, Fats?" I asked.

"You bet your booties I do!" Fats said.

That would show Schachter, I thought. But a few days later, when I asked Fats for an example of a time when it was particularly hard for him to avoid eating, he said, "Tonight when I passed that pizza stand on Eighth Street that has great frozen custard, it almost killed me." External cue.

My discussion with Fats about hunger began at the Gaiety Delicatessan on Lexington Avenue, where he goes every day for a kind of lunchtime breakfast. Having been terrified by Schachter, I ordered the tuna-fish-salad plate with double coleslaw, hold the potato salad, and a low-calorie cream soda. Fats ate two scrambled eggs, sausages, a bagel with cream cheese, and four cups of coffee with a total of eight packets of sugar. "A fat man's got to have something to look forward to," Fats said. "When I'm reading in bed late at night, I think about being able to have this bagel and cream cheese the next day." Underlying the Fats Goldberg system of weight control is more or less the same philosophy that led to the great Russian purge trials of the thirties—deviation is the treason. His Gaiety meal varies daily only in how the eggs are done. In the evening, he has either a steak or half a chicken, baked in the pizza oven. (He is always careful to cut the chicken in half before baking and to put the unneeded half back in the refrigerator. "You have to pre-plan," he says. "A fat man always cleans his plate.") On Sunday night he permits himself a quarter of a small sausage pizza in place of the steak or chicken, but then he works at the ovens trying to sweat it off. On Monday he cheats to the extent of some bread or maybe a piece of pie. The schedule is maintained only in New York, of course. Kansas City remains a free zone for Fats. He says that in the earlier years of his thinness a week's trip to Kansas City to visit his family would mean gaining seventeen pounds. Lately, restraint has begun to creep into his Kansas City binges. The week's eating he was about to start when I saw him on the Kansas City plane cost him only ten pounds.

A few days after our meeting at the Gaiety, Fats happened to drop by my house. It had been a difficult few days for me: Schachter's theories were still fresh in my mind, and St. Anthony's, my favorite Italian street fair, was being held so close to my house that I had been able to convince myself that I could smell the patently irresistible aroma of frying sausages—Italian sausages, frying on a griddle right next to the peppers and onions that always accompany them. I have looked all over the country for a sausage I don't like, trying them all along the way. In the course of my research, I have tested country patties in Mississippi and Cuban chorizos in Tampa and bratwurst in Yorkville and Swedish potato sausages in Kansas (yes, Kansas) and garlic sausages in Romanian restaurants in New York and just about everything else that has ever been through a sausage grinder. So far, I love them all. I even like English bangers. I look on the bright side; with all that bread in them, they couldn't possibly cause heartburn.

Trying, I think, to keep my mind off my own problems, I mentioned to Fats that a doctor I knew had said that in order to gain even fourteen pounds a week in Kansas City it would be necessary for Fats to consume an additional seventy-two hundred calories a day—or the equivalent of fifteen or twenty Winstead's cheeseburgers.

Fats considered that for a while. He didn't seem shocked.

"Just what *did* you eat on a big day in Kansas City the week you gained seventeen pounds?" I asked. I prepared to make a list.

"Well, for breakfast I'd have two eggs, six biscuits with butter and jelly, half a quart of milk, six link sausages, six strips of bacon, and a couple of home-made cinnamon rolls," Fats said. "Then I'd hit MacLean's Bakery. They have a kind of fried cinnamon roll I love. Maybe I'd have two or three of them. Then, on the way downtown to have lunch with somebody, I might stop at Kresge's and have two chili dogs and a couple of root beers. Ever had their chili dogs?"

I shook my head.

"Greasiest chili dogs in the world," Fats said. "I love 'em. Then I'd go to lunch. What I really like for lunch is something like a hot beef sandwich or a hot turkey sandwich. Open-faced, loaded with that flour gravy. With mashed potatoes. Then Dutch apple pie. Kansas City is big on Dutch apple pie. Here they call it apple crumb or something. Then, sometimes in the afternoon, I'd pick up a pie—just an ordinary nine-inch pie—and go to my friend Matt Flynn's house, and we'd cut the pie down the middle and put half in a bowl for each of us and then take a quart of ice cream and cut that down the middle and put it on top of the pie. We'd wash it down with Pepsi-Cola. Sometimes Matt couldn't finish his and I'd have to finish it for him. Then that would be it until I stopped at my sister's house. She's very big on crunchy peanut butter. She even has peanut butter and jelly already mixed. They didn't have that when I was a kid. Then for dinner we'd maybe go to Charlie Bryant's or one of the barbecues out on the highway. At the movies I'd always have a bag of corn and a big Coke and knock off a Payday candy bar. Payday is still my favorite candy bar. They're hard to get here, but they have a very big distribution in Kansas City. Then we'd always end up at Winstead's, of course. Two double cheeseburgers with everything but onions, a fresh-lime Coke, and a Frosty Malt. If it was before eleven, I'd stop at the Zarda Dairy for one of their 49-cent banana splits. Then when I'd get home maybe some cherry pie and a 16-ounce Pepsi."

And so to bed. I looked at the list. "To tell you the truth, Fats, I'm afraid to add it all up," I said. I looked at the list again. Something on it had reminded me of sausages. It must have been the mention of Bryant's, which used to have barbecue sausages but quit serving them before I had a chance to try them—a situation that has always made me feel like an archaeologist who arrived at the tomb just a few days after the locals began to use the best pot for a football. I decided that I would walk over to the fair later and have just one sausage sandwich with peppers and onions— saving a few calories by having a barbecued rather than a fried sausage. If things got out of hand, I figured, I could always go on one of those diets that allow you as much as you want to eat as long as you eat only Brussels sprouts, quinces and summer squash. I had mentioned the fair to Fats, but he couldn't go. It wasn't on a Monday.

"Is life worth living, Fats?" I asked.

"Well, I figure that in my first twenty-five years I ate enough for four normal lifetimes," Fats said. "So I get along. But there is a lot of pain involved. A lot of pain. I can't stress that enough."

NOTE: Alas, Fats is longer with us, and neither is Goldberg's Pizzeria.

IT'S NOT MOM'S, BUT IT'S PRETTY GOOD

Dennis Getto

I've had lots of fabulous frozen custard, sausages and even some great Serbian food in Milwaukee, but I've never had pizza there. According to Dennis Getto, restaurant critic of the Milwaukee Sentinel, *I missed out.*

I'm the son of a first-generation Calabrese mother whose knack for Italian flavors combined with a deep desire to pass for American. The result was home-cooked, crisp-crust pizzas made from scratch, slathered with her homemade, slightly sweet tomato sauce and dotted with sausage, onions and both mozzarella and Parmesan cheese. She made them in the broiler.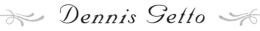

Ann's Italian Restaurant, 5969 South 108th Place, Hales Corners, WI, 414-425- 5040.
Everything I'm looking for in a Midwestern pizza done perfectly: crisp crust; fresh, fenneled sausage; crunchy vegetables; restrained tomato; and a blanket of silky, seductive mozzarella.

Louise's Trattoria, 275 Regency Court, Brookfield, WI, 262-784-4275.
The wood-fired oven here puts a hint of smoke into the crust; toppings range from traditional to designer. My favorite? Slightly sweet, barbecued-chicken pizza.

Trattoria di Carlo, 8469 South Howell Avenue, Oak Creek, WI, 414-768-0001.
The only thicker, Sicilian-style pizza that wows me by capturing Mediterranean sunshine on a thicker crust with tart tomato, mature Parmesan and little bursts of artichoke.

OMAHA!

Ed Delmont

I put out an APB to quite a few restaurant critics across the Midwest look-ing for pizza communiqués. Ed Delmont, restaurant critic of the Omaha News-Herald, *responded quickly with this report about pizza in Omaha.*

I THINK THE BEST PIZZA IN OMAHA IS ZIO'S "NEW YORK–STYLE" pizza, basically a thin crust with lots of available toppings—some of which are a bit exotic (Thai, etc.)—that keep customers happy. Usha Sherman oversees sev-eral Zio's locations and maintains a high level of quality control. Godfather's also does a very succulent, if thicker and gooier pizza. Their meat pies are excellent. Zio's and Godfather's beat the competition (most of which are national chains).

A local spot with a huge following, offering big, gooey, everything-added pizzas is Big Fred's. Other longtime spots are Lansky's, Sgt. Peffer's and La Casa Pizzaria.

I distinctly recall my first tangy, tomato-cheese pizza, sampled in Chicago when I was a boy in 1954 (I had no idea what was meant by "tomato pie"). At that time, hometown Minneapolis had no pizza parlors, though they arrived and multiplied soon after. 🍕

Big Fred's Pizza Garden, 1101 South 119th Street, Omaha, NE, 402-333-4414.

Godfather's Pizza, 4727 South 24th Street, Omaha, NE, 402-733-5577 (21 additional locations).

La Casa Pizzaria, 8216 Grover Street, Omaha, NE, 402-391-6300. 4432 Leavenworth Street, Omaha, NE, 402-556-6464.

Lansky's Pizza, 50th and L Street, Omaha, NE, 402-731-1919.

Sgt. Peffer Restaurant, 1501 North Saddle Creek Road, Omaha, NE, 402-558-7717.

Zio's, 7924 West Dodge Road, Omaha, NE, 402-391-1881.

CHAPTER
11

*California
and
West Coast
Pizza*

CALIFORNIA AND WEST COAST PIZZA

CALIFORNIA IS, ON THE WHOLE, A LOUSY PIZZA STATE. HOW DO I know? I've lived in both Los Angeles and San Francisco, and I've spent a fair amount of time driving around looking for a worthy slice. I am not alone in this assessment. Jonathan Gold, restaurant critic for both *LA Weekly* and *Los Angeles Magazine* and the author of *Counter Intelligence: Where To Eat In the Real Los Angeles*, writes about only two pizzerias in his book, which features 252 reviews. Compare that to the forty-one Mexican and thirty-one Chinese restaurants he reviews, and you can conclude that Gold does not think much of pizza in Los Angeles. The situation is no better in San Francisco. Patricia Unterman, in her five-hundred-page *San Francisco Food Lover's Guide*, reviews all of three pizza places.

When I asked *San Francisco Chronicle* restaurant critic Michael Bauer and his *Los Angeles Times* counterpart S. Irene Virbila to weigh in on where to find the best pizza in their respective cities, they agreed to do so only after telling me there wasn't much in the way of good pizza in their towns.

How did this sad state of pizza affairs come to be in a state filled with food lovers, great chefs and the best raw materials any cook could hope for? The answer lies partly in tracing Italian immigration in California. In *The World on a Plate*, his book about American ethnic food origins, Joel Denker notes that "California had America's largest Italian population (2,805) in 1860." He then goes on to say that "unlike the waves of southern Italians who swept into America during the late nineteenth and early twentieth century, California's frontiersmen were primarily northerners from Liguria and Tuscany." That explains why you can get fantastic focaccia (a Ligurian specialty) at the Liguria Bakery in San Francisco's traditionally Italian North Beach neighborhood, and a lot of lousy pizza elsewhere in the city. A Neapolitan immigrant named Frankie

Cantalupo did swim against the Ligurian tide when he opened California's first pizzeria, Lupo's (with a wood-burning oven, no less), in North Beach in 1935. In what can be described as a quintessentially Californian transaction, Lupo's became Tommaso's in 1971 when Cantalupo sold everything to his Chinese-American pizzaiolo, Tommie Chin, except the name. Chin was no dummy. He knew that a pizzeria named Chin's was going to have a rough time attracting customers, so he renamed it Tommaso's, which was Cantalupo's nickname for him.

But unlike Lombardi's in New York and Pepe's in New Haven, Tommaso's didn't breed a generation of pizza-makers in California. As Nora Ephron notes (see page 245), pizza was a scarce commodity in Los Angeles until the late fifties. When pizza did take hold in California in the late sixties and early seventies, chains and mediocre New York slicerias predominated. There were two pizza places I went to with my high school friends in 1969: Two Guys from Italy, one of many ersatz New York pizza places that dotted the minimalls of southern California; and Shakey's, on Olympic Boulevard, actually part of a Portland-based pizza chain that still exists. The idea that my friends and I chose to eat there more than once is deeply embarrassing to me.

California has contributed something of note to the pizza culture: the so-called designer pizza, made with nontraditional toppings such as goat cheese, spring onions and *merguez* (Moroccan lamb sausage). Inspired by some fantastic pizza she'd eaten in Torino, Italy, in 1979, Alice Waters installed a wood-burning oven at Chez Panisse, her groundbreaking restaurant in Berkeley, California. She topped her pies with locally grown vegetables, herbs, the best mozzarella she could find in the Bay Area and traditional toppings such as anchovies and sausage. Alice Waters may have been the first important chef in California to serve pizza with unconventional toppings in a serious restaurant, but it didn't really become a sensation until 1982, when Wolfgang Puck hired a pizzaiolo named Ed LaDou to be the pizza chef at the original Spago on Hollywood's Sunset Strip. Working with Puck's chef Mark Peel, LaDou came up with the idea for his now-famous barbecued-chicken pizza, made with barbecue sauce, red onion, cilantro, mozzarella and smoked Gouda cheese. Finally, California had a pizza culture to call its own. LaDou, dismayed by the credit and the attention Puck was receiving for *his* invention, left Spago and developed the menu for the first California Pizza Kitchen, which became a chain that introduced truly awful versions of California pizza to the rest of the country. Determined to be his own boss, LaDou opened his own place in Laurel Canyon in 1987 and then moved it to its current location in Studio City in 1993.

There are some hopeful signs for pizza in California. A Los Angeles–based Italian restaurateur named Peppe Miele introduced southern Californians to authentic Neapolitan pizza in 1992 at his Antica Pizzeria. Though that branch subsequently closed, in 1997 he opened another on the second floor of a minimall in Marina del Rey. In addition, a new breed of young and dedicated American chefs are studying Neapolitan pizza-making techniques and putting their own spin on it. These talented cooks are serving it in their restaurants and opening up pizzerias as well. Christophe Hille turns out beautiful Neapolitan pies in his two wood-burning pizza ovens at A16. Craig Stoll, chef/owner of Delfina, a terrific San Francisco trattoria, is about to take over an adjoining space to open a pizzeria. And Charlie Hallowell, a cook at Chez Panisse who treasured his time working the pizza station there, is opening Pizzaiolo on Telegraph Hill in San Francisco. He's even ventured to Phoenix to talk to Chris Bianco. All of these developments can only lead to more worthy pizza in the land of Schwarzenegger. Who knows? Maybe one day we'll be talking about pizza in California the same way we talk about Mexican and Chinese food there. I, for one, can't wait.

MY FIRST TIME

Nora Ephron

Writer and film director Nora Ephron responded almost immediately to my e-mailed request for a contribution to A Slice of Heaven. *Ephron, in her usual fashion, points out a fundamental truth about the perils of eating pizza.*

I FEEL THAT SOMEONE SHOULD POINT OUT THAT PIZZA WASN'T always with us. Like Saran Wrap, it turned up some time in the 1950s. (I was unbelievably irritated watching *A Beautiful Mind* when Russell Crowe ordered takeout pizza in Princeton in the late forties. Not possible.) The place you went for pizza in Los Angeles—and as far as I can remember, the only place—was called Miceli's Pizza Parlor, on La Cienega Boulevard, in the middle of what was known (then and now) as Restaurant Row. They made the pizza right in the window, and twirled the dough in the air. Crowds watched in wonderment.

Anyway, here is the point: I had never had pizza. It was not part of my family diet. When we went out to dinner we had Chinese. Pizza was something you had on a date, after a movie, at Miceli's. But, and here is the real point: I had never been on a date. And I was terrified—my best friend Marina Semenov's bossy older sister, Debbie, had drilled it into me there was only one way to eat pizza—with your hands—and that it was a fairly difficult skill possibly requiring you to fold the tip end of the pizza back over itself just slightly so that the oil and sauce didn't drip on your chin and your clothing. I was positive that if I ever had a date, and was ever taken to Miceli's, I would somehow eat the pizza the wrong way, and my date would know the horrible truth about me—that it was my first time. But eventually, I went on a date, I went to Miceli's, and eating pizza turned out to be a great deal easier than I had been led to believe.

Miceli's Pizza Parlor, 1646 North Las Palmas Avenue, Los Angeles, CA, 323-466-3438.

A16 | When the owners of A16 (it's named after the autostrada that runs through Campania) were shopping around San Francisco, looking for a chef to open their Campanian restaurant/pizzeria, they decided on a most unlikely candidate, Christophe Hille. Hille is a classically trained chef who cut his culinary teeth at such high-end restaurants as Campton Place and Charles Nob Hill. It turned out to be a great call. Hille spent five months cooking in Campania, the area around Naples that includes the Amalfi Coast and Capri. He became certified by the VPN American honcho, Peppe Miele, by spending three days at Miele's pizzeria in Marina del Ray. Hille is a very fine cook who makes lots of interesting, soulful Campanian food such as braised pork breast and tuna, confit style, but I refused to let those dishes distract me from the pizzas, which are among the best pies to be found in the Bay Area. Anyone craving the perfect Margherita pie in San Francisco could confine his search to A16. Hille has two wood-burning ovens, one for pizzas and one used for finishing the restaurant's meat dishes. He uses almond wood, which is quite plentiful in California. The mozzarella, which he ships from Casaficcio Joya, a cheese purveyor in the Los Angeles suburb of Gardena, is creamy and smooth. He uses San Marzano tomatoes and double-zero flour from Italy. His pies are sparsely and perfectly dressed, with just the right amount of mozzarella and sauce. Hille also had just the right amount of char on the crust—little dots of black and brown. He says the char depends on the nature of the fire in the oven. "It's the flame coming off the logs of wood that gives you the blistering. If you had just embers, the end result would be like bread." Hille also says the dough proofing is the most important thing in making great pizza. "The ideal temperature for dough is between 65 and 75°F." The ideal place for eating pizza in San Francisco is the counter at A16, where you can watch Hille and his merry band of cooks do their thing.

A16

2355 Chestnut Street (between Scott and Divisadero Streets), San Francisco, CA, 415-771-2216, www.a16sf.com.

RATING: ⊛ ⊛ ⊛ ◖

> **NOTE:** Go to A16 for lunch, when the noise level is tolerable, even pleasant. If you go at dinner, you may feel as if you're driving down A16 in a convertible with the top down.

  ALTO PALATO | I asked southern California native and current *Los Angeles Times* restaurant critic S. Irene Virbila to weigh in on her three favorite pizzerias in Los Angeles. Two of her choices were Angelini Osteria and Antica Pizzeria. For the third she chose the pizza Margherita at Alto Palato, a spot that I was sorry I missed the last time I was in Los Angeles. She wrote, "Thin-crusted and slightly smoky from the oven, it's the real thing, as spare and elegant as an Armani suit. The sauce is fresh and loose with none of the telltale bitterness of tomato paste, the mozzarella is fresh and the sole decoration is a few jaunty leaves of sweet basil. The minute the pie arrives, snatch it up from the plate, fold it over itself and devour it in eager bites.

"The most basic and delicious of pizza works only when the texture and flavor of the dough is right and the ingredients are in perfect balance. You can't make a Margherita with commercial mozzarella or an indifferent sauce. The quality has to be there in the simplest elements or it doesn't taste like anything at all. That's a principle Alto Palato's founder Mauro Vincenti instinctively understood. I also love the potato and rosemary pizza."

Alto Palato
755 North La Cienega Boulevard (between Santa Monica Boulevard and Sherwood Drive), West Hollywood, CA, 310-657-9271, www.alto-palato.com.

ANGELINI OSTERIA | All of Los Angeles clamors to get into this authentic osteria at dinner, when it wouldn't feel right to order just a pizza and a glass of wine. But at lunch, when it's less crowded, sidle up to the elegant little counter and do just that, as I did one glorious spring day. In a nifty little gas-burning oven that can't be seen, Chef Gino Angelini is making the Rimini-style pizza he learned to make as a teenager in Italy. It has a slightly thicker-than-cracker-thin crust that crunches when you bite into it. My two favorite pizzas here are the one with blobs of burrata cheese barely melted on top and the pie topped with mozzarella, cherry tomatoes and leaves of arugula straight from the Hollywood farmer's market.

Angelini Osteria
7313 Beverly Boulevard (at Poinsetta Place), Los Angeles, CA, 323-297-0070, www.angeliniosteria.com.

RATING:

🍴 ANTICA PIZZERIA | Antica Pizzeria wins the prize for the weirdest location for a good pizzeria in this country. It's in a mini–shopping mall in Marina del Rey, above a gourmet supermarket. It's worth searching out, however, because owner Peppe Miele, founding father of the VPN movement in this country, turns out exemplary Neapolitan-style pies. His crusts have a lovely raised lip and just the right amount of char from the wood-burning oven located just inside the door of the restaurant. The mozzarella that barely dots the Margherita pizza is made in-house, and the sauce is simply strained Italian tomatoes. Don't be put off by the atmosphere of Antica Pizzeria. It may look like a fast-food prototype (which in fact it is), but the pizza turned out by Miele and company is very serious indeed. Just go on a nice day, sit on the outdoor patio, and order a Margherita and a glass of wine.

Antica Pizzeria
13455 Maxella Avenue (2nd floor, Marina Villa Marketplace), Marina del Rey, CA, 310-577-8182.
RATING: 🍊 🍊 🍊

THE CAFÉ AT CHEZ PANISSE | I don't love salad, but I admit

that pizza and salad are a most felicitous combination. That being the case, I would rate The Café at Chez Panisse just a small notch below Pizzeria Bianco as the world's greatest pizza-and-salad restaurant. I've always had really friendly servers at the Café, and they've never given me a hard time about ordering just pizza and salad for a light and quick dinner. All right, I also get dessert, but sometimes it's just fresh fruit. On my last visit, I had the Riverdog Farm asparagus salad with prosciutto di Parma and almonds, a leek-and-beet salad with mustard vinaigrette and the baked Sonoma goat cheese with garden lettuces. The greens tasted of the sun and the earth, and the asparagus were tender and spritely. The beets were so sweet they could have been part of the dessert menu.

We ordered the two pizzas on the menu that night—one with spring onions and herbs, the other with tomato sauce, anchovy and capers. Neither was a classic Neapolitan combination, but both were very fine, indeed. The crusts were thin, chewy and pliable, if a little wan for my taste. The mix of mozzarella and fontina was inspired and perfectly proportioned, and didn't overwhelm the pie. The spring onions and fresh herbs were a perfect combination in late April. The anchovies were minced, rather than whole, and they blended beautifully with the capers and tomato sauce.

The Café at Chez Panisse
1517 Shattuck Avenue (between Cedar and Vine Streets), Berkeley, CA, 510-548-5049,
www.chezpanisse.com.
RATING: ⊛ ⊛ ⊛

CAIOTI PIZZA CAFÉ | As I mentioned in the beginning of this

chapter, Caioti Pizza Café's Ed LaDou is a certified California pizza pioneer. He moved his nondescript, unassuming pizzeria from Laurel Canyon to its current Studio City location a few years ago, and he's never looked back. LaDou is a pizza toppings master. His barbecued chicken pizza will make it impossible to eat the pale imitation at a California Pizza Kitchen ever again. His toppings, which feature roast garlic, bacon, shallots and lamb sausage, let you know that there is a serious culinary mind at work here. The only thing that's slightly disappointing at Caioti is the crust. It's a perfectly okay, thinnish crust that somewhat surprisingly comes out of a conventional gas-fired oven, but it's not unlike crust you've had at many other pizza places. Toppings this good created by someone as talented as LaDou deserve a better crust.

Caioti Pizza Café
4346 Tujunga Avenue, Studio City, CA, 818-761-3588.
RATING: ⊛ ⊛ (for the crust)   ⊛ ⊛ ⊛ ⊛ (for the toppings)

NIZZA LA BELLA | Evelyne Slomon, chef/co-owner of Nizza La Bella, wrote a truly great pizza tome, *The Pizza Book*, which is tragically out of print (see her fascinating account of the history of Lombardi's on page 87). She also knows a great deal about *making* great pizza, having studied at the feet of two legendary New York pizzaioli, Pete Castellano of John's and Anthony Pero of Totonno's. Those two demanding taskmasters would be proud of the pies Slomon makes in her wood-burning oven here. Her crust is medium-thin with just enough puffy chewiness. Her sauce tastes of ripe tomatoes and little else, and she uses the highest-quality mozzarella she can get her hands on. The New York–style pizza isn't even on the menu, but the regulars know that Slomon is thrilled to be able to show what she has learned from her teachers.

Nizza La Bella
825 San Pablo Avenue (between Castro and Garfield Avenues), Albany, CA, 510-526-2552.
RATING: ⊛ ⊛ ⊛ ◖

> NOTE: Occasionally, when Slomon is taking a day off, the pizzas come out of the oven with a completely charred bottom.

🍴 PIZZETTA 211 | I love the idea of Pizzetta 211. Two young, passionate

San Franciscans set up shop in a tiny storefront on a side street in the Richmond district, armed with a desire to turn out perfect pizzas from a conventional gas pizza oven, along with salads that utilize the abundance of fresh local ingredients. They've succeeded, for the most part. The pizzas here are carefully made with well thought-out toppings, but I wish their crusts were a little less crisp, and a little more pliant and puffy. The salads are minimally dressed and excellent, and there's always a selection of fine artisanal cheeses from the Artisan Cheese Shop. They even make a pretty swell flourless chocolate cake using Scharffenberger chocolate.

Pizzetta 211
211 23rd Avenue (between California and Clement Streets), San Francisco, CA, 415-668-8998.
RATING:

🍴 TOMMASO'S | Agostino Crotty, coowner of Tommaso's, is a dedicated

pizzaiolo and restaurateur. Every night, customers see him tending to the seventy-year-old, wood-burning oven in the right-hand corner of the restaurant. He's a hard-working man turning out an honest pie. The crust has a nice yeasty flavor and a fine raised lip and flattens out considerably the further toward the center of the pie you go, leaving the crust a little gummy. The Italian sausage, from Molinari's down the street, is a little bland. I love sitting in one of the white wooden booths that line both sides of Tommaso's, ordering a pizza and staring at the murals while I wait for my pie. Tommaso's doesn't make the pizza of my dreams, but in a city lacking many quality pizzerias, Tommaso's is a worthwhile destination.

Tommaso's
1042 Kearny Street (at Pacific Avenue), San Francisco, CA, 415-398-9696.
RATING: ⊛ ⊛ ◖

NOTE: Tommaso's is actually a full-service, Italian-American restaurant with an extensive menu. The one item to be found on everyone's table is a pizza.

We're Not in Kansas Anymore

Michael Bauer

Michael Bauer, restaurant critic and food editor of the San Francisco Chronicle, *is always elegantly attired, even in all-day business meetings. But after receiving his account of San Francisco (and Kansas) pizza, I can only surmise he's ruined an awful lot of ties eating pizza.*

GROWING UP IN A SMALL TOWN IN KANSAS, I CAN'T SAY I HAVE A long history ferreting out great pizza. I remember our next-door neighbor started a pizza restaurant on Main Street with red vinyl tablecloths on each table and the "Girl from Ipanema" on a continuous loop on the stereo. The pizza was thick and gloppy; double cheese was standard and most patrons wanted even more. It was practically impossible to hoist it into your mouth without prior weight training.

When I moved to California, I rejected that style completely for the thin blistered crust that can only be achieved in a hot wood oven. A slice of pizza needs to stand at attention from the minute you pick it up until you savor the last bite of warm yeasty crust. I'm a fool for "designer" pizza, whether it's something from the brick oven at The Café at Chez Panisse in Berkeley, or the smoked-salmon pizza in the lounge at Postrio in San Francisco. When I'm in a hurry I'll pick up a pizza at Firewood, with several locations around the city, always getting the version with paper-thin slices of prosciutto and leaves of peppery arugula. I also love the blistered crust slathered with thyme-scented tomato sauce with mozzarella and pancetta at RNM. I still dream about the version I had at Manzanita in Healdsburg, topped with white anchovies, celery leaves and preserved lemon, and the one at Bistro Don Giovanni's in Napa that's topped with an egg and truffles. When I have a craving for something more substantial, I'll head to Pauline's, home of the cornmeal crust.

Bistro Don Giovanni's, 4110 Howard Lane, Napa, CA, 707-224-3300.

Firewood, 620 West Field Road, San Francisco, CA, 650-588-8464 (with five additional locations).

Manzanita, 336 Healdsburg Avenue, Healdsburg, CA, 707-433-8111.

Pauline's, 260 Valencia Street, San Francisco, CA, 415-552-2050.

Postrio, 545 Post Street, San Francisco, CA, 415-776-7825.

RNM, 598 Haight Street, San Francisco, CA, 415-551-7900.

In Defense of Designer Pizza

Brian Koppelman

When Brian Koppelman, coscreenwriter of Rounders *and* Runaway Jury, *moved into our building, he, his wife, Amy, and their two children, Sam and Anna, became active participants in* A Slice of Heaven. *Eight-year-old Sam in particular had strong opinions about pizza that he was not reluctant to voice. Brian, likewise, loves to dish about pizza. He also loves pizza with designer toppings, for which he gives an impassioned defense.*

MY FATHER, WHO FIRST INTRODUCED ME TO PIZZA, IS A PURIST. To him, a pie isn't legit unless it's built like the ones he ate during his high school years in Far Rockaway, Queens. Out there, amongst the row houses by the Atlantic Ocean, the neighborhood joints served it straight up: crisp crust, tomato sauce, fresh mozzarella. Maybe a sprinkle of Parmesan. That's all. No pesto. No goat cheese. Definitely no pineapple. That's how my old man liked it. He's still a no-nonsense guy; I, however, am a fop hooked on "gourmet" pizza.

Give me a pie like the ones they make at Joanne's on route 25A in Manhasset, Long Island—either dotted with pieces of sweet honey-Dijon chicken, or chunks of chicken wings, with the whole pizza slathered in hot sauce and blue cheese, or even stacked high with bread-crumbed baked clams and roasted garlic or one like Mark Strausman's white pizza drizzled with aged balsamic vinegar at Fred's at Barney's on Madison Avenue in Manhattan—and you won't hear another word from me until the entire thing is gone.

It's not only my father who looks down on the rococo pies I dig so much, but also people of taste throughout the food world. It's as if I were professing a love for jazz-fusion, or the art of Thomas Kinkade, or line dancing. There's even a moniker for this funky pizza, an in-the-know word used by foodies to classify and mock: designer. "Designer pizza isn't pizza," they say, "it's casserole." In Italy, the legislative body has even proposed a law to codify that which can be called pizza, relegating all nonconforming pies to the gray market, I suppose, where dealers will skirt the law and slip you a shrimp-scampi slice at their own risk of prosecution.

That's fine with me. Let Italy protect Old World tradition. The way I see it, gourmet pizza hews to a particularly American ethos: Take a classic and make it better by adding, taking away, adapting it to the times.

This is not to say that I don't like the original. I understand the need for pizza that shows its *terroir*, its ecological pedigree. A well-prepared slice of basic pizza is an example of perfect simplicity, the sauce, cheese and crust as satisfying as great three-chord rock and roll. But just as much as recent-vintage, three-chord rock has lost the spark of the original and now sounds redundant, imitative and boring, much of the pizza that you will find being sold in street-corner parlors is served stale, with fake cheese and watery tomato sauce, crust either brittle and overcooked or reheated and soggy.

If, however, you walk into Giorgio's on Second Avenue in Manhattan, where the awning advertises "gourmet pizza by the slice," you will find pizza good enough to stand up to the contempt of the pizza police. They serve one slice in particular—the Giorgio roasted garlic, spinach and ricotta slice—that epitomizes all that I find compelling about gourmet 'za.

The crust at Giorgio's is thin but substantial, and always crisp without being flaky. They use a sweeter sauce than is traditional, and that tastes not merely of sugar, but also of tomatoes picked at the very height of flavor. The mellow roasted garlic, along with the ricotta and slightly bitter spinach, cut the sweetness of the sauce, enhancing the richness and depth of the slice. All of the ingredients used in this slice are, taken separately, fairly common in Italian restaurants and pizzerias, but when combined in this distinctive manner they truly rise to the ideal of the gourmet.

It is this notion, that there can be *gourmet,* not merely *designer* pizza, that I find animating. Why should this most egalitarian food be limited by any constraints? Why shouldn't innovation, imagination and creativity be encouraged, rewarded? Yes, many of the attempts to make brilliant, new pizza have failed. For every wonderfully exciting pie there are twelve that should have been thrown out the moment they came out of the oven (starting with the Tandori Chicken pie at California Pizza Kitchen). Still, I look forward to discovering my next gourmet pizza obsession. Will it be a cheeseburger-and-bacon slice with jalapeños in Boston, or an heirloom-tomato-and-Stilton combination outside of London, or a sea-urchin-and-wasabe slice with rice-infused crust right here in New York? I don't know, but I can't wait to find out.

Fred's at Barney's, 660 Madison Avenue, New York, NY, 212-833-2220.

Giorgio's, 1343 Second Avenue, New York, NY, 212-628-8419.

Joanne's, 1067 Northern Boulevard, Roslyn, NY, 516-869-8686.

ON THE PROWL FOR PIZZA

Karen Brooks

Karen Brooks, of the Oregonian, *was so dedicated to her Portland Pizza Report that she kept resubmitting her entry with updated information. Who knows, by the time you read this, she'll have discovered someplace new.*

CRACKER-THIN CRUST CUT INTO OBSESSIVELY NEAT SQUARES WITH a sweet-salty-tangy sauce and a bizarro but addictive sticky-gooey cheese called Provel. Profound regional pizza . . . or malpractice? Depending where you're from, it's both. I grew up on it, so "St. Louis–style" pizza, like Proust's madeline, is still as powerful as a whiff of truth serum. Pizza does not drive date books in Portland, where the approaches run from East Coast–School hopefuls to wacky West Coast—overweight pies piled with organic things or odd topping combos begging the question: Does broccoli, much less Thai BBQ chicken, belong on a pizza, even if you are saving the planet? That said, the restaurant Café Castagna makes a fine pie Italians would recognize: thin and super crispy, with impressive, minimal toppings, such as asparagus and eggs with a knock of Cacio de Roma cheese. I happily take the twenty mile drive from Portland to the new Scholls Public House, a funky country place serving the kind of blistery, brick-oven pizza with things like homemade pork sausage and a buttery, muscular dough that has fanatics whispering. And if I'm acting like a native, it's Hot Lips Pizza, a homegrown chain where pies come with the likes of wild-catch sockeye salmon or River Run Farm beef and delivery is by bike or electric car.

Café Castagna, 1758 Southeast Hawthorne Boulevard, Portland, OR, 503-231-9959.
Hot Lips Pizza, 721 Northwest Ninth Avenue, Portland, OR, 503-595-2342.
Scholls Public House, 24485 Southwest Scholls Ferry Road, Hillsboro, OR, 503-628-1904.

FAR-FLUNG PIES

 Nancy Leson

I've spent a fair amount of time in Seattle working on a cookbook with my friend Tom Douglas. I must admit I've never had pizza there. To my rescue comes Nancy Leson, restaurant critic for the Seattle Times *and a passionate pizza eater with whom I've shared many a slice.*

WHAT CAN YOU SAY ABOUT A GIRL FROM PHILADELPHIA WHO EATS pizza? That she moved to Seattle and married a guy from Chicago? That she still prefers her pizza thin-crusted, cheese-laden and oily? Damn straight. And while the Chicago connection has me eating Lou Malnati's deep-dish specials Fed-Ex'd frozen from the Windy City, my heart still beats for the pies of my youth: namely, Joseph's Pizza in Northeast Philly (with a cherry pepper–fueled cheese steak on the side), its yeasty-scented confines still etched in my old hunger memory bank.

Here in Seattle, I turn to Piecora's, where the staff's New York attitude goes a long way toward making these royal rounds taste the way they should. And I'll gladly drive the distance to tantalize my tastebuds at VPN-recognized Tutta Bella, where high-quality toppings take as their canvas a slender, beautifully blistered, silky-textured crust. But when it's time to let my fingers do the walking—and someone else do the driving—it's all about Pagliacci Pizza, whose "Philadelphia-style" recipe (who knew?) and far-flung delivery outlets have made this pizza purveyor a Seattle favorite for twenty-five years.

Pagliacci Pizza, 550 Queen Ann Avenue North, Seattle, WA, 206-285-1232.
Piecora's, 1401 East Madison Street, Seattle, WA, 206-322-9411.
Tutta Bella, 4918 Rainier Avenue South, Seattle, WA, 206-721-3501.

Hawaii Pizza

Honolulu Magazine

The following report came via e-mail from writer/editors Joan Namkoony and John Heckathorn. I love the idea of professional wrestler-driven pizza.

To determine the best pizza in town, we ordered almost all of them—fourteen to be precise. We picked up pizza pies from Kähala to Mäpunapuna and brought them all back to the office for a side-by-side comparison (a.k.a. a pizza party). We weren't looking for newfangled pizzas with goat cheese, peanut sauce or caramelized pears. We wanted real pizza—tomato sauce, pepperoni and cheese piled atop a crispy crust. The result surprised us. We discovered that some of our personal favorites didn't taste nearly as good as they did in the restaurant. A few of these pizzas were so good, we wondered why we hadn't tried them before.

Our top pick: Antonio's New York Pizzeria. Cousins Joe Tramontano and Anthony Romano bought the restaurant about a year ago. After tweaking the original owner's recipe, they noticed a spike in business. "We actually make it the exact way they make it in New York," says Tramontano, who moved to Hawaii from the East Coast about sixteen years ago. "We import the flour and cheese and get vegetables delivered fresh daily. All of our meat is cut on a slicer here. Nothing comes from a can, so this is food that's fresh." Antonio's pizza looks unassuming, but it's got a nice texture, lively sauce and plenty of cheese. The cousins' secret? "It's made by real Italians," says Tramontano. "You wouldn't buy your lau lau from an Italian, would you?"

If Tramontano looks familiar, you might recognize him as local prowrestler JT Wolfen, who last year won the NWA North American Heavyweight Title.

Antonio's New York Pizzeria, 4120 Waialae Avenue (across from the Kahala Mall), Suite 109B, Honolulu, HI, 808-737-3333, www.antoniosnypizza.com.

CHAPTER

12

Bar Pizza

Bar Pizza

Bar (or tavern) pizza is an entity unto itself within the pizza realm. It's been around at least since Prohibition ended in 1933, but who knows, maybe there was a speakeasy serving pizza. It is served all over the country, although I have found a preponderance of bar pizza in New Jersey, Staten Island, Chicago and Connecticut.

What defines a bar pizzeria? They're usually family-run businesses that have been passed down from generation to generation. It's pizza served in a bar (of course), which means minors are not let in unaccompanied by adults. At Vito & Nick's on Chicago's far South Side, a sign on the door greets all perspective customers with that very message. Bar pizza is served by waiters, waitresses and bartenders who, let's just say, have been around the pizza oven more than a few times. They may make you feel welcome, but only after sizing you up for a full minute. They usually have a twinkle in their eye that's not immediately discernible, and more than a little bit of attitude. A bar pizzeria likely has plastic tablecloths if it has any tablecloths at all. There's a good chance that the choicest tables are booths.

What is bar pizza like? It's usually very thin-crusted to (I'm guessing) leave plenty of room in the eater's stomach for beer. It's baked in a gas oven that may have replaced a coal oven if the bar is old enough. Bar pizza is made with decent, commercial, aged mozzarella, and comes topped with canned mushrooms, standard pepperoni and, if you're lucky, house-made sausage. You will not find any fancypants ingredients or toppings in or on a bar pizza, though at the Brü Rm. at Bar in New Haven they have created a yuppie, postmodern bar pizzeria that serves things like mashed-potato pizza and Blonde Ale. It's actually good pizza and good beer, but somehow it seems antithetical to the original idea of bar pizza.

In the last twenty years, a new kind of bar pizza has cropped up—a decidedly fancypants pie, served in the bars of serious restaurants all over the country. Chef/proprietors such as Alice Waters and Wolfgang Puck wouldn't deign to serve pizza in their formal dining rooms at dinner alongside the foie gras and caviar but, like the rest of us, they love pizza and wanted to figure out a way to serve it in their restaurants. For more about the chef-pizza phenomenon, turn to page 284.

I ate more than my fair share of working-man's bar pizza in writing *A Slice of Heaven*. Here are my favorites.

Boonton (New Jersey) Bar Pizza

RESERVOIR TAVERN | With its low ceilings adorned with stained acoustical tile, the Reservoir Tavern needs only a Knock Hockey set and a ping-pong table to be the rec room all of us wanted to have growing up. The Bevacqua family has been turning out pizzas and other homey Italian-American fare since 1937. The pizza here comes out of a bread oven with rotating shelves that looks very much like the oven at Santarpio's in Boston. The pies are hearty, fairly thick-crusted and have a great crunch when you bite into them. The sausage is made in-house, and though they use standard aged mozzarella on their pies, they will substitute fresh mozzarella on request. The potato-and-bacon pizza would be spectacular if they used thinner potato slices.

Reservoir Tavern
90 Parsippany Boulevard (Route 287), Boonton, NJ, 973-334-5708.
RATING: ⊛ ⊛ ⊛

Boston Bar Pizza

SANTARPIO'S | Santarpio's opened as a bread bakery in the same East Boston location in 1910. In 1933, after Prohibition was lifted, the Santarpio family took over the pool hall next door and started serving pizza, pasta and grilled lamb-and-pork sausage skewers to the Italian laborers who worked and lived in East Boston. Why the unlikely combination of pizza and grilled meat? Because, as current owner Frank Santarpio remembers with a chuckle, "Our neighbors and customers, Italian laborers, worked hard and drank hard, and they wanted filling, cheap food and a piece of meat." The pizzas were made in a coal-fired brick oven until 1952, when, according to Santarpio, "the thing just fell apart, and they had to replace it with a Reed gas bread oven, which had five shelves that could hold eight pizzas each." The crust at Santarpio's has plenty of crunch and char, although Santarpio says, "A lot of people these days want it more like the chains, so if they want it not too crispy, we'll give it to them. But if we make it for 'em the way I like it, it will be the best pizza they ever ate, as long as they have good teeth."

Santarpio's
111 Chelsea Street (at Porter Street), East Boston, MA, 617-567-9871.
RATING: ✷ ✷ ✷

Chicago Bar Pizza

 VITO & NICK'S | In 1952 Vito Barraco and his son Nick began serving thin-crusted pizza at their tavern at 79th and Carpenter. It (and they) would eventually become famous all over the South Side of Chicago. Thirteen years later, the Barracos moved to their current location, a low-slung building on the corner of 84th and Pulaski. The Barracos use excellent local sausage on their pizza and, much like Stamford's Colony Grill, their hot oil spices up the pizza considerably.

Vito & Nick's, See page 217.

New Haven Bar Pizza

🍴 BRÜ RM. AT BAR | Bar is the quintessential yuppie tavern pizzeria. When you walk in you're confronted by big copper beer tanks and a huge gas-fired brick oven. Bar doesn't deviate too much from New Haven pizza tradition. They serve their pies on metal rectangular trays just the way they do it on Wooster Street. Bar's clam pie has just enough fresh briny clams on a slightly charred and crisp crust, and their more conventional pies like sausage and mozzarella aren't too shabby either. Bar devotees swear by the designer toppings, but I say when in New Haven, eat New Haven pizza. That means no mashed potatoes on your pie.

Brü Rm. at Bar
254 Crown Street (between College and High Streets), New Haven, CT, 203-495-1111.
RATING: ⊛ ⊛ ⊛ ◖

New Hyde Park (New York) Bar Pizza

🍴 EDDIE'S | I'm not a big fan of cracker-thin pizza crust, so I was pleasantly surprised by how much I liked Eddie's pizza, which features a crust not much thicker than one of those pieces of cardboard sandwiched inside my laundered shirts. Though the crust is cracker-thin, it's surprisingly pliant. You can fold a slice of Eddie's pizza. Through five owners and seventy-three years, Eddie's has been pleasing Nassau County residents determined to save the bulk of the room in their stomachs for beer, not pizza.

Eddie's
2048 Hillside Avenue (at Denton Avenue), New Hyde Park, NY, 516-354-9780.
RATING: ⊛ ⊛ ◖

Stamford (Connecticut) Bar Pizza

COLONY GRILL | I was turned on to Colony Grill by a pizza-loving patron of Sally's Apizza in New Haven. He said that although he loved Sally's, the one pizza he could not do without is Colony Grill's. It's the oldest establishment serving food in Stamford, Connecticut, having opened in 1840. The only thing on the menu is pizza: small, round pies baked in a pan. The crust is the quintessential ultrathin, crackerish bar pizza crust, and the sausage may be made in-house. The pièce de résistance at Colony, its reason for being, is the spritz of hot pepper oil they'll add to the top of your pie if you so desire. Make sure you have a full mug of beer when you bite into the hot-oil pizza . . . you will need it.

Colony Grill
172 Myrtle Avenue, Stamford, CT, 203-359-2184.
RATING: ◉ ◉ ◖

Staten Island Bar Pizza

DENINO'S | At Denino's, the pizza box says it all: IN CRUST WE TRUST. They should trust their crust, because it is light and crisp and pliant. Denino's is a classic red-brick tavern pizzeria (with a separate dining room), but it is just as welcoming to kids after a little league game as it is to middle-aged softball players coming in for a pie and a brew after a game. I'm crazy about Denino's sausage pie, which features fine sweet Italian sausage made fresh every day by a local butcher. If you want to go vegetarian, try the white pie, made with mozzarella, onions, fresh garlic and a splash of olive oil. After fifty-three years you might think the Denino family has gotten bored with making pizza. Not so, according to third-generation coowner Michael Denino: "We still put our heart and soul into every pie."

Denino's
524 Richmond Avenue (at Hooker Place), Staten Island, NY, 718-442-9401.
RATING: ◉

CHAPTER
13

*Chain, Frozen
and
Internet
Pizza*

Chain Pizza

IS CHAIN PIZZA AS BAD AS SERIOUS FOOD PEOPLE SAY IT IS? I WAS determined to find out . . . and determined to give chain pizza a fair shake. So I resolved to eat only chain pizza for dinner for a period of one week. I would limit myself to one chain pizza a day (though I was sorely tempted to get all the chain pizza eating out of the way in an afternoon). My wife, son and friends were horrified by this regimen, and reminded me of the fate of the man who attempted to eat nothing but McDonald's food for a month. But if I wasn't willing to die for my art, at the very least I was willing to get a little sick for it. What did I find? Chain pizza is for the most part awful stuff. No news here. How is it awful? Why is it awful? What does it mean for pizza-eating people everywhere that it's awful? These are the essential questions that must be answered in any thorough examination of pizza.

First things first. As a discerning eater I found all elements of chain pizza wanting. The crust is characterless, tasteless and lacks even the merest trace of salt and yeast. Chain pizza sauce invariably tastes of tomato paste and sugar. Chain pizza cheese is inferior-quality mozzarella that resembles a yellow blob of melted goop. Toppings are made of inferior ingredients, typically watery canned mushrooms or porklike sausage pellets overwhelmed by the awful dried herbs and spices that go into them.

Why is chain pizza so awful? Many, many reasons. The pizza chains were all started by business people, as opposed to individuals interested in food. Go to the web site of Little Caesar's or Pizza Hut or Papa John's. You'll find heartwarming stories of young people who overcame their modest circumstances to achieve great wealth and build big, successful businesses. You won't find the stories of passionate pizza makers determined to bring their fabulous pizza to every corner of the world.

All "Quick Service Restaurant" businesses are built on the same fundamental tenets:

1. Standardize your product. Make sure the pizza tastes the same in Omaha as it does in Anchorage. For pizza, this means that the dough, sauce, cheese and toppings are made in central locations for maximum shelf life, and then distributed to the franchisees. Even if a Pizza Hut franchisee decided to use fresh mozzarella on even one pizza, company rules would prohibit it. Freshness is an obvious casualty of this approach.

2. Control costs and minimize waste. Chain pizzas make pizza a commodity. That means the major chains compete on price, because the market for commodities is by definition price driven. That's why I can buy a large sausage pizza at Little Caesar's for $7.99. Low prices mean low food costs, and low food costs mean low-quality ingredients.

3. Minimize labor costs. Pizza-making is labor intensive, so pizza chains find the lowest-cost labor they can find. These poorly paid workers are given scant training, and what training they are given is not geared to the overall quality of the pizza they are making. After all, the managers themselves have never been shown how to make great pizza.

The result is that most pizza chains are staffed with poorly trained and paid pizzaioli supervised by people more concerned with the bottom line than the bottom crust. This is not the stuff of great pizza.

What's particularly disturbing about all this is that pizza is made with relatively inexpensive ingredients: water, flour, canned tomatoes, yeast, salt, mozzarella cheese and olive oil. Even the costliest ingredients on that list are not absurdly expensive. Good fresh mozzarella is three dollars a pound, good Italian packaged tomatoes are a couple of bucks a can and you can find good-quality, extra-virgin olive oil for eight dollars a liter. So it should be possible to make a better-tasting pizza using good ingredients without spending an exorbitant amount. A pizza at Pizzeria Bianco is less than fifteen dollars. But the crucial ingredients Chris Bianco adds to his pizza are sadly lacking at the chains: skill, passion and pride.

Those come from the top, and until someone starts a pizza chain with those ingredients, we are all going to have to go elsewhere for great pizza.

> **NOTE:** Bertucci's is a chain with close to a hundred locations. They use good ovens and fresh mozzarella in their pizza and, as I discovered, the results are promising. A large Margherita at Bertucci's costs $17.99. That's a lot more than at the other chains, but Bertucci's pizza is exponentially superior. So if chains are your only option, and you can afford it, head for Bertucci's.

BERTUCCI'S

"Hi, welcome to Bertucci's. My name is Johnny, and I'll be your server today." When I heard that, I knew I had wandered into a different kind of pizza chain. The state of the art Woodstone brick oven I was staring at across from our table was another giveaway. It's fueled by gas, though there are other Bertucci's locations with wood-burning ovens. The first Bertucci's opened in 1981 in Somerville, Massachusetts. At one point Bertucci's had even received certification from the VPN. These days its membership has been suspended, because as VPN America founder Peppe Miele explained, "They went around me to Italy for their certification. We can't allow that."

Undeterred by their American VPN suspension, Bertucci's has persevered, and after a few missteps caused by too rapid expansion, has positioned itself as a low-priced, more authentic alternative to Olive Garden.

I of course had no interest in anything on the very large menu other than pizza. We ordered a large Margherita with sausage on half. My man Johnny brought over some warm rolls and a plate of olive oil with fresh rosemary, oregano and red pepper flakes floating in it. The rolls tasted like Tuscan brown-and-serve rolls, but they were warm and actually quite satisfying once dipped into the flavored olive oil. Our complimentary salad tasted like it was dressed with a bad, bottled "Eye-talian" dressing.

The pizza arrived at the table five minutes later. I grabbed a piece of the plain half and took a bite. The yeasty crust was pretty darn good. It had a decent lip and was nicely charred. I ripped off an edge of the crust and put it in my mouth. It wasn't world-class pizza crust, but it was certainly way better than any chain pizza I had tasted. The dots of white cheese on the pizza were obviously fresh mozzarella, a pleasant surprise. The sauce was a deep red. It looked more like a cooked pasta sauce and, although it tasted okay, there was way too much of it on the pizza. The oddly seasoned sausage came atop the pizza in large pelletlike chunks that had no discernible pork or fennel flavor. The next time I go to a Bertucci's I would order a plain Margherita, easy on the sauce.

The pizza at Bertucci's is good enough to give me hope for the future of chain pizza. It's not the pizza of my dreams, but it's certainly way better than Domino's, Little Caesar's, Pizza Hut or Papa John's. In fact, it's one small step for pizza-kind.

CALIFORNIA PIZZA KITCHEN

I have had a number of pizzas at CPKs all over the country in the last ten years, and though the pizza was never better than acceptable, I wasn't prepared for just how awful the pizza would be when I went into the only Manhattan location in June for a late lunch. We ordered the pizza that made CPK founders Rick Rosenfeld and Larry Flax rich and almost famous, the Original BBQ Chicken pizza, and a Margherita, described on the menu as authentic thin-crusted pizza made with both aged and fresh mozzarella.

The toppings on the Original BBQ Chicken pizza—smoked Gouda, red onions, cilantro and barbecue sauce—were actually quite tasty. But the crust was limp and flaccid. It had no charred black or brown spots. In true California fashion it was blonde. It also had no hole structure and no yeasty flavor. The Margherita was no better. It had a few browned edges, but was still as soft and puffy as a cotton ball. Next time around I will opt for a salad. California Salad Kitchen. Now that's got a nice ring to it.

DOMINO'S

The clock was about to strike six when I called Domino's. I ordered a large Classic Hand-Tossed Italian sausage and cheese. The woman who took my order was exceedingly polite, and said my pizza would be $12.45, and would take thirty minutes to arrive. I checked my watch a number of times, and then, like magic, at exactly 6:29, our doorbell rang. How did she know it would take exactly thirty minutes? What could Domino's possibly teach its employees in order for them to be able to tell me to the minute when my pizza would arrive? Or had the delivery guy been standing outside my door for the last eight minutes, waiting for the magic thirty-minute signal to finally ring the bell?

"CAUTION," warned the box in white letters on a red background. "Hot! CAUTION: Hot! CAUTION: Hot!" The pizza was in fact hot when I opened the lid. I tried the plain slice first. The outer rim of the crust, what the Neapolitans call *cornicione,* had a couple of big air bubbles, and fairly decent hole structure. The cheese was a predictable blanket with browned spots on top. It had no discernible taste. The sauce tasted of sugar and dried herbs and hardly at all of tomato. The Italian sausage had the merest hint of dried fennel. Assessed individually, the ingredients of a large Domino's Classic Hand-Tossed pizza with Italian sausage don't amount to much. But because it was still melted cheese on warm bread, it was kind of satisfying.

I was satisfied enough not to take Domino's up on its Total Satisfaction Guarantee: "If you are not completely satisfied with your Domino's Pizza experience, we will make it right or refund your money. Guaranteed." How can the company make that guarantee in New York, where there are scores of top-notch, by-the-slice places, not to mention coal-fired, brick-oven stalwarts like Totonno's and Lombardi's? Maybe that guarantee holds up in Ann Arbor. But surely in the Big Apple, where pizza is king, no one ends up paying for a Domino's Pizza.

LITTLE CAESAR'S

Things must not be going so well for Little Caesar's in New York. When I walked into its Greenwich Village location, I found myself in a cavernous space that spanned an entire city block. Most of the space, however, was devoted to computers. I had wandered into a Little Caesar's Internet café. I ordered my pizza at a little counter right off the front entrance. There were stacks of already-made pizzas ready to be eaten behind the young man who took my order. When I told him I wanted a large pie with Italian sausage, he said that would take twenty minutes. I e-mailed Will from one of the computers and told him I would be home soon, pizza in hand. Twenty minutes later the counterman announced that my pie was ready. It was still warm when I walked into the house fifteen minutes after that. The cheese was the usual sludge, the sauce had no discernible tomato flavor, the sausage was the usual chain pellets and the crust was rescued by the large amount of oil in the dough. It turns out that the Internet service was better than the pizza.

PAPA JOHN'S

It was Saturday night, and I was excited. I was going to have my first ever Papa John's pizza. Of all the big pizza chains, only Papa John's has staked out a position based on taste. Its motto is "Better Ingredients. Better Pizza." According to its website, "As a high school student working at a local pizza pub in Jeffersonville, Indiana, Papa John's founder John Schnatter realized there was something missing from national pizza chains: a superior-quality traditional pizza delivered to the customer's door. His dream was to one day open a pizza restaurant that would fill that void. In 1984 'Papa' John Schnatter knocked out a broom closet located in the back of his father's tavern (Mick's Lounge), sold his prized 1972 Z28 Camaro, purchased $1,600 worth of used restaurant equipment and began selling his pizza to the tavern's customers." Sounds like my kind of guy; he actually wanted to make good pizza.

I ordered my regular test pizza, a large half-sausage, half-plain pizza. The counterperson asked me if I wanted regular sausage or Italian sausage. I said Italian and, because they had pizza by the slice as well, I ordered a slice of half regular sausage, half hamburger while I waited. The "regular" sausage (what exactly *is* regular sausage?) tasted like bad breakfast sausage. I got into a cab and arrived home while the pizza was still hot. The pie came with a container of garlic sauce, which I guess was meant for dipping. There's a rule of thumb that's generally followed all over the world: Pizza should not be served with dipping sauce. I shook well and opened it up. It was a shade of yellow not found in nature. It looked positively radioactive. I turned off the lights. Thankfully, it didn't glow in the dark, but it did taste awful.

I brought the pizza to my office, where I had downloaded and printed out Papa John's story and surprisingly elaborate description of ingredients. I took a bite of a slice, and began to read about what I was chewing. The dough is made at regional quality-control centers with proprietary flour and specially filtered water, and then shipped fresh (never frozen) to its restaurants, allowing it to proof slowly and naturally. I must admit the dough is lighter and tastier than the dough at most other chains. It tasted as though it might have sugar in it, and not nearly enough salt. The sauce is made from canned tomatoes that go from the vine to the can in an average of six hours. The sauce wasn't bad, though it was a little sweet for my taste. The cheese is 100-percent mozzarella made by one of America's finest cheese producers, not available to any other pizza company. I couldn't discern any difference between it and the other chains' cheese. The Italian sausage is made from 100-percent pork and seasonings. It tasted porklike, with an unpleasantly peppery finish. I think Papa John's may indeed make a slightly better pizza than its competitors, but if I were John, I would have kept the Z28.

PIZZA HUT

I don't know why, but somehow I thought I was going to get a good pizza from Pizza Hut. Maybe it was the fact that Consumer Reports pronounced Pizza Hut the best all-around chain pizza in 2002.

I went to the Pizza Hut at 50th and Broadway—in one of those mini–food courts that dot Manhattan. This particular one had a KFC and a Dunkin' Donuts in addition to the Pizza Hut. I ordered my large regular pie with sausage, and was told to come back in fifteen minutes. I contemplated getting some fried chicken in the meantime (I'm actually quite fond of Kentucky Fried Chicken). Then I started thinking about my diet, and I concluded that there was no diet in the world that would sanction a dinner of sausage pizza and fried chicken.

Now I must tell you that the mini–food courts in Manhattan are a little weird when it comes to pizza. The ovens are not in plain sight. All I could see behind the counter at this particular Pizza Hut was one of the shelves where they line up the already baked personal pizzas. I began to worry that my pizza had been made at Pizza Hut World Headquarters in Wichita, Kansas, and then had been shipped to New York City. I asked the person behind the counter if I could see the oven. She shook her head emphatically. No. Request denied. It was as if I had asked to see one of the terrorist prisoners in Guantánamo.

As promised, fifteen minutes later the counterperson brought my pizza to the counter and lifted the box top to show me my dinner. It was then that I noticed white stuff oozing out of the crust. I said, "This isn't a stuffed-crust pizza, is it? Because I asked for a regular-crusted pizza." She replied, "Yes, it's a stuffed crust. Eat this one, it will take another fifteen minutes to make another pizza." I acquiesced, not wanting to wait.

Remarkably, the pizza was still intact when I got home fifteen minutes later. To paraphrase cereal-box language, the contents of my pizza box had shifted slightly during shipment, but only slightly. My stuffed-crust pizza was still warm. Maybe all that cheese functions as insulation, like quilting in a winter jacket. I put a slice on a plate and sat down to eat. I know this sounds all too predictable, but the slice was unspeakably awful. The crust was oily, had that grid on the bottom that indicates it was premade in a rack oven, and was positively oozing an off-white cheesy substance. The sausage looked like bird-feed pellets and tasted worse. The sauce was sweet and yucky.

Well, I thought to myself. At least my son will eat it. He'll eat almost anything that doesn't have mushrooms or green peppers in it. Just then, Will waltzed through the front door. "Hey, Will," I called out warmly. "I got a stuffed-crust sausage pizza for dinner."

He walked into the kitchen. "Stuffed-crust pizza. Those are nasty, Dad. Even my friends won't eat those. That's as low on the food chain as you can get."

Oh, well. Taken in again by those do-gooders from *Consumer Reports*. I put the stuffed-crust pizza on top of the *CR*-recommended air-conditioner that is so loud it drowns out helicopters, and announced that, from now on, that corner of the room would be known as the *Consumer Reports* shrine.

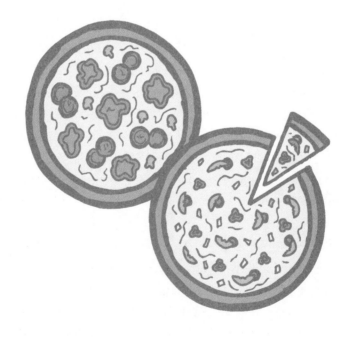

FROZEN PIZZA

I'VE ALWAYS HAD A THING FOR FROZEN PIZZA. AS A KID, I devoured box after box of Pizza Fours, individual snack-sized pies that unsurprisingly came four to a box. By the time I got to college, I had kicked the frozen-pizza habit, mostly because we could buy pizza pretty late into the evening at Pagliai's and Ahrvano's. It wasn't the greatest pizza in the world, but I was in Grinnell, Iowa. I needed sustenance, and it was cheap and filling.

Frozen pizza has come a long way since my Pizza Four days. In fact, according to an article written in the *New York Times* Sunday business section, "In strictly frozen-pizza terms, the year 1995 was every bit as momentous as 1066 or 1492. Before that date, frozen pizza was a gourmand's worst nightmare: overly chewy crusts topped with bland sauce, rubbery cheese and meat specks tougher than jerky." In 1995, Kraft Foods came out with the first DiGiorno pizza, featuring a rising crust.

According to Brendan Koerner in the aforementioned *Times* story, rising crust was a "food technology coup. Kraft's researchers were inspired in large part by three patents taken out in 1983 by General Foods of White Plains, which combined with Kraft in 1989. The patents covered the preparation and safe storage of frozen, yeast-leavened dough, a complex process involving the meticulous addition of hydrophilic colloids for stability and surfactants to 'facilitate flour hydration and initial dough development.' Kraft also developed modified atmospheric packaging, which keeps the pies bathed in inert gas rather than oxygen, which erodes the dough."

My son, Will, has introduced me to DiGiorno Rising Crust Pizzas (and their fierce competitor, Freschetta, which introduced a similar product a year later, in 1996) and while they are marginally better than the Pizza Fours of my youth, they are not as good as the slices I can get from any of a dozen pizzerias within three blocks of my Manhattan apartment. But, as someone who works at Freschetta told me, New York is the single worst frozen-pizza market in the country, because of the number of high-quality, independently owned pizza shops in Gotham.

In 2004, Schwan, which was sued by Kraft for allegedly obtaining vital pizza secrets by hiring a former Kraft contractor (the suit was settled in 2001), upped the ante in the frozen pizza category with the introduction of a line of "Brick Oven" pizzas made with a "fire baked crust." DiGiorno has responded with "Thin Crispy Crust" pizza. It seems to me that both companies are hoping these pies will satisfy customers looking for a crisp-crusted, New York–style slice anywhere in the country.

In addition to these two new entries from the industry leaders, other companies are also coming out with upscale, gourmet pizza, some of which are made with supposedly more healthful ingredients. To sort out this Darwinian struggle for frozen pizza supremacy, I enlisted the aid of my friend and colleague Jeffrey Steingarten, *Vogue* magazine's food critic and the most relentlessly curious food person I know. Jeff and I (along with his assistants Jeanne Koenig and Elizabeth Alsop) endeavored to taste seven brands of frozen pizza in his loft, which is filled, floor to ceiling, with every foodstuff, cooking gadget and food book and periodical imaginable. Steingarten has a decidedly scientific bent when it comes to food, so I figured I could arouse his curiosity by alerting him to all the new technology going into frozen pizzas.

I arrived one beautiful late spring day, laden with seven kinds of frozen pizza. Jeffrey was ravenously hungry (as usual), but was not looking forward to our lunch. "Ed," he announced, "perhaps—and I'm only speculating here—if I was in a spaceship on the way to Mars, and the only food at my disposal was a frozen pizza floating tantalizingly close to my nose, I might—just might—eat one or two of them."

Elizabeth had preheated the oven and a pizza stone, so we immediately popped in the DiGiorno Thin Crispy Crust Four Cheese Pizza. When Elizabeth took it out of the oven, the crust was golden brown and the cheese was molten. Elizabeth cut the rectangular-shaped pizza into little pieces with scissors, which turns out to be the best way to cut a pizza. I was really hungry, and immediately took a bite of my piece. Big mistake. Not only did I get pizza burn on the roof of my mouth, but also I was immediately admonished by Steingarten. "Ed, surely you must know it's far more accurate to taste things when they're closer to body temperature." I waited a minute, then took another bite. The crust was crisp, all right, but it didn't have much flavor. It was salty. It tasted like bad crackers.

Freschetta's 5 Italian Cheese Brick Oven Pizza was next. I liked the fact that there were discrete areas of sauce and cheese, and the crust was again crisp but completely lacking in flavor. Elizabeth said it tasted like Pizza Goldfish. She was right, but I kind of like Pizza Goldfish.

American Flatbread's Organic Tomato Sauce and Three Cheese Pizza, made in a stone-and-clay oven fired with wood in Waitsfield, Vermont, actually had a pliant and chewy crust that tasted good on its own, even though it was made with whole wheat. Its crust had hole structure the way a good crust should. The only slightly strange aspect of this pizza was its sweet smell. "It smells like French Toast," Jeanne said. Sure enough, when we looked on the box for ingredients, there it was, pretty high up on the ingredient list: pure Vermont maple syrup.

Whole Food Market's 365 Four Cheese was pretty awful. It was thick and unappetizing with a cheesy sludge on top. Jeanne said, "Even when really drunk I don't think I could eat this."

Amy's Cheese Pizza, made with organic tomatoes and flour, had a crisp crust and a vaguely sweet aftertaste, perhaps from the honey listed in the ingredients.

California Pizza Kitchen's Five Cheese & Tomato Pizza claimed it had a fresh-baked restaurant taste. The crust puffed up like a proud father's chest at his daughter's wedding, and the whole thing was quite tasty in a bad-food way. Elizabeth put her finger on it: "It tastes like cheese sticks or that cheesy bread you get at chain pizzerias." Jeffrey also liked the CPK pizza, which had chunks of tomato rather than tomato sauce, but he didn't understand Elizabeth's cheesy bread analogy, never having eaten at a pizza chain in his life. He said, "This isn't bad, but there's something about the cheese I don't like. It tastes like unripe cheese, which could mean something is wrong with the whey solids." Once again Steingarten had me scrambling for old chemistry textbooks. But there they were, on the list of ingredients, whey solids.

A new brand, Linda McCartney, was our final pizza. Before she died, she and Paul launched a line of frozen foods. The pizza was described on the box as a Stone-Fired Crust Cheese Pizza, made with mozzarella and Romano cheese and a zesty tomato sauce. It was by far the worst pizza we tried. It had a crust that looked and tasted like cardboard, with a yucky, pseudo-tangy topping. Just as Paul needed John Lennon to make truly inspired music, maybe Linda needed Yoko to make a decent-tasting frozen pizza.

I asked Steingarten if he was impressed with the new technology. He thought for a moment before giving me a most unscientific answer. "Ed," he announced, "there's an extremely technical term for the new frozen pizza technology: ca-ca."

INTERNET PIZZA

(and Overnight Pizza)

WITHOUT THE INTERNET IT WOULD HAVE BEEN VERY DIFFICULT TO write *A Slice of Heaven*. On the web I found addresses and phone numbers, old reviews of pizzerias and lists of every city's best pizza places. But like just about everything else on the Internet, the real gems to be unearthed are the quirky, idiosyncratic and impassioned blogs and web sites. Want to know weird and fun facts about pizza, try pizzaware.com. Everything you need or want to know about pizza is right at your fingertips.

I have fallen in love with a couple of sites, ones I check out even when I'm not writing about pizza. Slicenyc.com is a pizza blog. It's funny, well-written and infused with pizza passion and knowledge. PizzaTherapy.com comes from the pizza-possessed brain of Albert Grande, a Hawaiian whose motto is "Pizza on Earth, Good Will to All." PizzaTherapy has a log of user-generated pizza faves in all fifty states. I don't agree with all of the picks, but it's certainly a handy service to have if you're desperate for pizza in Mobile, Alabama, or Davenport, Iowa. PizzaTherapy.com also has a pretty complete list of pizza links on the web. From that list I found the website of a truly obsessed Pepe's maven, Howard Goldbaum of Las Vegas, Nevada. Log onto his website at www.unr.edu/goldbaum/travelblog/pizza/, and you'll find a feature-length documentary about Pepe's.

As far as ordering pizza on-line and over the phone for overnight delivery, there is no shortage of options. Chicago pizzerias Gino's East and Lou Malnati's both ship, as does Imo's in St. Louis. But be aware that very few of the pizzerias I write about in *A Slice of Heaven* offer shipping all over the country. None of the "Keepers of the Flame," for example (see chapter 17), will ship their pizzas directly from their places of business. In fact, many of the pizzaioli chronicled here are such sticklers for freshness that they don't like to sell their pizzas to go, because a box ends up steaming the pizza and makes the crust less crisp. So my advice to anyone wanting to savor the taste of a Pizzeria Bianco pizza or a Sally's or Pepe's tomato pie is to befriend someone living in Phoenix or New Haven and ask him to buy a pizza for you and send it overnight. If you don't know anyone in those two cities, befriend someone on-line who lives there and ask him to do you a favor. Pizza enthusiasts are a tribe, and they will often go to great lengths to make fellow tribe members happy.

CHAPTER
14

*Chefs and
Pizza*

CHEFS AND PIZZA

COOKING IS EASY. PIZZA IS HARD. THAT'S THE PREVAILING SENTIMENT among the many serious chefs across America who tackle pizza in their restaurants. What used to be the province of slice counters and "red sauce" Italian-American restaurants has now become required eating at many of the seminal American restaurants in this country. From Alice Waters to Wolfgang Puck in California, to Todd English and George Germon in New England, it seems you can't find a chef who's not crazy about pizza.

How did this come to be? Why would men and women who have spent years behind a stove mastering sautéing and braising and making sauces bother with something so simple and plebian as pizza? Alice Waters became enamored with the idea of making pizza after a trip to Torino, Italy, in 1979. "I loved the elegant simplicity of the pizzas that came out of a wood-burning oven at this trattoria in Torino. When you eat pizza you get the experience of eating warm bread topped by all these lovely little tastes." When she returned she installed a wood-burning oven at The Café at Chez Panisse. The wood-burning oven is another reason she and other chefs love the idea of making pizza. "When you get to see the fire it connects to the experience of the hearth. Not to mention the incredible smell that goes with it. Plus, pizza is incredibly affordable and adaptable."

The "chef-pizza" craze kicked into high gear in 1982, when Wolfgang Puck opened Spago. There, pizza chef Ed LaDou (now of Caioti Pizza Café) expanded the range of toppings to include barbecued chicken, *merguez* (lamb sausage), smoked salmon and crème fraiche and Peking duck. According to LaDou, "The pizzas at Spago were initially expected to be a complement, almost the equivalent of appetizers, to the entrees and pastas that would showcase the artistry of Puck and his executive chef Mark Peel." Instead they became the signature dish of the restaurant. As Puck wrote in his book *Pizza, Pasta, and More,* "When the restaurant [the original Spago] finally opened, we could barely keep up: pizza was the most frequently ordered item on the menu."

LaDou eventually developed 250 different pizzas for Spago. Pizza became critically important to Puck for another reason: When the kitchen was backed up, he would send out a pizza gratis to tide his ravenous customers over.

The same year that Spago opened, George Germon, a former professor at the Rhode Island School of Design turned chef/restaurateur, invented his now-famous grilled pizza at Al Forno in Providence. He began experimenting with soaking pizza dough in olive oil and then stretching and grilling it. "I have always been mesmerized by fire. I love cooking on it, and I love watching it. Cooking over a live fire is a challenging thing, an event. We cook our pizzas three inches over the coals. Our grill generates an incredibly fierce heat. Right over the coals it's 1100°F." Germon's sparsely topped pizza is unique and absolutely wonderful. It's crispy, chewy and just oily enough, a perfect confluence of tastes and textures. When I eat at Al Forno I have to stop myself from ordering more than just a couple of pizzas and two or three of Germon's wife Joanne Killeen's made-to-order desserts, which are as mind-bogglingly good as Germon's pizzas.

For Germon, the decision to make pizza in his informal but very serious restaurant was a difficult one. As he told author Peter Reinhart (see page 206) in his book *American Pie,* "I'm working it out, I guess. When I first told my dad we were opening a restaurant, he complained, 'Now you'll be just like any other Greek, making pizza.' I explained we weren't going to make pizza, but then a couple of years later we figured out a way to do these grilled pizzas, and you know, you have to take what life gives you and go with it."

In Boston ten years later, a pizza-obsessed former baseball catcher, Todd English, started making oddly shaped pizzas at his Charlestown restaurant Olives. Having grown up in southern Connecticut, English's life changed when he had his first clam pizza at Pepe's. "I love food that you can eat with your hands. And I'm fascinated by pizza." A playful, irreverent chef who is constantly pushing the envelope, English began making pizzas both fanciful and classic at Olives. Fig jam, Gorgonzola, prosciutto and rosemary is a signature pizza at English's restaurant, Figs. A pie topped by carpaccio, arugula, Gorgonzola and garlic aioli sounds silly, but is delicious. Traditionalists can easily make do with a pepperoni, marinara and *mozzarella di bufala* pizza or what English calls a Classico, shaved Parmigiano-Reggiano and tomato.

So if all these supremely talented chefs are taking pizza so seriously, why is it so hard? It's because chefs like Alice Waters, George Germon and Todd English are not actually cooking in their restaurants most nights, so it is up to them to transmit their knowledge and their passion to their cooks. At The Café at Chez Panisse, Al Forno and Olives, pizza is just another station through which the cooks at these restaurants must rotate, and it's often the kitchen stepchild. Waters says, "You really need someone who's passionate and professional. It's not easy; you're dealing with a lot of unpredictable elements and variables like dough and a live fire. A lot of cooks say or at least think that making pizza is demeaning. They want to show me how they can really cook at a stove. It's about finding a person who has the right disposition for it."

One Chez Panisse cook who has the passion and the fire has just opened Pizzaiolo on Telegraph Hill in San Francisco, with Waters's blessing and assistance. Meanwhile, the cooks keep cycling through the pizza station at The Café at Chez Panisse, and as a result the pizza there has its ups and downs. The toppings are always delicious, but the crust can be beautifully brown and blistered one day, wan and flat the next.

Germon says he tries to find cooks on his staff who have a natural affinity for grilling pizza. "Once I identify someone who gets it, I watch him or her carefully. I try to build pride and dignity into the pizza-making process. To make it work, the pizza cook has to make the station his or her own." His method is effective. The pizza cooks work incredibly hard making something that almost every table orders at Al Forno. As a result the pizza is quite consistent at Al Forno.

What Alice Waters at Chez Panisse and George Germon at Al Forno started more than twenty years ago has now become a full-fledged trend. Many talented young chefs are mastering different aspects of pizza-making and making the medium their own.

As you're about to read, Mario Batali went through many ups and downs when he opened his pizzeria/enoteca Otto. Christophe Hille, a classically trained chef, went to Italy for six months before opening A16, where he makes very fine Neapolitan-style pizza. Vincent Scotto took his Al Forno pizza training and fashioned a thinner, crisper grilled pizza at Gonzo in New York.

Andrew Feinberg and his wife, Franny, opened Franny's in Brooklyn with a simple desire to make first-rate pizza using great ingredients. Craig Stoll, chef/owner of Delfina, a fine trattoria in San Francisco, is about to open a pizzeria next door. And leading the chef-pizza charge is Phoenix's Chris Bianco, who in his own poetic way has shown all of us, chefs and pizza lovers alike, what pizza can be in the twenty-first century. Alice Waters says the most exciting, uplifting thing she sees happening in food right now is chefs opening small places so that they can get back to cooking themselves. Many of those small places are turning out to be pizzerias.

In an unpublished manuscript Ed LaDou wrote something about the pizza at Spago that best explains the relationship chefs have to their slices of heaven: "There was something about the pizzas that just hit the right note at the right time. They were sophisticated without being pompous. They were friendly and familiar, yet interesting and creative. Chefs loved them as a respite from the intricacies of many of their own creations. Finally, the pizzas tapped into childhood associations we all have about pizza." Alice Waters puts a more mystical spin on why chefs are attracted to pizza: "Pizza is an immediate kind of pleasure; its got chi, this life force, to it."

Al Forno, See page 292.

The Café at Chez Panisse, See page 250.

Olives/Figs, There are numerous Olives across the country as well as four Figs in Boston that serve Todd English's pizzas. Though Todd is a very talented chef, even he has not figured out how to be in every location at the same time. That said, I have eaten Todd's pizza in Boston, New York and Washington, and have found it to be consistently good.

It's Not Easy Makin' Pizza in the Heart of the City

Mario Batali

Über-chef/restaurateur and television personality Mario Batali found out the hard way that even for famous chefs, cooking is easy and pizza is hard. I asked him to write about the difficulties of a well-known chef opening a pizzeria.

I'D ALWAYS WANTED TO MAKE PIZZA—NOT THE REGULAR, GREAT New York City slices like the ones I eat at Joe's, right around the corner from two of our restaurants, Babbo and Lupa, or the great whole pies made in coal-fired brick ovens like the one at Totonno's in Coney Island, where we eat when Susi and I take the kids to the aquarium. Instead, Joe Bastianich and I decided we'd do a pizzeria and enoteca that would feature Sardinian flat bread, more like cracker or a lavash, that would be charred on a griddle. It'd be faster, different and easier to do. Or so we thought.

Otto opened on January 8, 2003. The first griddle we bought and installed was unusable. It had too many hot spots. But that didn't stop the people from coming. The second Saturday we were open we served almost a thousand people. Plus, we had every freakin' critic coming through the doors, and I found myself on the line burning pizzas on one side of the griddle and leaving them cold on the other. We weren't quite ready for the crowds in other ways as well. My dough recipe was enough for twenty pounds of dough, and the first weekend we opened we needed eight hundred pounds. A slight miscalculation. I was trying to make a classic Neapolitan dough using fresh yeast. Among other things, I misinterpreted the mixing time and the intensity of gluten development of all-purpose flour. I was hoping to develop a firm, chewy crust, more crisp than elastic. Unfortunately, it came out hard, not crisp, when it came off the griddle. As it cooled it got worse. We knew we were still in the process of fixing it, and we also knew the other things on the menu, the calzones, the vegetables, the antipasto items, were all killer. And every day the pizzas were getting a little better. But with everything coming at us, the crowds, the critics, it was virtually impossible for us to step back and look at the pizza objectively. We were too inside the process to know exactly how to fix it right away. We started fanning out to any place that made pizza, looking for clues to pizza. We went to New Haven, Providence and all kinds of places around New York, like Little Frankie's.

We were really up against it. I lost my confidence a little bit, but I didn't lose my resolve. Who knew there were sixteen million pizza experts in New York City? But pizza is one of those foods that everyone grows up with and has strong taste memories of. Danny Meyer went through the same thing when he opened his barbecue joint, Blue Smoke. But I think it was even a little worse for us at Otto because pizza is one of those things everyone north, south, east and west grew up with.

The food press had always been very good to us, but the pizza at Otto gave people a good opportunity to take a shot at us. Some of it was deserved, and some was a little gratuitous. William Grimes gave us a glowing, two star review in the *Times,* which of course we deeply appreciated. But even the headline of his review read, "A Pizzeria Where Pizza Is Not the Main Thing."

Our colleagues also weighed in with suggestions. It turns out that anyone who's handled any kind of dough thinks they know about pizza dough. Although it was hard to listen to sometimes, I think just about everyone was well-intentioned. And some were genuinely helpful. Jim Lahey from Sullivan Street Bakery did give us the idea to stop mixing the dough so much. So we cut the mixing time to four minutes from twelve minutes, and that worked wonders. We also started proofing the dough whole instead of in little balls, and that helped a lot as well. Finally we added a little more olive oil to the dough.

In the end what did I learn? I learned I wasn't bulletproof. I learned that it's hard to go up against people's taste expectations about a food that everyone has tasted a thousand times in their lives. I had never staked my reputation on dishes that everyone knows and loves. Nobody has ever walked up to me after eating at Babbo and said, "I've had goose liver ravioli with balsamic vinegar, and you're not making it right." Or, "That beef cheek ravioli you make is not the way my mother made it."

And you know what? Our pizza is really good right now. We fixed the crust, and the toppings are out of control. The pizza at Otto is not definitive or earth-shattering. But it's pretty damned delicious.

Otto, 1 Fifth Avenue (at the corner of 8th Street), New York, NY, 212-995-9559.

My Take on Otto
Ed Levine

I WAS ONE OF THE MANY WELL-INTENTIONED PEOPLE
offering advice when Otto first opened.

The crust was hard when they first started, and when it cooled (like by the second slice) it got even harder. But two pizzas I had with friends recently proved to me that Batali and company had indeed fixed the problem. In fact my pepperoni pizza was the first pepperoni pizza I'd ever loved. That's because the pepperoni is made in-house, and it tastes like the crispiest, porkiest salami ever put on a pizza. The fresh mozzarella from neighboring Joe's Dairy was creamy and lovely, and the Italian Pomi tomato sauce is naturally sweet. And the crust, the bane of Batali's existence, was crispy and pliant.

In the true test of any pizza crust, the third slice tasted as good as the first.

After pizza, I had some of Otto pastry chef Meredith Kurtzman's gelati, which are sensational. The coffee ice cream was strong, not too sweet and very creamy, and the avocado ice cream was positively dreamy.

ODE TO AL FORNO

Corby Kummer

My friend Corby Kummer, managing editor of Atlantic Monthly *and restaurant critic for* Boston Magazine, *is one of those suspiciously thin food writers, but I've seen him polish off a whole pie without blinking. I've had the pagnotielli at Da Ettore that Corby describes below and they alone are worth a trip to Naples.*

THE ROAD TO HELL WAS PAVED WITH PIZZA IN THE KOSHER HOUSE I grew up in—or at least the road to unkosher food on our own table, which to my brother and sister and me seemed like heaven. We looked with envy on the Salisbury steak TV dinners and sausage grinders our cousins could take home at will. Our cousins and their parents looked on us as quaint if not peculiar, my mother's extended and assimilated family having long abandoned all but gestures to Jewish food (let alone to religious observance). Our mother agreed to keep kosher perhaps in recognition of my father's settling in the small Connecticut town where her family had had a strong presence for generations; his family viewed him as practically marrying out. Like most Jews who kept kosher in my pre–religious reawakening generation, as soon as we shut the doors of my father's Electra 225 (Cadillacs were too showy) we headed straight for spaghetti and meatballs and lobster fra diavolo at the "authentic" Italian restaurants Italian immigrants had opened.

But we could open steaming, sturdy square boxes from Steve 'n' Tom's right on our white Formica table, after phoning in orders and lining up at the pizzeria, which always had a line out the door Sunday nights at six. Practically no one ate on the premises. That would seem somehow sordid, as if you had no home to go to, or lived in an apartment, which amounted to the same thing.

Viewed from the side the pizza could be carpet squares, with strata of thick crust, tomato sauce and melted mozzarella and provolone so dense but pliable they could pave a handball court. From above the squares resembled the confetti-patterned linoleum tiles that covered our cellar floor, with big squares of green pepper for color. What has become of oversized green bell peppers? They were the Italian vegetable of my youth, right for stuffing with hamburger and rice and tomato sauce, and the sole color on pizza if you weren't ordering nitrate-red, always misspelled "peperoni" because your family inconveniently kept kosher. Peppers and the pepperoni helped make Italian food seem really Italian, an experience intimately connected with heartburn (which connected Italian with Jewish food). Now green peppers are hidden from sight, crude and acidic victims of fashion that dictates wimpily sweet hothouse peppers in red, yellow and orange.

I now recognize the Steve 'n' Tom's pizza as a version of the southern Italian *pizza rustica,* which is meant to be a hot meal on a plate like a casserole. The crust was too thick, yes—but right for a pizza rustica, which needs a strong support and is conceived more as a one-crust pie than a pizza. The cheese came from a Mafia factory turning out hardballs for the American food-service industry. But the tomato sauce was honest and fresh, and the almost-uncooked green pepper gave coolish crunch and tang to the otherwise warm, squishy pie. There was nothing wrong with Steve 'n' Tom's pizza. There still isn't, if you don't think of it as pizza.

As for what we now consider to be authentic Italian pizza, good luck finding it. Chefs out of cooking school and European apprenticeship, lacking the confidence of Italian-Americans who cheerfully Americanized their families' already Americanized palate, turn out hot sauced lavash in an attempt to be more Italian than the Italians. And in Italy you can spend a lifetime searching out the right crust—chewy and soft rather than brittle, yet not much more than $\frac{3}{16}$th-inch thick—and the right proportions of sauce and cheese.

Even in Naples I'm often disappointed by the blandness of the crust. You have to like soft, underrisen bread to love Neapolitan pizza, which is fired so quickly that there should only be a few small, blackened spots to show the right heat of the brick-floored, wood-fired oven. It's not supposed to be crisp, burnt toast, delicious as

I would find that. A Neapolitan pizza is judged done when the mozzarella (cow's milk, buffalo being both wasteful and watery) is just melting at the edges. The center usually tastes chewy and underbaked, and the cheese slides all over the place when you take a knife and fork to it, the way decorous Italians approach pizza.

Neapolitans, masters of one of the world's great cuisines, have found ways around this. At Da Ettore, an extremely popular restaurant near the Naples opera house and the great hotels commanding views of the bay and Vesuvius, waiters sail through the crowds bearing aloft trays covered with what look like pita sandwiches half wrapped in white paper napkins. These are *pagnotielli*, the word derived from *pagnotta*, for "large loaf." Da Ettore makes excellent pizza, as any casual restaurant in Naples feeding crowds of opera-goers (and creators) and well-heeled international guests must. It has the obligatory wood-fired pizza oven at the back, in a room with brown paneling and kitschy Bay of Naples prints that would fit right into the Italian restaurants of my childhood.

The specialty, though, is the *pagnotiello*, which is a round of untopped pizza dough baked until it puffs up like a pita and sliced open. When an order comes in the pizza chef fills the pocket with the requested ingredients, usually similar to a pizza—mozzarella, halved cherry tomatoes rather than sauce, arugula or similar wild greens, prosciutto—and slides it back into the oven until the cheese starts to melt. The result is fully baked crust, with superior texture and flavor for its double heating, and a fresh-flavored but not scalding or soppy filling that stays where it's supposed to, so you get filling and bread in every bite. (It's a different animal from the calzone, which is filled unbaked and almost by definition has a soggy bottom crust and big tough walls of undercooked dough where the edges are sealed.) No wonder the *pagnotiello* always seems to outsell the pizza.

I confess to preferring the warm fresh crackerbread that is often served as designer pizza to the underdone-in-the-middle real thing. I know everything will be cooked through, and even if the dough is underrisen it won't be underbaked. This is why my favorite pizza in America is grilled pizza at Al Forno, in Providence, with paper-thin, beautifully flavored dough guaranteed cooked by the time it spends on the grill. The grill also guarantees delicious charring—

though never quite enough, for my taste, and the kitchen of late seems to take a focaccia approach of bathing a thin layer of bread in olive oil. When the kitchen goes light on the oil and keeps the big thin square on the grill an extra few seonds, this is a great pizza experience, authentic or inauthentic.

And perhaps a very thin crust is kosher, even in the Bay of Naples. The best pizza I ever had was served at a welcoming party given near Sorrento by a friend of Tony May, the Naples-born restaurateur who did more to introduce true Italian food and ingredients to New York and by extension America than anyone else, for my money. May had taken a group of restaurateur friends on an annual jaunt, and his friend's hillside villa had on one of its several terraces a beehive-domed pizza oven. Out of it came long rectangles of very thin-crusted pizza, covered with nothing more than fresh tomatoes someone had crushed by hand and wiped over the dough, fruity southern Italian olive oil, very few polka dots of cow's-milk mozzarella and maybe a basil leaf or two. It was sliced into wide ribbons and though the chefs kept sliding the ladder-sized wooden peels into the oven for the better part of two hours, there was never enough.

I don't expect Steve 'n' Tom's, which still exists though in a larger, minimall setting, to drive ninety minutes to Providence and copy Al Forno. And I guess I would be disappointed if the new generation decided to be Italian, turning away from the Italian-American tradition that merits a place of respect. I'd rather know I can still burn the roof of my mouth on the plasticized mozzarella still hot when it gets to our kitchen table, which is still kosher in the capable hands of my Yankee step-mother. And it's been too long since I've had a big, sharp chunk of green pepper.

Al Forno, 577 South Main Street, Providence, RI, 401-273-9760.

AIRPORT PIZZA

PIZZA IS SOMETHING I'VE FOUND AT VIRTUALLY EVERY MAJOR airport in the country. Most airport pizza is pretty dreadful, with cardboardlike crust, a blanket of cheese that glows under the heat lamp, and generic toppings. One vendor in the Detroit airport offers six flavored crusts to choose from. Yuck! But chefs are trying to come to our rescue as we fly. The airport pizzas at Wolfgang Puck's Pizza Express shops, found at Denver International Airport, Los Angeles's LAX, and Chicago's O'Hare, are certainly a cut above what I've just described. The crust has a pleasant chewy puffiness, and the cheese isn't too thick. It's not great pizza, but it will do if you're hungry and have a chance to grab one before getting on a plane. The clear winner of the airport pizza derby is Todd English. At LaGuardia Airport in New York, he has opened a Figs that serves pizza almost worth missing your flight for (I guess it all depends on what you were planning to eat once you reach your destination). You can't go wrong with the Classico (see page 284) or the fig-and-prosciutto pizza.

Figs, LaGuardia Airport, Queens, NY, 718-446-7600.

CHAPTER
15

Planet Pizza

PLANET PIZZA

AS THE TWENTY-FIRST CENTURY UNFOLDS, PIZZA HAS NO PASSPORT. What was the provenance of the Neapolitans in the late eighteenth century, which the American chains built into a megabusiness in the sixties, has now become a staple worldwide. Google any city or country, and you'd be amazed at what you come up with. In Shanghai, for example, you can get a slice for the equivalent of $1.20 at Pizza Italia, where the Italian pizzaiolo makes use of a wood-fired brick oven. In Bangkok you can do the same at Diulio's or the aptly named Calzone. In Kenya, pie lovers flock to The Flame Tree or La Scala. And in Moscow they go in droves to Pizza Amore or Pinocchio. The basics remain the same: crust, cheese and tomato sauce. The toppings are another matter. In Russia, they like their pizza topped with *mockba*, not the rock band, but a combination of sardines, tuna, mackerel, salmon and onion, or just red herring straight up. In Japan, which has nine establishments recognized by the VPN, eel and squid and Jaga, a combination of mayonnaise, potato and bacon, are the preferred toppings. In Brazil, they like their pizza topped with green peas. Shanghai pizza enthusiasts have their pie topped with sliced duck, green onions and hoisin sauce.

There's even a VPN member, Lombardi, in Budapest. When you get a hankering for traditional Neapolitan pizza in Sydney, go to Pizzeria Mario. Pizza has become a local food no matter where you go in the world.

UNIVERSAL PIZZA TRUTHS

Robb Walsh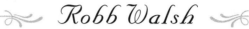

Pizza lover and Houston Press *restaurant critic Robb Walsh is willing to go to the ends of the earth (in this case, Argentina) in search of a good slice, only to find a fellow Pepe's fan.*

THE BAKER SLIDES HIS LONG WOODEN PADDLE UNDER OUR PIZZA and pulls it steaming from the oven. Above his head, the sign in Spanish reads: "El Cuartito, 1934–1994, 60th Anniversary of Great Pizza—Thanks to you, your parents and your grandparents." The ceiling fans turn slowly over the crowded wooden tables where we're sitting. As the waiter rounds the corner with our pizza, I notice that the *terrazo* floor is worn all the way down to the cement along the path he treads.

The El Cuartito Special, topped with tomato sauce, ham, mozzarella, fresh tomato slices, red peppers and green olives with a sunny-side up egg baked in the middle, is quite a meal. Although it is piled high with ingredients, the crust is still crisp on the bottom. The patina of history that covers the walls and floors and ancient stand-up counters at El Cuartito not only adds to the flavor of your pizza-eating experience, it also reminds you that pizza is a very old tradition in Buenos Aires.

If you ranked the cities of the world according to how hard it is to find a street corner without a pizzeria, Buenos Aires would be right up there with Naples and Brooklyn. And, like pizza-lovers the world over, *porteños*, as the citizens of Buenos Aires are known, are fiercely loyal to their favorites. They claim their city's pizzerias rank with the best in the world. And as a pizza zealot in my own right, I intend to put their claims to the test.

If a Latin American country with a pizza tradition sounds odd, consider that the Buenos Aires phone book contains more Italian surnames than Spanish ones. With its ubiquitous espresso bars, trattorias, pizzerias and a language that is supposed to be Spanish, but sounds like Italian, Buenos Aires recalls an earlier meaning of the word Latin—somebody from Rome.

Rome is easy to picture as my girlfriend Marion and I check out the famous pizzerias along Avenida Corrientes, downtown's main drag. At Pizzeria Guerrin, Luciano Pavarotti's twin brother is sitting at a table in the dining room washing down his pizza with a quart of beer. An elegantly attired little old lady who must be in her eighties is eating a slice with a knife and fork at the shiny marble counter. The cashier is wrapping up boxes of pizzas to go in elaborate purple paper decorated with gold Guerrin logos. The perfume of pizza is all around us as we trade bites from a garlicky, rich slice with spinach and white sauce and an anchovy-and-tomato slice that tastes like one of Philadelphia's tomato pies.

Farther down Corrientes, we recognize the famous Café Los Inmortales by the huge poster of Gardel that towers above it. Gardel was the most popular tango singer in Buenos Aires early in the century. I once saw a black-and-white photo of Café Los Inmortales that was dated 1910, and I've been eager to eat in this historic landmark ever since.

"I'll have what Gardel had," I tell the waiter when he comes to our table. "Gardel never ate here," he says. "This place didn't open until 1950." "But the old photos—I thought this place was Gardel's hangout," I mumble in miserable Spanish. The original Café Los Inmortales is long gone, he explains. This place is a modern recreation. He grows increasingly impatient as we look at the menu. There are pages and pages of pizzas—plain pizzas, combination pizzas, artichoke pizzas, eggplant pizzas, *fugazzas*, *fugazzettas* and more. We hastily order a Roquefort *fugazzetta*, a tomato-and-hearts-of-palm salad and a bottle of Sangiovese. *Fugazza* is something like Italy's focaccia, but here the flat crusty bread is topped with mozzarella and onions. *Fugazzetta* is a crust with cheese.

"I'll have what Gardel had," Marion mimics cruelly after the waiter leaves. I drink my wine and fume. When the *fugazzetta* arrives, we are overwhelmed. We both like Roquefort, but this is ridiculous—it is melted in a pool that must be a half-inch deep.

"It's good, but one slice is all I can eat," I tell Marion. So we sit and drink our wine, write a few postcards and watch the *porteños* come and go. I nibble at another slice, only because the Roquefort goes so well with the salad and the wine. By the time the wine is gone, I am surprised to realize that we have eaten the whole *fugazzetta*.

After eating another half dozen pizzas over the course of a week, I am ready to make some judgments. My favorite pizzeria in Buenos Aires is a little neighborhood café called Romario on Calle Cabello where they bake the pizzas in a brick oven with a roaring wood fire. The olive oil–coated crusts come out of the brick oven with a deep-fried sort of crunchiness, and the wood fire gives the toppings a rustic, smoky flavor.

As I try to express my conclusions, Marion and I get into our usual pizza fight. As good as the crust at Romario is, I say that I don't like the texture as much as, say, the yeasty, brick-oven crust at Pepe's in New Haven. Marion accuses me of being hopelessly pizza-centric. If I had grown up in Buenos Aires, I would call this the best pizza in the world. If I'd grown up in Chicago, the best in the world would surely be a deep dish. But just because I grew up in Connecticut, I have this stupid prejudice in favor of Frank Pepe's. That's why rankings are ridiculous, she says.

And so is the whole food-writer schtick of going around the world rating things, proclaiming this the best chocolate and that the best coffee . . . I shrink a little in my chair. Maybe Marion's right. Maybe ranking foreign foods by home-town American standards really is redneck chauvinism . . . But then again, she's never been to Pepe's.

On the way home from Buenos Aires, we stop in Punta del Este, a beach resort in Uruguay. In a beautiful little Italian deli called Tutto Sapori, the owner, Frank Cinquegrana, hears our accents and comes over to introduce himself. He speaks great American English.

We talk a little about Italian food around the world. Frank knows Buenos Aires pizza, New York pizza and Neapolitan pizza, too. "I go to Italy four or five times a year, and I used to live in New York," he says. "My son still lives in Connecticut." A smile crosses my face at the mention of my former home state, and I take a chance.

"So where's the best pizza in the world, Frank?"

"I'll tell you what I told them in Italy," he says waving one finger in the air. "They may have invented pizza in Naples, but the best pizza in the world is Frank Pepe's in New Haven, Connecticut."

Marion is speechless, and I can't stop laughing.

C'EST UNE PIZZA QUI VIVE

~ *Daniel Young* ~

Writer and critic Daniel Young, author of Made in Marseille, *is one of my pizza oracles. When he was at the* New York Daily News, *I would savor every word of his pizza reporting and writing. Dan spends half of the year in France these days, writing and researching his cookbooks, but he's stayed in touch with his inner pizza by searching out great pizza all over the south of France and Paris (see page 311).*

FRANCIS CRESCI'S DECISION TO BAN MOZZARELLA AT LA PIZZA, the pizzeria restaurant he opened on the French Riviera in 1956, was less a matter of taste than conviction, echoing as it did the insistence of his grandfather, an immigrant from Umbria, that nary a word of Italian be heard in the family's new home in Nice. The young, assimilated Cresci—that's KRE-see, *s'il vous plaît*, the French pronunciation long ago replacing the Italian KRE-shee—thought his pizzas should speak either French or, like his grandfather, Nissart, a local dialect with Italian, Provençal and French influences. "In every region of Europe the locals were eating foods produced on their land," recalled Mr. Cresci, then seventy-eight, his reasoning dating back to the preglobalization 1950s. "I reckoned there was enough cheese to choose from in France." The nutty, buttery flavor of semi-hard French cheeses such as Emmental or Cantal, Cresci's cheese of choice, distinguishes much French pizza from Neapolitan-styled pies made only with milky mozzarella. When the cheese is of above-average grade, spread over a thin round of dough coated with tomato and herbs, and then subjected to the relentless whoosh of intense heat circulating through a properly fired and ventilated brick oven, the result is a juicy (referring to the melted cheese, and not the tomato sauce), bubbling, molten masterpiece.

"*C'est une pizza qui vive*," boasts Ludovic Cresci, who now oversees his father's business. Sure enough, that pizza is alive.

To a foreigner, the tremendous thrill when first encountering such an enticingly animate pie is all the greater because it's so unexpected. You don't anticipate finding memorably good pizza in France. You're certainly not supposed to hunt for it. A well-traveled gourmet might even regard the suggestion of seeking out pizza in Provence of all places as the faux pas equivalent of going out for Chinese food in Bologna. Indeed, my girlfriend began to question my judgment on all matters of taste when I, the passionate follower of Zola, Truffaut, Brassens, bistro collectibles, *profiteroles au chocolat* and the Tour de France, as well as the author of two French cookbooks and dozens of articles of French cuisine, ordered pizza three times during the first five days of our Côte d'Azur vacation in July 2003.

The Crescis were hardly the first to top their pizzas with French *fromage*, nor were they the first to maintain they did so for reasons other than to save money. (And money is certainly an important factor: Francis Cresci won't splurge for pricey Comte cheese, though he admits it's a superior pizza cheese to Cantal and Emmental.) A decade earlier the great Marseille pizzeria Chez Etienne began employing a bottom layer of shredded Emmental over its sensational crust. According to owner Etienne Cassaro, the easy-melting—and easy-on-the-wallet—cheese helped the overlay of sliced mozzarella spread out over the surface of the crust as it baked. Much of the mozzarella sold in France, like inferior supermarket mozzarella in the United States, is rather hard and rubbery and doesn't loosen up all that much when baked.

The unhappy irony of the domestic cheese policy is that it is partly responsible for some of the worst pizza in Western Europe. France may be the proud land of Camembert, Roquefort and enough fine cheeses to fill the days of a thirteen-month calendar, but its citizens tolerate globs of generic grated cheese, processed cheese, even adhesive "delivery" cheese (it doesn't slide around in a cardboard box) on their pizza.

"Many of the people who go into the business are only looking at the profit margins," laments Julien Panet, president of L'Association de Pizzerias Françaises and director of www.pizza.fr. "They see it as investment requiring minimal investment and savoir faire. There's no pride, there's no passion for culinary art."

Mr. Panet speculates that pizza is generally superior in the south of France, especially in Provence and along the Côte d'Azur, because the southerners know and expect more. First, they're raised on a Mediterranean diet. They understand tomatoes, basil, olive oil and anchovies. Second, the region's proximity to Italy and influxes of Italian immigrants, vacationers and retirees have, over the decades, provided a steady supply of pizza cognoscenti. There's no better source of quality control.

Maybe there is also something in the rocks and the trees. The custom-made ovens first installed beside the entrance of the original La Pizza on the rue Massena in the heart of Nice, and a second, four-hundred-seat locale that opened on the quai Saint-Pierre in the Old Port section of Cannes in 1960, the year *La Dolce Vita* won the Palme d'Or at the Cannes Film Festival, turned those meccas of people-watching into ones of pizza-watching. Their baking stones were constructed, like many of France's finest bread ovens, with volcanic ash quarried in the village of Biot, midway between Nice and Cannes. Their fires were set ablaze with logs from the lush pine groves and forests that evoke the jazzy Riviera of the Fitzgeralds—Scott, Zelda and, years later, Ella.

The divinely thin crusts baked in such ovens constitute the hallmark of the best wood-fired French pizza, the revered pizza *au feu de bois*: crisp but neither hard nor dense, delicate but not brittle, charred but not burned, flour-dusted but not dry. They may be sampled not only at landmarks such as La Pizza and Chez Etienne but also in the most unlikely of spots, be they brick-oven-equipped pizza trucks parked near the *corniche* or main-square bistros in Provençal villages such as Vence and Joucas.

Hidden amid the Near Eastern, African and Vietnamese markets in the Noailles quarter of Marseille is a small, unsung pizzeria to rival Chez Etienne both in age and art. At Pizzeria au Feu de Bois, which opened in 1943 under the name

Sauveur back when immigrant Italian shops and vendors crowded the quarter, owner Michel Gilabert feeds his oven two woods: quick-burning pine to get the fire going and smoky oak to cook the pizza. He offers two first-rate cheeses, a mozzarella and an Emmental, and makes his sauce from scratch with fresh tomatoes.

The setting of Le Vesuvio on the palm-lined coast of Cannes is every bit as incongruous. The garishly lit and decorated—the best word for it might be "cheesy"—establishment is situated among a Rodeo Drive–like strip of grotesquely expensive designer boutiques on the storied boulevard de la Croisette. Its next-door neighbor is the Hotel Martinez, an opulent Art Deco palace built in 1929. Though mostly a sit-down pizza and Italian restaurant, Le Vesuvio does a brisk takeout business: Its puffy, smallish, artfully crisped, nearly weightless, Cantal-draped ten-euro Margherita has climbed to the $18,000-a-night Presidential Suite at the Martinez. Now that's upward mobility!

Spilling out into the cours Saleya, site of the celebrated flower and food markets of Old Nice, the terraced brasserie Le Safari serves chops, pasta, seafood, Niçoise specialties and, almost as an afterthought, outstanding pizza. Its outdoor tables are popular with tourists. Famous artists, movie stars and politicians hang out instead in the rear dining room. Originally an African restaurant, Le Safari was reworked in 1973 by new owners Gaston Bargioni and Henri Gastaud, a childhood friend of Francis Cresci. Mr. Bargioni had no experience as a pizza baker but rolled out Le Safari's first pies anyhow.

"Everyone knows pizza in Nice," says Mr. Bargioni. The Pizza César—no relation to the salad—is a Le Safari specialty designed by César (Baldaccini), the late French sculptor and first-name-only celebrity best known for the junked cars he compressed into solid blocks. The Marseille native's tastes in pizza were somewhat easier to digest. He envisioned a simple pie of tomato, black olives and a certain green sauce that now does double duty atop the Pizza Provençale (tomato sauce, ham, herbes de Provence, Cantal). As the Provençale bakes in the brasserie's 750°F oven, olive oil slowly seeps out of the green sauce, from which it has acquired an emerald tint, and into the lavalike Cantal, a dreamy interplay of pizza toppings. Talk about a pizza that's alive.

So what's in that sauce? It's listed as just basil in one part of the menu and a *persillade* (chopped parsley and garlic) in another. Mr. Bargioni says it's a combination of the two and then backs off from that assertion when challenged on it for the fourth time. My visit to the pizza kitchen and my conversation with the current pizzaiolo, Lotfi Mahjoub, revealed its true contents: basil, garlic and extra-virgin olive oil. Essentially it is a sauce *au pistou*, the Provençal and Niçoise counterpart to Italy's pesto. Yes, Le Safari's pizza speaks French, too.

- **Chez Etienne**, 43, rue Lorette, Marseille, no phone.
- **La Pizza**, 3, quai Saint-Pierre, Cannes, 04-93-39-22-56.
- **La Pizza**, 34, rue Massena, Nice, 04-93-87-70-29.
- **Le Safari**, 1, cours Saleya, Nice, 04-93-80-18-44.
- **Le Vesuvio**, 65, boulevard de la Croisette, Cannes, 04-93-94-43-52.
- **Pizzeria au Feu de Bois**, 10, rue d'Aubagne, Marseille, 04-91-54-33-96.

PISSALADIÈRE TRUCK

 Eric Karpeles

Friend and artist Eric Karpeles is an incredibly talented painter (go see his Mary and Laurance S. Rockefeller Chapel of Hope and Remembrance at the HealthCare Chaplaincy, 307 East 60th Street, in New York). He is also a passionate eater, cook and gardener. After reading about the pissaladière truck he discovered, I wanted to board a plane for Nice immediately.

IT WAS THE SUMMER AFTER FINISHING COLLEGE. I HAD STUMBLED miraculously upon a room at the Château Noir just outside Aix-en-Provence, where Cézanne had worked, and was living and painting there, amidst the twisted pines, under the deep blue Mediterranean sky, in full view of Mont Sainte-Victoire. I was both footloose and foot-dependent. To get anywhere I had to walk. Twice a week, on market days, I would go to town, four or five miles away, stock up, and tote my groceries home. But it was the walk in the opposite direction, away from Aix, that holds the fondest memories for me.

Two miles east of the Château Noir is the crossroads of le Tholonet. (To call it a town would be misleading. There is the office of *le mairie* and there is the café, *toute simple*.) I would often hike this halcyon stretch of road in the early summer evening. In a small clearing just before le Tholonet, I would find a *camionette*, a little truck, parked off the road. Here, in the back of the truck, replete with a wood-burning oven, a handsome young couple made sumptuous *pissaladière*. As I approached, my appetite was primed by the smell of woodsmoke and the Midi's ubiquitous aroma of wild thyme. The *pissaladière* was made from scratch in individual servings, and after I placed my order I would stroll to a nearby *allée* of plane trees a quarter-mile long. These were magnificently mature, seventy-foot-tall trees whose upper limbs entwined so as to make a verdant tunnel. (Cézanne painted these very trees.) I would wander up one length, then down the other, and by the time I returned my pizza was ready. I would be hungry and the first bite was always the best. Just so slightly burned, the thin crust provided an undertaste of char that ruggedly set off the sweet and pungent onion-and-herb mixture, which in turn gave way to the tang of niçoise olives and the final salt thrill of anchovy. The texture was one of crunch and chewiness. The explosion of flavors was complex and robust, and the hot, just-out-of-the-oven temperature forged a gustatory sensation—sophisticated, satisfying and affordable—in which I frequently indulged and never forgot, never bettered.

Love the One You're With

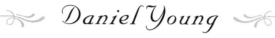

Daniel Young

Dan Young weighs in again, this time on pizza in his adopted second home, the City of Lights.

MY REMARKABLY MATURE APPROACH TO PIZZA LOVE IS SUMMED up by paraphrasing an E. Yip Harburg lyric from the 1947 show *Finian's Rainbow:* "When I'm not near the pizza I love, I love the pizza I'm near." In case you're wondering, Yip was writing about girls and no, I don't regard them as interchangeable with pizza. How could I when it's obvious I loved pizza before I loved my sixth-grade sweetheart, that it took me thirty years to get over the closing of Luigino's and the disappearance of its charred, bubbly, molten masterpizzas and only eleven minutes to forget Mindy Rosenberg?

The problem with growing up on New York City pizza, not only Luigino's but also, in my case, the dependable slice shops of Queens—Lorenzo's, Centre, Gloria—is that you're spoiled for life. When you're away from the pizza you love you're always lonely and disappointed. Pies baked on distant shores, meaning east of exit 40 of the Long Island Expressway, never measure up. Who knows? A particular style might be worthy of praise. It might even be superior in certain respects to my hometown's method, as much as I doubt that. Regardless, there is little if any good New York pizza outside New York. Searching for it, as I did during my college days in Montreal and subsequent travels around the U.S. and in Europe, is a masochistic endeavor.

For my own emotional well-being I had to force myself to judge and appreciate the away team's pizza on its own merits. There is, for example, no crusty, hard-to-the-chew pizza in Paris, a largely mediocre pizza town with a couple of nice churches and a good restaurant or two where I now live half of the year. There is almost no pizza made with high-quality, Italian plum tomatoes.

But what you do find in many parts of the French capital are ultrathin crusts baked to a browned but not blistered crisp in blazing, wood-fired brick ovens. (How, I ask myself, can dough exposed to such violent heat bake to such lightness and delicacy? *Magnifique!*) Moreover, you're assured of getting hot chile oil drizzled on your pie. And in three select Parisian pizzerias you will encounter cheese meltdown so extreme it challenges the laws of physics. I still can't figure out what prevents the melted mozzarella and liquified Cantal from spilling off their pies and dripping down onto your shoes.

The main attraction at Da Mimmo, a kitsch-congested trattoria, is not the mural of Naples. It's Erico the pizzaiolo. Because his workspace is too narrow for even his pizza peel, little Erico must dip, bend, twist and twirl just to lodge a single small pie in the brick oven. His magic hands flatten out a dough that produces a weightless crust. The man is an artist.

La Scuderia del Mulino, near the Moulin Rouge, is the sort of nondescript place knowing Parisians and worldly travelers instantly dismiss as a tourist trap. Too bad. The straying Italians who fill the place know better. Everything is Italian-made: the tomatoes, the milky mozzarella, the custom-ground flour, even the revolving brick oven. I'm not kidding. The pizza stone revolves so that the pies are evenly cooked.

I like Amici Miei best when I'm homesick. The crust is nearly hard and bubbly enough to remind me of Queens and the toppings are superb. The place is packed elbow-to-elbow and so you're always enveloped by pizzas, pastas, Sangiovese reds and happy people. Best of all, the guys give you a nod of approval for ordering the plainest of pizzas, the Margherita. They realize you're revisiting your first love.

Amici Miei, 53, boulevard Beaumarchais (3rd arrond.), Paris, 01-42-71-82-62.
Da Mimmo, 39, boulevard de Magenta (10th arrond.), Paris, 01-42-06-44-37.
La Scuderia del Mulino, 106, boulevard de Clichy (3rd arrond.), Paris, 01-42-62-38-31.

PIZZA? WHICH PIZZA?

David Downie

> *Dan Young suggested I get in touch with his friend David Downie to write something about pizza in Rome and Liguria. Downie has written books about both places:* Cooking the Roman Way *and* Enchanted Liguria. *He divides his time between France and Italy.*

IT MUST HAVE BEEN BACK IN THE EARLY 1970S. I WAS STANDING on a corner in San Francisco's North Beach neighborhood, outside an Italian-American bakery. When my mother handed me the slice of focaccia the olive oil that dribbled off it stained a pair of bell-bottoms I'd bought on Telegraph Avenue in Berkeley.

"It's Genoese pizza," she said in Italian. "*Assaggia!* Taste it . . . "

I chewed with something less than alacrity, wondering how a transplanted Roman such as she had deigned to buy greasy, salty fraudulent pizza such as this. It was nothing like the luscious tomato-sauced *pizza rossa* I'd eaten in Rome when we lived there in the mid-1960s, or the lavish American equivalent of the same I gobbled while growing up in the Bay Area. To me, pizza was something soft, usually round and doughy, with red sauce. Sure, it could also be plain and white—meaning no tomatoes—and more or less flat, as in Roman pizza bianca. But pizza bianca wasn't pizza in the normal, Neapolitan sense, rather a kind of chewy, porous olive-oil based bread, like a cross between a low *ciabatta* loaf and the "Genoese pizza" I was experiencing now for the first time in North Beach.

My mother could tell I wasn't happy. "When your father and I took the ship from Genoa to California they served focaccia on board," she sighed.

Nostalgia. I remember thinking, "Boy, the stuff must've been better in Genoa." And I couldn't help wondering what my meat-and-potatoes father from Garden Grove must've thought back then, in 1950, of this strange pockmarked, salty, oily pizza-bread.

Fifty-odd years after my parents' freighter docked in San Pedro, California, pizza joints have sprung up in every mall in the land. Flanking the all-American deep-dish pizza pies, you can also get so-called focaccia too. Focaccia crops up in bakeries, sandwich shops, delis and restaurants including, no doubt, a couple in Garden Grove, which is way too close to Disneyland for comfort.

More often than not the New World focaccia I've tried is fancy pseudopizza without tomato sauce. It comes studded or heaped with fistfuls of rosemary or sage, with grated Parmigiano mixed into the dough then scattered on top, not to mention everything from grilled eggplant and sun-dried tomatoes to olive paste, capers and white truffle oil, arugula, curried chicken breast, Mongolian beef and "shrimp scampi" as the "cuppa-coffee" waitresses of old used to call prawns.

These bounteous faux-focaccias are hybrids—*pizzaccias* or maybe pizza *biancaccias*. They're easier on the teeth than the leathery 1970s North Beach variety of focaccia. But they've got little to do with the authentic, austere item as made in Liguria, that mysterious seaboard region of northwestern Italy more commonly known as the Italian Riviera, where my wife and I spend several months each year.

Liguria is where I fell in love with true focaccia, and Genoa, the unsung city of Christopher Columbus, is the regional capital. So rewind again, this time to 1976 and a café in Genoa's medieval port. "Try that," I said to my traveling companion from Berkeley, sure he'd hate the unfamiliar, dimpled, oily bread that everyone was wolfing. My pal grimaced just as I had a few years earlier in North Beach. "It's Genoese pizza," I said. The moist, olive-scented dough and crunchy coarse sea salt took him by surprise. But soon he was chewing a second slice. "Grease bread" is what he dubbed it, though I explained that focaccia is made not with grease but with wholesome olive oil, a staple in this mountainous olive-growing region.

"Grease bread, grease bread," he sang as we hoofed around the perched seaside villages of the Cinque Terre, and the celebrated horseshoe-shaped harbor of Portofino, "get me more grease bread!"

On that culinary coming-of-age trip I remember recording the well-known fact that the most lusciously porous and tender focaccia came from a twenty-mile stretch of rocky coast southeast of Genoa, roughly between the villages of Sori and Sestri Levante. It still does. The excellence of the focaccia of the eastern Riviera derives, I suppose, from the combination of fruity Ligurian oil, the yeast cultures clinging to old bakery walls, the local water, the microclimate, heat and salty air of this breezy, cliff-hedged seaboard, plus the peculiar fingertip-kneading technique used by bakers to give their focaccia its telltale moonscape surface.

It's not that Ligurians don't eat normal pizza—meaning Margherita (it gets a capital M because it's named after a queen), Napoletana, *quattro stagioni* and so forth. They do and how. Nowadays they even make Genoese basil pesto pizza, which, though heavy on the oil, is better than you might think (the combination is so plausible that when you type "pesto pizza" using Microsoft Word, Bill Gates's automatic spell-checker doesn't even underline it). I've enjoyed memorable pesto pizza at a place called Bedin in central Genoa, and at Pizzeria Aurelia in Ruta di Camogli, where it comes with nice chunks of mozzarella and lots of whole pine nuts.

Normal pizza—even pesto pizza—is one thing to the Genoese, however. Focaccia is another. My mother, the transplanted Roman, didn't understand that or she'd never have called focaccia "Genoese pizza." Focaccia is focaccia. Period. Over the last thirty years I've learned that wherever they live along the Riviera, Ligurians hold their pockmarked, pre-Columbian flatbread sacred, just as Neapolitans venerate round red pizza.

More than mere foods, these are cultural ID cards. For instance, Ligurians recognize each other amid the summer Riviera tourist crowds by the way they order and eat focaccia. *Fugassa* is their name for it and if you're not Ligurian you'll never get the slippery pronunciation right. The Ligurians' favorite breakfast is a slice of *fugassa* baked with a sweet white-onion topping and washed down with a tepid cappuccino. At other times of day they eat plain *fugassa* made with flour, water, yeast, salt and olive oil, nothing more. The herb-scented varieties found in a handful of Genoa snack joints are for out-of-towners and foreigners. And despite raging globalization you still won't encounter a Ligurian *fugassa* flecked with Parmigiano or topped with eggplant, capers, truffles or chicken curry. The simplicity is divine.

That same simplicity is what makes Roman pizza bianca so irresistible—and impossible to counterfeit, as I discovered a couple of years ago while recipe testing for a cookbook called *Cooking the Roman Way*. Of the thousand or so bakers in Rome a handful make great pizza bianca. I put on several pounds finding the top half dozen then pestered them until they revealed their secrets, or at least gave me a few hints. The most helpful and forthcoming baker of all was young Pierluigi Roscioli at the cult bakery Antico Forno Marco Roscioli, which hides its storefront on an alley between the Campo de' Fiori and the Ghetto. Pierluigi took me into the backroom several times, showing me from scratch how he made pizza bianca dough. I'd go home each time to my rented apartment in Trastevere, across the Tiber River and, using the same flour and yeast as Pierluigi, fail over and over again.

Pizza bianca is diabolically difficult to make, a papillary paradox: it should be firm and crisp yet moist and airy, olive oil-perfumed yet never greasy. Finally, after a dozen tries, and having consulted other fine Roman bakers, I figured out how to make good pizza bianca at home, in Rome. Then I started all over again in America, enlisting the aid of renowned chefs and cookbook writers. People often ask me, is it possible to make good Roman pizza bianca outside Rome? Certainly. Good, not great.

As with the Neapolitans and their thin, damp, sauce-swirled pizzas, or the Ligurians and their dimpled focaccia, the Romans build culinary altars and sacrifice their dearest delicacies to the god of pizza bianca. When in Rome you wish to express the opinion that things are hunky-dory or that people get along like peas in a pod, you say "*come pizza e fichi*"—like pizza (bianca) and figs. A ripe, peeled, split fig placed spread-eagle atop a translucent slice of Parma ham, itself riding a slice of pizza bianca, is the ultimate manifestation of hunky-dory and very delicious indeed.

Another way a Rome native asserts his identity is by asking the baker to slather a slice of pizza bianca with olive oil. All Roman bakeries worth their sea salt keep a bowl of oil and a pastry brush under the counter, at the ready.

Not long ago the Rosciolis perfected the fancy pizza bianca by crowning it with mozzarella, zucchini flowers and anchovies—an unlikely cornucopia even by American standards and surprisingly good.

Pizza bianca dough is also what many bakers use to make *rustici*—filled turnovers related to the southern Italian calzone. In Rome the filling can be anything from spinach and ricotta to diced braised artichokes, spicy garlicky sautéed chicory, or ham, mushrooms and cheese.

Romans don't seem to have a problem with the fact that the term "pizza" means many things, referring not only to local pizza bianca and what we think of as classic, thin round Neapolitan red-sauced pizza, or deep-dish *pizza a taglio* (thick pizza sold by the slice and usually *rossa*—red with tomatoes). In Rome and certain other parts of central Italy you also find *pizza pasquale*, an Eastertide loaf with grated pecorino cheese in it; *pizza lievitata*, a similar leavened loaf that might contain olives, bacon and cheese; and even *pizza dolce*, a slightly sweet brioche-style cake sometimes flavored with fennel seeds.

It was when I learned just how ambiguous a term "pizza" is in Rome that I finally understood why my mother all those years ago called focaccia "Genoese pizza." To her it *was* a kind of pizza. By the same token, most Romans don't necessarily think of pizza and Naples as a binomial. For instance, order a pizza Napoletana in Rome and you'll get what the Neapolitans disparagingly call a pizza Romana with tomato sauce, mozzarella and anchovies. And if you ever suggest to real *Romani de' Roma*—people whose families have lived in the capital for hundreds, even thousands of years—that pizza is a Neapolitan invention, they'll probably smile and quip, "Naples was Greek and Roman long before it ever became Neapolitan."

Rome Pizza

▓ ACCHIAPPAFANTASMI | The name means ghostbusters, the pizza is Calabrian or, rather, the people who run the place are from Calabria, and they like their pizza thin and crisp.

66, Via dei Cappellari, Rome, 06-687-3462.

▓ DA BAFFETTO | *Da leccarsi i baffi* means whisker-lickin' good, which is at least as good as finger-lickin' good. The name "Baffetto" and the pizza—the same classic Roman/Neapolitan pizza dished out here since the 1960s—makes me want to lick my whiskers.

114, Via del Governo Vecchio, Rome, 06-686-1617.

▓ RISTORANTE PIZZERIA DA SABATINO | The pizza is fine—not the best in Rome but certainly not the worst, let's say above average. But the setting? Fantastic. This pizzeria/restaurant (also known as Le Cave di Sant'Ignazio) draws locals and tourists in equal numbers, spilling its tables into Piazza Sant'Ignazio, a baroque-rococo stage set bounded on one side by the soaring Jesuit church dedicated to the inflammable saint, and on the other three by matching palazzi.

169, Piazza Sant'Ignazio, Rome, 06-679-7821.

LIGURIA FOCACCIA AND PIZZA

BEDIN | This century-old restaurant (not always in the same location) in downtown Genoa serves some of the region's best chickpea *farinata*—plain or with fresh herbs. They claim to have invented the pesto pizza, a specialty with a small but faithful following in Liguria.

56r, Via Dante, Genoa, 010-58-09-96.

PANIFICIO DAMA | All kinds of focaccia, all of them good, though the traditional ones are best . . . on the narrow central *carugio* (alleyway) of one of the best food towns on the eastern Riviera.

34, Via Palestro, Santa Margherita Ligure (GE), 0185-28-65-09.

PANIFICIO-PASTICCERIA MOLTEDO | Lorenzo Moltedo and his family not only make what is probably the best *focaccia al formaggio* in Liguria, a Recco specialty, but also excel with plain focaccia and focaccia with onions.

2/4, Via XX Settembre, Recco (GE), 0185-74-046.

PANIFICIO ROCCO RIZZI | Rocco is Pugliese and I can already hear the Genoese screaming . . . but his plain or onion focaccia is pretty darn good, and even the hard-to-please Camogliesi seem to agree.

126, Via della Repubblica, Camogli (GE), 0185-77-02-47.

NOTE: GE = province of Genoa

FROMAGE DOMMAGE

Lesley Chesterman

When my family was visiting Montreal, Lesley Chesterman, restaurant critic for the Montreal Gazette, was gracious, helpful and exceedingly generous with her time. She never took us for pizza, though. I guess she was holding something back.

HAVING BEEN WEANED ON SPONGY, GREEN-PEPPER-LADEN PIZZAS, this Montrealer has long considered a Godsend the thin-crust pies topped with pancetta and Parmesan at Little Italy's Pizzeria Napolitana. Then there's the hip pizza parlor Pizzedelic, where square, cracker-thin pizzas are piled high with arugula, and La Piazzetta, whose seventeen-inch pies include gourmet toppings such as escargots and white-wine-marinated onions. Yet the one area in which Montreal pizza suffers is cheese. Though over three hundred varieties of fromage are produced in the region, not one local cheesemaker has yet produced a mozzarella to rival that of Naples or New York. Quel Dommage!

La Piazzetta, 4097 Saint-Denis Street, Montreal, Canada, 514-847-0184.
Pizzedelic, 3509 St. Laurent Boulevard, Montreal, Canada, 514-282-6784 (with additional locations).
Pizzeria Napolitana, 189 Dante Street, Montreal, Canada, 514-276-8226.

CHAPTER
16

*The Pizza
Police*

THE PIZZA POLICE

I FIRST BECAME AWARE OF VERA PIZZA NAPOLETANA (VPN), sometimes referred to as the Pizza Police, after I wrote a piece about pizza in the *New York Times* (see page 69). I received a letter from well-known Italian-born restaurateur Tony May, who informed me in no uncertain terms that I was misinformed about many aspects of pizza. He wrote, "Having read your article, I think I should bring a couple of points to your attention. First: it's not buffalo, it's *bufala!* The topping for pizza is not a sauce but 'marinated raw tomatoes with the desired spices, depending on the type one wishes to make,' and never cooked." The last line of his letter read, "I hope the above proves useful to you for future enjoyment of pizza." Enclosed in the letter were the Rules of Neapolitan Pizza Making, as put forth by Vera Pizza Napoletana, "an organization started in Italy in 1984 by Antonio Pace to promote the culinary tradition of Neapolitan pizza. To this end, we provide training in the production of Neapolitan pizza and certification for those pizzerias/restaurants which produce Neapolitan pizza."

A Los Angeles restaurateur, Peppe Miele, founded the American branch of the VPN in 1998. There are now twelve pizzerias in America that belong to the VPN, which suggests that given the fact that there are approximately 61,269 pizzerias in this country, the VPN is catching on rather slowly.

There are so many things to object to about the VPN. It implies that Neapolitan pizza is the only kind of pizza worth eating. As my travels around the world for this book have shown me, that is not true. In fact, as I point out in Chapter 2, a lot of Neapolitan pizza is simply too wet and too soft and bready for my taste. None of the great New Haven pizzerias belong, or could even join for that matter. They use coal-fired ovens (or oil-fired, in the case of Modern Apizza), the pies can be crusty, their borders are not high and soft and their pizzas don't even have a true diameter, as they're not round. Chris Bianco, certainly a passionate, dedicated pizzaiolo, doesn't belong, though his pizza does in fact adhere to

The Rules of Neapolitan Pizza Making

The denomination of VERA PIZZA NAPOLETANA (True Neapolitan Pizza) is reserved exclusively to pizza made according to the following rules:

- It must be made only with flour, natural yeast or brewer's yeast, salt to taste and water as needed. All types of fat are absolutely forbidden from inclusion in the pizza dough.
- The diameter of the pizza should never exceed 30 centimeters (10–12 inches).
- The dough must be kneaded by hand or by approved mixers that do not cause the dough to overheat. (If the dough overheats, it speeds up the fermentation process.)
- The dough must be punched down by hand and not by mechanical means (never use a rolling pin, etc.).
- The cooking is done directly on the floor of the oven (the use of sheet pans or other containers is not allowed).
- The oven must be of brick and *materiale refrattario* (refractory material similar to volcanic stone) and must be fired with wood. (The selection of wood is the operator's choice.)
- The oven temperature must be at least 400˚ Centigrade or 750–800˚ Fahrenheit.
- The classic pizza ingredients are:
  Marinara: tomato, oregano, garlic, olive oil, salt
  Margherita: tomato, mozzarella, olive oil, basil, salt
  Al Formaggio: grated Parmigiano, lard, garlic, basil, salt (tomato optional)
  Calzone: stuffed with ricotta, salami, olive oil, salt
  Variations on the classics that are inspired by tradition and fantasy are accepted, provided they are not in conflict with the rules of good taste and culinary laws.
- The pizza must have the following characteristics: not crusty, well done and fragrant with the border *(cornicione)* high and soft.

The above rules are set by the association of "Vera Pizza Napoletana," which is part of the Association of Pizzaioli Europei and Sustaining Members.

most of the rules (the exceptions being that his pizza can border on the crusty, and his border is not particularly soft). Nick Angelis of Nick's Pizza could not be a member, as he uses gas ovens. Lawrence and Cookie Ciminieri of Totonno's don't and couldn't belong, as they use the same coal-fired brick ovens Totonno's founder, Anthony Pero, did. None of these people need the rigid guidelines and standards of the VPN to make great pizza. They have their own dedication, and their own passion, to fuel their own standards, which in many ways are more rigorous and more demanding than the VPN's.

This kind of rigid silliness does have its upside. I've tasted first-rate pies from all the United States members. In some cases the members have introduced excellent pizza to cities that many people would say did not have a tradition of pizza excellence, such as Minnesota, Pittsburgh and Sheboygan.

But the real question is: Where does all this craziness stop? The Italian government recently weighed in with its own rigid set of standards. But as Al Baker points out, many of the classic Neapolitan pizzerias in Italy fall short of the standards laid out and, perhaps more important, there are no penalties for violating the standards. As for this country, well, I shudder to think what's in store for us, the ultimate pizza-loving nation. Perhaps the New Haven Chamber of Commerce should weigh in by designating certain pizzerias as Vera Pizza New Havenana. Phoenix should follow suit by designating Pizzeria Bianco Vera Pizza Bianco. The Brooklyn Borough President could introduce the Vera Pizza Brooklynana designation. Or maybe, just maybe, we can let our taste buds set the standards. Mine dictate that the crust be chewy, pliant and slightly puffy, the mozzarella fresh and the sauce uncooked canned tomatoes with very few spices added. Vera Pizza Levinana, anyone? I'm going to be tough. I'm going to demand an inspector on-site for each pizzeria, just like the USDA has at sausage-making facilities. And I'm going to have stiff penalties for anyone not living up to my standards. For the initial offense, the pizza criminal will be forced to eat at Pizza Hut every day for a month. For the second offense, I will force him to wear an ankle bracelet monitoring his every movement, like pizza parolees. Pizza Prison, a lifetime of eating only at the worst chains, awaits the third-time offender. Three strikes and you are *so* out of good pizza. 🍕

VPN Members Listing

HERE IS A LIST OF ALL THE PIZZERIAS AROUND THE WORLD that belong to the VPN. Although I obviously have some reservations about the organization, there can be no doubt that you'll get a good pizza at any pizzeria that belongs. In the last year I have eaten at all of the VPN pizzerias in this country. And when I make it to Japan and Australia I look forward to eating a pizza Margherita at one of the VPN pizzerias there, as one cannot live by sushi or shrimp "on the barbie" alone. In Budapest, I will take a break from goulash and eat at the Lombardi's there (no relation to the U.S. Lombardi's).

USA

Antica Pizzeria
13455 Maxella Ave.,
Ste. 201
Marina Del Rey, CA
Tel. (310) 577-8182

Café Niebaum-Coppola
417 University Ave.
(at Cowper Street)
Palo Alto, CA
Tel. (650) 752-0350

Il Pizzaiolo
703 Washington Rd.
Mt. Lebanon, PA
Tel. (412) 344-4123

Il Ritrovo
515 South 8th St.
Sheboygan, WI
Tel. (920) 803-7510

La Pizza Fresca
31 East 20th St.
New York, NY
Tel. (212) 598-0141

Naples 45
200 Park Ave.
New York, NY
Tel. (212) 972-7000

Punch Neapolitan Pizza
704 Cleveland Ave. South
St. Paul, MN
Tel. (651) 696-1066

Regina Margherita Pizzeria
516 Lincoln Ave.
Bellevue, PA
Tel. (412) 761-1077

Tutta Bella Neapolitan Pizzeria
4918 Rainier Ave. South
Seattle, WA
Tel. (206) 721-3501

2 Amys
3715 Macomb Street NW
Washington, D.C.
Tel. (202) 885-5700

JAPAN

Diaz
Sakashita Itabashi
Tokyo

Marechiaro
New Pier Takeshiba
South Tower 105
Tokyo
Tel. 3 54 67 85 38

Partenope
(two locations)
5-15-25 Minami Azabu
Tokyo
Tel. 57 98 33 55

1-22-20 Ebisu
Tokyo
Tel. 57 91 56 63

Piccola Tavola
4-2-4 Eifukucho Suginami-ku
Tokyo
Tel. 59 30 00 08

Samurai Pizzaiolo
6-2 Kariya Ako Hyogo
Karyiaminami

Ristorante e Pizzeria Santa Lucia
1-9-17 Nishiku
Kyomachibori
Osaka

AUSTRALIA

Pizzeria Mario
38 Yurone Street
East Sydney
Tel. 06 12 93 31 49 45

CANADA

Il Fornello
214 King Street West
Toronto, Ontario
Tel. (416) 977-2855

GERMANY

Pergola
Mauerstettnerstrasse 50
Kaufbeuren
Tel. 83 41 99 39 07

FRANCE

Bella Napoli
Avenue Michel Jourdan
Le Cannet

ITALY

Abruzzo

Taddei Evandro
Via Saline Nord
Sant'Angelo, Pescara

Calabria

Moderno
Terme Luigione Cosenza

Elba

Pizza In
6, Via Marconi
Marina di Campo
Tel. 056 597 7496

Friuli

Vulcano
4, Via Nazario Sauro
Trieste
Tel. 040 30 33 11

Ischia

Ristorante da Cecilia
9, Via Emilio Cortese
Ischia
Tel. 081 99 18 50

Lazio

La Rosetta
37, Via Duomo
Alatri
Tel. 077 543 4568

Pizza Doc
276, Via Ardeatina
Anzio
Tel. 069 87 31 43

Lombardy

El Merendero
Via della Volta
Brescia

Naples and Campania

Addo Guaglione
Via Consalvo
Naples

Angelo
112, Corso Italia
Naples

Antica Pizzeria Port'Alba
18, Via Port'Alba
Naples
Tel. 081 45 97 13

Arcadia
5, Via Nicolardi
Naples
Tel. 081 743 0300

Cafasso
72, Via Giulio Cesare
Naples
Tel. 081 239 5281

Capasso
2-3, Via Fuori Porta San Gennaro
Naples
Tel. 081 45 64 21

Capatosta
30, Via Marconi
Recale, Caserta
Tel. 08 23 49 31 88

Cinque Vie
Via Provinciale Cicciano
Naples

Ciro a Santa Brigida
71, Via Santa Brigida
Naples
Tel. 081 552 4072

Ciro a Santa Lucia
29/30, Via Luculliana
Naples
Tel. 081 764 6006

Da Mario
2, Via Cavalleggeri d'Aosta
Naples

De Vito
San Sebastiano al Vesuvio

Di Matteo
94, Via Tribunali
Naples
Tel. 081 45 52 62

Don Salvatore
Via Mergellina
Naples
Tel. 081 68 18 17

Gianni al Vesuvio
8, Via Vesuvio
Herculaneum
Tel. 081 777 3738

Jossa
Piazzetta Nilo
Naples

La Brace Ristorante e Pizzeria
14, Via Spaventa
Naples
Tel. 081 26 12 60

La Caraffa
41/47, Via Piave
Naples
Tel. 081 64 06 34

La Locanda
284, Corso Italia
Quarto
Tel. 081 876 8771

La Spaghettata
81a, Via G. Doria
Naples
Tel. 081 556 0892

Lo Scugnizzo
Via D. Menichini
Barra

Lombardi
59, Via Benedetto Croce
Naples
Tel. 081 552 0780

Lombardi
12, Via Foria
Naples
Tel. 081 45 62 20

Macondo
74, Via Torregaveta
Monte di Procida

Marino
118, Via Santa Lucia
Naples
Tel. 081 762 2280

Mattozzi
2, Piazza Carità
Naples
Tel. 08 15 52 43 22

Megaron
Via Fornace
Paternopoli
Tel. 082 77 15 88

'O Calamaro
30a, Via Campi Flegrei
Naples
Tel. 081 570 4387 or
081 570 9738

**Pizzeria Abate
Gaetano**
75, Via Cassano
Naples
Tel. 081 738 2835

Pizzeria Alba
14a, Piazza Immacolata
Naples
Tel. 081 578 7800

Pizzeria Bikini
SS 145
Vico Equense
Tel. 081 801 6222

Pizzeria Diaz
119, Via A. Diaz
Naples
Tel. 08 17 76 29 87

**Pizzeria Fiorenzano
D'Elia Ciro**
1/2/3, Via Ninni
Naples
Tel. 081 551 2788

Pizzeria La Pergola
58, Via Litoranea
Torre Del Greco
Tel. 081 883 2431

Pizzeria Pirozzi
26, Via Seminario
Ischia Ponte
Tel. 081 99 11 21

**Pizzeria Vittoria di
Capobianco Mariano**
34, Via Piscicelli Maurizio
Naples
Tel. 081 579 5771

Qui La Pizza
Via Trav. Provinciale
Pianura, Naples

**Ristorante Al Ragno
D'Oro**
Via Niutta Vincenzo
Naples
Tel. 081 556 4031

Renzo e Lucia
Via Tito Angelini
Naples

Rocco e I Suoi Fratelli
155, Via S. Giacomo dei Capri
Naples
Tel. 081 546 5302

Salvatore alla Riviera
91, Via Riviera di Chiaia
Naples
Tel. 081 68 04 90

Scarlatti Pizza
Via Scarlatti
Naples

Tonino
270, Via Cilea
Naples
Tel. 081 64 09 01

Tortora
Via Agnano
Naples

Villa Meridiane
Via Montagna Spaccata
Pianura, Naples

Zio Enrico
9, Via Figurella
Barra

Sardinia

Dante
Località Sottovento
Porto Cervo, Sardinia
Tel. 078 99 24 74

Pape Satan
Santa Teresa di Gallura
Sassari

Trentino Alto-Adige

**Pizzeria Da Zio
Alfonso**
50, Viale Druso
Bolzano
Tel. 047 127 3466 or
047 128 6160

Umbria

Topgest
Via Larga Perugia
Brescia

Veneto

Moment's Pizza
10, Corso Venezia
Caorle
Tel. 042 12 61 66 00

Pizzeria Bella Napoli
144, Via Quadri Giovanni
Battista
Vicenza
Tel. 044 450 4171

For the addresses of these
VPN-certified pizzerias,
please consult a local
telephone directory or
your hotel concierge.

JAPAN

Alberbello

O'Pulcinella

FRANCE

Megaride

Scarpati

HUNGARY

Lombardi

ITALIAN GOVERNMENT "BRANDED" PIZZA

Al Baker

In 2004 the Italian government issued a set of national pizza standards that all pizzerias in Italy were supposed to follow. Or else? This kind of pseudoauthentic silliness caused an uproar, even in pizza-crazed Naples. Al Baker of the New York Times immediately weighed in on this critically important topic.

THE THING ABOUT NEAPOLITAN PIZZA, ONE AXIOM GOES, IS THAT THE higher the grade of the olive oil, the better the thread-count of the proprietor's clothes.

So while a new national law mandates what can authentically be called Neapolitan pizza, the legislation also exposes a deeper, ages-old rift about whether pizza is best served to the masses or the classes.

Italian pizza makers, politicians and the modern-day proletariat had set aside a century's worth of squabbling over tomatoes, basil, cheese and oil to focus on a larger topic that threatened them all: Neapolitan pizza was under attack, facing impostors worldwide.

As one local pizza maker, Alfonso Cucciniello, put it: "Everyone in the world is trying to do this type of pizza. In Japan, in China, in the United States, in Miami.

"Pizza with pineapples?" he asked. "That's a cake."

At the behest of the Association of Real Neapolitan Pizza [VPN], a group with 2,500 members worldwide, lawmakers and officials of the administration of Prime Minister Silvio Berlusconi recently acted to put some political weight behind an ancient dish made with green, red and white ingredients, the colors of the Italian flag. A law was passed. A nation of pizza makers gave thanks.

The European Union may follow suit. As the continent is homogenized, the new law is a marketing tool to brand Naples forever as the cradle of pizza. Pizzerias that serve the approved brand are now stamped official.

Then details of the new national standards slowly started to be digested. Under them, the pizza must be round, no more than 35 centimeters (13.8 inches) in diameter. The crust cannot be too high. The dough must be kneaded by hand. Only certain flour, salt and yeast can be used. Extra-virgin olive oil is a must, as are tomatoes from the Mount Vesuvius region and buffalo mozzarella (*mozzarella di bufala*). For cooking the classic pizza Margherita, only mozzarella from the southern Apennine Mountains is allowed.

But here in the sun-blessed hills near the Sorrento peninsula, where the locals say pizza was invented, an almost improbable mini-melodrama is being played out. The pizza made by Mr. Cucciniello is no longer officially Neapolitan.

Mr. Cucciniello runs Da Michele pizzeria on the same gritty street in the working-class Forcella quarter where his wife's grandfather, Michele Condurro, first started baking pizzas, a bit larger in size than the average dinner plate, in the late 19th century.

Da Michele's pizza breaks the new rules in several ways. It uses vegetable oil, not the more expensive extra-virgin olive oil; cow's-milk mozzarella, not the moister, costlier variety made from the milk of a water buffalo; and small, sweet San Marzano tomatoes, grown in the nearby Sarno Valley, not the ones that come from the soil around Mount Vesuvius.

Yet Mr. Cucciniello, draping his thick forearms over the cash register one recent night, said the pizza in Rome is being made by foreigners and is not authentic.

"It's not Italian," said Mr. Cucciniello, who wears blue jeans and serves his pizza with paper napkins and plastic cups to hordes of adoring Italians. "It's not the Italian pizza."

Rosa Russo Iervolino, the mayor of Naples, praised the new law. "It is a guarantee for Naples pizza, just as there are guarantees for other Italian brands, like Parmesan cheese," she said recently. "It is important to recognize where certain foods come from and protect them from impostors."

Across town from Da Michele, in a more refined dining setting in a more opulent neighborhood, Carmine Stentardo, who runs Ciro a Santa Brigida, a pizzeria where diners can get an award-winning pizza as well as a variety of fancier dishes—antipasti, vegetables, pasta, fish and desserts—said he could not agree more. It was his pizza association, after all, that had its standards codified in the new pizza law. Those ingredients are used in the pizzas on his menu. "Now this product is protected," Mr. Stentardo said with an air of self-satisfaction.

He is a tan, white-haired man who dresses in sport coats and leather shoes the complexion of his skin. His grandfather started serving the pizzas he serves in 1932.

"It's protected as a brand-name product," he added as he sat in a lacquered wooden chair in a dining room of tables with glinting silverware and heavy cloth napkins.

Once the law passed, Mr. Stentardo, Mr. Cucciniello and others seemed only too happy to pick up where they left off with the honored pastime of bickering over just the right ingredients for the pizza.

Of the pizzas made at Da Michele, and at another popular pizzeria that claims to be the birthplace of the Margherita, Antica Pizzeria Brandi della Regina d'Italia, Mr. Stentardo said they use the wrong foods to be considered real Neapolitan pizzas.

"They don't make good pizza," he said of those places. "They make a cheaper pizza."

But no one is fretting too much. The law has no real teeth. It comes with no sanctions.

Eduardo Pagnani is the owner of Pizzeria Brandi, where, he said, the pizza Margherita was invented in 1889 and named after Queen Margherita of the House of Savoy. He said that pizza may be named for nobles, but that it has always been more about the people.

Indeed, here in famously passionate Naples, where garbage mounts in fetid mounds and moped drivers zoom the wrong way up one-way streets, there seems a certain pride in ignoring the new law—of course, only after it has been passed.

"We'll start a mini-federation," Mr. Pagnani said, laughing. "We'll be outlaws."

🍴 IL RITROVO | Il Ritrovo chef and owner Stefano Viglietti was leading a

staff trip in Italy from his other Sheboygan restaurant when he met pizzaiolo Peppe Staiano in Agerola, outside Naples, in 1999. Staiano became his pizza muse, first teaching Viglietti the essentials of Neapolitan pizza making in Italy, then coming back to the States to help Viglietti open Il Ritrovo in 2000. Staiano is now in Italy, but he left his imprimatur on the superb pizza served at Il Ritrovo. The crust is indeed slightly bready and clearly inspired by Naples, but it has just enough brown and black spots to add the slightest bit of crunch when you bite into it. The tomatoes used on the pies here are sweet DOP San Marzanos from Italy, with just a pinch of sea salt added. Viglietti imports *mozzarella di bufala* for his Margherita DOC pizza, and uses a Grande loaf mozzarella for his other pies. His fabulous fennel sausage is made by a local butcher shop founded by his great grandfather. As a chef, Viglietti understands the sanctity of using great ingredients for his pizza. He says, "When you have something so simple, you must pray to the ingredient gods." Just as important, the ingredients at Il Ritrovo are used sparingly and in the right proportions. As Viglietti himself points out, "Balance is everything in pizza."

Il Ritrovo
515 South Eighth Street, Sheboygan, WI, 920-965-2289.
RATING: 🍊 🍊 🍊 ◖

🍴 LA PIZZA FRESCA | La Pizza Fresca makes a really big deal about the

authenticity of its pizza. A laminated card on each table carefully explains the vagaries of real Neapolitan pizza. All this solemn talk about authenticity strikes me as a little self-important, but I have to admit that Pizza Fresca turns out fine Neapolitan-style pies in a gorgeous wood-burning oven located in the back of the restaurant. I usually stick with the Margherita, made with a spritely tomato sauce, imported *mozzarella di bufala* and, in a surprising departure from Neopolitan pizza orthodoxy, a little olive oil and a sprinkling of Parmigiano-Reggiano. The crust is chewy and soft enough to, as the table card explains, "pass this test—the pizza can be folded in half and then folded again, into a quarter, without breaking the crust. This is contrary to a belief held in America that Neapolitan pizza is thin and crisp but not chewy."

La Pizza Fresca
31 East 20th Street (between Park Avenue and Broadway), New York, NY, 212-598-0141, www.lapizzafresca.com.
RATING: ◉ ◉ ◖

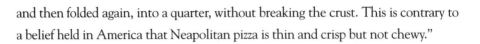 **NAPLES 45** | By all rights, Naples 45 should not serve some of New York's best pizzas. It's owned by a corporate entity, Restaurant Associates. It's located in the decidedly unquaint and unromantic MetLife Building next to Grand Central Terminal, and on a busy day the hustling pizzaioli churn out five hundred pizzas a day. And yet Naples 45 is one of the best, most consistent pizzerias to be found anywhere in America. Head Pizzaiolo Charlie Restivo started making pizza in a slice shop in Queens at age thirteen, spent five years making pizza and other dishes at Mezzaluna and Mezzogiorno, and has been at Naples 45 since it opened in 1996.

Restivo does everything right. He uses a combination of 85 percent low-gluten Italian flour (Caputo Red), and 15 percent high-gluten Italian flour (Caputo Blue), water, salt and brewer's yeast to make his dough, which proofs for twenty-four hours. The fresh mozzarella arrives daily from Giuseppe Luomo in New Jersey, and the tomatoes are not DOP San Marzanos, but they are sweet, imported Italian beauties. He has two wood-burning ovens that bake the pizzas between 600°F and 700°F in two minutes flat.

The result is a pizza that has a not-too-thick, not-too-thin, raised and pliant crust, with just enough char on top and bottom and excellent hole structure. He uses enough cheese so that you get a little in every bite without the pies becoming soggy. At Naples 45 my pie of choice is topped with prosciutto and fresh arugula, which are placed on the pie after they come out of the oven.

Restivo may not preside over ovens as romantic as those you can find in Naples, and, yes, he's working for Restaurant Associates, but he is making better pies than you can find almost anywhere in Naples, the rest of Italy or America for that matter. There are a lot of pizza pretenders and poseurs all over America these days turning out supposedly authentic Italian pizzas, but very few of them turn out a pie as good as Restivo's.

Naples 45
MetLife Building, 200 Park Avenue (at 45th Street), New York, NY, 212-972-7001.
RATING: ◉ ◉ ◉ ◖

 PUNCH NEAPOLITAN PIZZA | Punch owner John Sorrano was born in the United States, but grew up in Milan (where he was known as Giovanni). There he started hanging out after school at a Neapolitan pizzeria called Da Gino. He would pester the pizzaiolo at Da Gino to show him how to make a true Neapolitan pizza. He and his family eventually moved back to Minneapolis, where he realized his dream by opening Punch in 1996. Sorrano doesn't just talk the Neapolitan pizza talk. His pizza is superb. Atop the blistered and blackened crust are San Marzano tomatoes, fresh mozzarella imported from an Italian section of Brooklyn and sea salt from Caserta that he spent half a year sourcing. For two bucks extra Sorrano will substitute *mozzarella di bufala* on your pizza. About his pizza Sorrano says, "We're kind of fanatical about what we do. I'm obsessed with pizza, as much now as when I was a boy in Milan." Though there are now three Punch locations in the Twin Cities, ultraperfectionist Sorrano has yet to retire from the ovens. "I still make pizza for at least three hours every night at one of our places. Our goal is to make our pizza 10 percent better every year." Sorrano is one of the first pizza purists to acknowledge the difference between Neapolitan pizza and American pizza. On his menu it says, "In Naples, people like their pizza 'wet.' Order any of our pizzas Neapolitan Style for an additional fifty cents and we will add more tomatoes and olive oil and serve it to you uncut."

Punch Neapolitan Pizza
804 Cleveland Avenue South, St. Paul, MN, 651-696-1066.
Prairie Center Drive (north of Highway 212), Eden Prairie, MN, 952-943-9557.
3226 West Lake Street, Calhoun Village Shopping Center, Minneapolis, MN, 612-929-0006.
RATING: ◉ ◉ ◉ ◖

🍴 REGINA MARGHERITA PIZZERIA | I first met Regina Margherita

owner Roberto Caporuscio in New York, where he was one of a number of serious pizzaioli invited to New York for a celebration of Neapolitan pizza at Naples 45. His pizza was fabulous, especially given that he was using an unfamiliar oven. Even more fabulous was his speech to the crowd: "This is a very important night for all of us. It makes us feel very special that you like our pizza so much," he said in halting English, and then started to cry. What's not to like about Caporuscio's pizza? I particularly love his Regina Margherita, which combines crushed tomatoes, *mozzarella di bufala*, basil, extra-virgin olive oil and cherry tomatoes. In true Neapolitan style, his Italian wood-fired brick oven cooks the pizza at 800°F in less than two minutes. Former Pittsburgh Steeler star Jack Ham once kiddingly called Roberto the "pizza Nazi," because Roberto refused to put artichokes in Ham's salad. "I told him I'm Italian," Caporuscio said with a laugh. "So if anything I'm a Pizza Fascist."

Regina Margherita Pizzeria
516 Lincoln Avenue, Bellevue, PA, 412-761-1077, www.reginamargheritapizzeria.com.
3801 Butler Street, Pittsburgh, PA, 412-622-0111

RATING:

CHAPTER
17

*The Keepers
of the
Flame*

THE KEEPERS OF THE FLAME

TWELVE MONTHS. A THOUSAND SLICES. WHAT HAVE I LEARNED? There's a lot of pizza out there. Pizza is a $32-*billion*-per-year industry. Americans eat three billion pizzas a year. That's one hundred acres of pizza every day, or about 350 slices per second. There are more than 62,000 pizzerias in the United States alone. My admittedly unscientific sampling indicates that most of them (61,000 or so) serve mediocre pizza at best. But as so many chefs, food writers and diners have told me, even bad pizza is pretty good—or certainly good enough to eat—and nobody would make a similar claim about bad hot dogs or hamburgers.

But in writing A *Slice of Heaven*, I wasn't looking for pizza that was merely good enough to eat. I was looking for pizza that would make my heart pound when I thought about it; transcendent pizza that could cause grown men and women to moan with pleasure in public without embarrassment. And I found a fair amount of it. Many of the places I knew about when I started my quest: Sally's, Pepe's and The Spot in New Haven; Totonno's in Coney Island, Brooklyn; Al Forno in Providence; and Nick's in Queens, Manhattan and Rockville Centre. But others I had the joy of discovering for the very first time in the last year: Pizzeria Bianco in Phoenix; Una Pizza Napoletana in Point Pleasant Beach, New Jersey; Franny's in Park Slope, Brooklyn; Regina Margherita in Pittsburgh; King Umberto's in Elmont, Long Island; and 2 Amys in Washington, D.C.

After a year of intense pizza eating, there were six people I couldn't get out of my mind. They comprise a diverse group, socioeconomically, and share a set of ideals and values when it comes to making pizza. They are people who understand that it takes an unlikely combination of skill, intelligence and passion to make great pizza day after day, night after night. They are kitchen artists who respect pizza-making tradition, yet are not slaves to it. They are chefs who have taken the time to master their craft and the nuances of live fire and flame in their ovens. They understand that pizza is such a simple and unadorned food that it demands superior ingredients: high-quality flour, fresh yeast and salt to make the dough; the best strained, drained and uncooked canned tomatoes (Italian or Californian) for the sauce; soft, tender fresh mozzarella made in-house or delivered fresh every day (except for Sally's, which uses aged mozzarella); spritely fresh basil for the Margherita; and coarsely ground and chunked fennel sausage again either made in-house or by a local purveyor who cares about his product as much as they do. These are obsessive people who can't bear to send out a substandard pizza, people who live and die with every pie.

These six pizza makers are The Keepers of the Flame. They have mastered Neapolitan and Neapolitan-American pizza-making traditions and techniques, and in some cases improved upon them. They do what they do because they love it, but also because they can't imagine doing anything else. Chris Bianco is a kid from the Bronx who inexplicably found himself making pizza in Phoenix, Arizona. He has the soul of a poet and a penchant for self-reflection. Anthony Mangieri is a Jersey kid tattooed from shoulder to hand on both arms, and so serious about pizza he refuses to put any toppings on his pies. Domenico DeMarco was born in Italy, learned his craft at an old-fashioned pizzeria/restaurant in downtown Brooklyn and is crazy enough to put *mozzarella di bufala* on pizza slices he sells for $2.50 at Di Fara in Midwood, Brooklyn. Nick Angelis is the son of a Greek immigrant whose idea of a good time was to load his family into the car and head to Totonno's to let his young children experience real pizza. Angelis learned at his father's feet well enough to be turning out world-class Neapolitan-American pies at his three pizzerias in the New York area. Flo Consiglio, at Sally's Apizza in New Haven, presides with steely resolve and a gentle smile over the dark, wood-paneled dining room that she and her husband opened sixty-six years ago. In that time only three people have ever made pizza there: her late husband, Sally, and her two sons, Richard and Robert. Lawrence Ciminieri was born into one of the nation's great pizza-making families, and initially rejected the pizzaiolo's way of life to move to Las Vegas and work at Caesar's Palace. But he couldn't resist the Siren call of pizza, and now lives in Coney Island, where he turns out great pies, using the same time-tested, coal-fired brick ovens his grandfather used.

In this chapter we will meet these obsessed perfectionists who, day in and day out, are setting the standard for pizza in this country . . . and the world. If you love pizza, as I do, you will adore these six originals. And if you are ever within a three-state vicinity of their wares, you will know what you need to do.

CHRIS BIANCO

of Pizzeria Bianco

"ALL WE CAN DO IS PUT UP SMOKE SIGNALS AND HOPE SOMEBODY reads them," Chris Bianco was saying. "That's all any of us can do. If the pizza guy is teaching you something, imagine what the smart people can do."

Mr. Bianco, chef and proprietor of Pizzeria Bianco in Phoenix, Arizona, and the only pizzaiolo to win the best regional chef designation of the James Beard Foundation, was searching for words to describe what he does. He presented the pizza-making craft in terms a Zen master might appreciate:

"There's no mystery to my pizza: Sicilian oregano, organic flour, San Marzano tomatoes, purified water, mozzarella I learned to make at Mike's Deli in the Bronx, sea salt, fresh yeast cake and a little bit of yesterday's dough. In the end, great pizza, like anything else, is all about balance. It's that simple."

But how did a nice Italian boy from the Bronx, a soulful high school dropout with a ferocious intellectual curiosity, end up making what just might be the best pizza in America in a city that by my count has more golf courses than pizzerias?

I posed that question, and a few others, as Mr. Bianco was in his usual place, making pizza in his restaurant in an old house in Phoenix's Heritage Square. His menu is disarmingly simple: one starter, *spiedini* (cheese wrapped in prosciutto); an antipasto plate; and two salads. One is a simple green salad while the other consists of whatever goodies one of his local suppliers drops off at his back door. That night, it was composed of juicy tangerines with a perfect sweet-and-acid balance, paper-thin slices of fresh fennel, a splash of fruity olive oil and some Malden sea salt.

Then there are Chris's pizzas. His crust is simultaneously thick and thin, puffy and crisp on the outside and softer and chewy on the inside, with hole structure like great bread. His mozzarella, which he and his staff make every morning, is creamy and slightly tart. The sauce tastes like the ripest tomatoes in concentrated form. His sausage tastes of fennel and pork, with just the right meat-to-fat ratio.

The Rosa, one of six pizzas, is made with red onion, Parmigiano-Reggiano, rosemary and Arizona pistachios, and is as multilayered and intense as Mr. Bianco himself. The Wiseguy pie has smoked mozzarella (he smokes it every morning in his wood-burning oven over pecan wood), roasted onions and fennel sausage.

My first bite of the Wiseguy melted in my mouth, as all great pizza does. The elements blended like a great jazz rhythm section.

"What I do is like a producer picking up the individual tracks of some unbelievable music," said Mr. Bianco, who often expresses himself in musical terms. "It could be Miles or Mozart. All I do is take it back to the studio and remix it."

Mr. Bianco lived in the Bronx until he was six, when his family moved to Ossining, New York. His mother worked at Saks Fifth Avenue in bridal design, and his father was a portrait painter who supported the family by designing wine and liquor labels. His father's paintings adorn the walls of the pizzeria and Bar Bianco, which are separated by a patch of grass and Mr. Bianco's herb garden. Pane Bianco, which serves four kinds of sandwiches a day on hot rolls baked in a wood-burning oven, is a couple of miles away.

Mr. Bianco had asthma as a child, forcing him to stay indoors and letting him spend hours watching his Aunt Margie cook. At thirteen, he was working at a local pizzeria and after the eleventh grade, he left school and went to work in restaurants. Cooking, he said, saved him.

"Most of my friends went one way, which turned out to be the wrong way," he said. "I went another."

In 1985, he won two plane tickets to anywhere in the United States, and he chose Phoenix. Why Phoenix? To this day, he does not know. "When I got here," he says, "somehow I felt connected to this place."

The young Bianco started making mozzarella in his apartment, and sold it to Italian restaurants at their back doors. Eventually, a specialty grocer in Phoenix, Guy Coscos, offered him a corner of his store to put in a wood-burning oven and to make and sell pizzas. Pizza became Mr. Bianco's obsession, with the following practical consideration: "I thought to myself that maybe I could make a living out of it."

A move to Sante Fe, New Mexico, in 1989 put him in the world of Deborah Madison, the vegetarian cookbook writer, and her sous-chef, David Tanis. "Their whole thing was about food and what made it special," he said.

At the same time, he found himself in the forefront of the American food revolution, which placed a premium on tradition, localism and craftsmanship. Finally, he was able to draw on his childhood experiences.

"At last I had something to offer from my past, a reverence for what my family had," he said. "I realized that what I had, what was in me, was something of value."

Armed with newfound confidence and a renewed sense of purpose, he opened Pizzeria Bianco in 1994.

Ten years on, pizza is still fraught with meaning, cosmic and otherwise, for Mr. Bianco. "I have invented nothing," he said. "I'm just trying to do something, one small thing, right. I'm on a mission, I have a responsibility, to do something with integrity and dignity.

"My menu might be small but, to me, it's the biggest thing in the world. Pizza inspires me, fascinates me and gives me hope."

Pizzeria Bianco

623 East Adams Street (Heritage Square), Phoenix, Arizona, 602-258-8300.

RATING: 🍊 🍊 🍊 🍊

ANTHONY MANGIERI

of Una Pizza Napoletana

WHEN YOU CALL UNA PIZZA NAPOLETANA AND OWNER/PIZZAIOLO Anthony Mangieri isn't there (which is most of the time), you get the following message: "Thank you for calling Una Pizza Napoletana. We're open Friday, Saturday and Sunday from around one in the afternoon until sold out of fresh dough." The obsessive, no-nonsense appeal of that message is why I found myself on a train one Sunday afternoon headed for Point Pleasant Beach on the Jersey Shore. The friend who'd discovered Una Pizza Napoletana, *Asbury Park Press* restaurant critic Andrea Clurfeld (see page 160), picked me up at the station and drove us to a nondescript minimall anchored by a 7-Eleven. Clurfeld, who has been writing about food and reporting in New Jersey for more than twenty years, had enticed me by saying. "The pizza at UPN is the single best thing I've ever eaten in the state of New Jersey." Now that's a big claim, coming from a restaurant critic who spends her evenings eating at New Jersey's best and fanciest restaurants.

We walked into the simple, whitewashed space with five tables and a bright red Vespa labeled Neapolitan Limousine. A classic Neapolitan wood-burning oven is tucked into the left-hand corner. Right under the mouth of the oven are wood shavings to stoke the fire. To the left is a pile of wood. Mangieri, a small, wiry man whose arms are completely covered with tattoos from shoulder to fingers, makes pizzas on a simple white counter. In front of him is a tray of dough balls, and metal bowls of *mozzarella di bufala*, DOP San Marzano tomatoes, fresh basil leaves, Sicilian sea salt and fresh halved cherry tomatoes. Those are all the ingredients Mangieri uses. No sausage, no pepperoni, no mushrooms, no peppers.

We asked for a menu, which at UPN has all of four items: a marinara, with San Marzano tomatoes, extra-virgin olive oil, oregano, fresh garlic, fresh basil and sea salt; a Margherita, which adds buffalo mozzarella and subtracts the fresh garlic; a bianca, which leaves out the tomatoes; and the Filetti, which has fresh cherry tomatoes along with every other ingredient in the house.

We ordered one of each. The Margherita came out first and was stunningly good. Mangieri's sourdough crust, made by hand with American flour and water and a little starter from the previous day's dough, was thinner than any I'd had in Naples, but still had perfect hole structure and a fantastic smoky tinge. It tasted like freshly baked bread. The buffalo mozzarella was tangy and creamy. The olive oil was poured generously, giving the pie a slightly fruity taste. Each bite melted in my mouth.

The marinara was next—a minimalist masterpiece. I didn't even miss the cheese. The bianca may have had a little too much olive oil, but I still couldn't stop eating it. Finally, the Filetti arrived. I should have resisted (I had already eaten a lot of pizza), but my willpower melted at the sight of this perfect pie, with halved cherry tomatoes topping the mozzarella just so.

I asked Mangieri why he does what he does. "I just wanted to do things the ancient way." In fact, I'd say he was setting the Neapolitan pizza industry back hundreds of years. I don't think anyone in Naples is still mixing his dough by hand, or eliminating toppings all together, or using no yeast. Mangieri, born into a Neapolitan-American family, had been going to Italy three or four times a year with his family. After high school his trips became more frequent, and he ended up spending time just observing in a bakery in the small town of Sant'Arsenio in Salerno. He opened a small Italian bakery in Asbury Park just before his twenty-first birthday. That lasted for five years, and when his landlord wanted to jack up his rent, he opened UPN in 1998.

Anthony told me that he was closing UPN in Point Pleasant, and was going to reopen in Manhattan's East Village, on 12th Street just west of First Avenue. I said surely he was going to add toppings and salads to the menu when he opened in New York. "Nope. I'm going to have exactly the same menu. It's what I know how to do."

Three weeks later I received an e-mail from Andrea Clurfeld:

"Hey. Don't know if you've caught up with Anthony, but:

1. The buyer for his place in Point backed out last week, so he's hanging in Point a few more weeks doing pies until the back-up deal goes through.

2. He was robbed in NYC last week, and bummed about it (he thinks it was the down-on-his-luck guy whom Anthony had hired to help him work on the NYC place). He's fine, though.

3. He and his girlfriend broke up last Friday, which is killing him."

I called Anthony to see how the New York pizzeria was progressing. He seemed quite upbeat, though he did mention that it was hard to realize his dream, opening his own pizzeria in New York, without his girlfriend. "She says that she's not sure she knows me. I don't get that. I'm the same guy I always was. I get up in the morning, and I make pizza. Believe me, that's never going to change. Pizza is what I do."

Anthony mentioned that he had seen the story I'd written about Chris Bianco in the *Times* (see page 339). Anthony had actually gone to Phoenix to eat at Pizzeria Bianco a few months before, but his shyness didn't allow him to strike up a conversation. His girlfriend said that she thought Anthony's pizza was better than Chris's, but in retrospect I think she was standing by her man. After reading my story, Anthony said to me, "Chris is just like me. I didn't think there was anyone else in the world who feels the way I do about pizza. But Chris does. I guess there are at least two of us in this world who live and die with every pie."

 Una Pizza Napoletana
349 East 12th Street (between First and Second Avenues), New York, NY, 212-477-9950.
RATING:

DOMENICO DeMARCO

of Di Fara Pizza

Jeff VanDam

*I was just about to start writing about Domenico DeMarco of Di Fara
Pizza, where for $2.50 anyone can buy his or her own slice of heaven,
when I picked up the New York Times. There in black and white was Jeff
VanDam's piece about DeMarco. VanDam just turned on his tape
recorder and let Domenico tell the story of his life as a pie man. I have
eaten hundreds of transcendent slices at Di Fara over the years, and tried
to engage him in conversation many times. He was never particularly
forthcoming, so when I saw that VanDam had actually gotten Domenico
to talk about why and what he did, I knew I had to include this piece, enti-
tled "Charred Bubbles, and Other Secrets of the Slice," in the book.*

FAME HAS COME LATE FOR DOMENICO DeMARCO, WHO FOR
forty years has operated Di Fara Pizza on Avenue J in Midwood, Brooklyn.
Since 1999, the year that a favorable review in a city guidebook put his pies on
the map, Mr. DeMarco has graced the cover of The Village Voice (the "Best
Italian Restaurants" issue in June 2004), and his restaurant has topped not only
the Zagat list of the city's best pizzerias but also those of countless other guides
to slice-related nirvana.

Through it all, Mr. DeMarco has changed very little. With his hair slicked
back and flour on his shoes, he has continued to make each pizza personally as
three of his seven children labor in the back. He maintains beds of basil and rosemary on the windowsill, and imports nearly every ingredient from such faraway
lands as Israel and the Netherlands. The man insists on no less than three different cheeses on each pizza, and chowhounds line up, sometimes for more than an

hour, to buy a regular slice for $2.50 or the Sicilian for $2.75. The city's reigning pizza deity is pleased by this sort of success, but he is hardly surprised.

I'm 67 years old. I've been in Brooklyn since 1959. I'm from Provincia di Caserta in Italy, near Napoli. When I got here, I spent three months in Long Island, in Huntington, working on a farm.

I stayed three months in Long Island, then I came back to Brooklyn, and my brother and I opened a pizzeria at Fourth Avenue and 59th Street in Sunset Park. The name was Little Venice, Piccola Venezia. We stayed there five years.

The neighborhood, it was mostly Irish. I wasn't happy over there. The people were cheap. If you raised it a nickel, they made a big deal out of that. There were a lot of break-ins, a lot of broken windows. I got a gun pointed at me one time.

So I sold, and I opened over here in 1964. I was supposed to open a pizzeria at 77th Street and 18th Avenue. But then somebody put a bug in my head and said there's a good spot on Avenue J. I didn't even know Avenue J existed. So I come over here with my accountant on a Saturday night, and this corner was for rent. It was so crowded, the street. So I take the phone number, I call the landlord, and he says to come see me Sunday, make sure you bring a deposit.

When I opened the store, my partner's name was Farina. My name is DeMarco. So when the lawyer made the paper, he put the two names together. Di Fara. Di for me, and Fara for him. I bought my partner out in 1978, I think. I kept the same name; I didn't bother changing it.

It was all Jewish then, but they weren't that religious. Then, little by little, it became very Orthodox. People, they got scared, and they all sold out their restaurants. I was left alone. And it was the best thing that could have happened.

Nobody taught me to make the pizza. You gotta pick it up for yourself. All of these 40 years, I keep experimenting. My pizza is good, because I use fresh tomatoes. They come from Italy, from Salerno. Then I started to get mozzarella from Italy, from my hometown in the province of Caserta. It's $8 a pound, and this Parmesan, it's $12. It comes twice a week. This might have been made two days ago, or three days ago.

I do this as an art. I don't look to make big money. If somebody comes over here and offers me a price for the store, there's no price. There's no money in the world they could pay me for it. I'm very proud of what I do. I don't have any employees; I use my kids.

You want to know something? A lot of people, they pay more for a slice than they have to. That guy David Blaine, the guy who does the magic tricks? He was over here the other day. His bill was $75, but he gave me $100. He comes here all the time.

I come over here at 8 o'clock in the morning, sometimes 7, because I use fresh dough. I come from Italy, and I go back there every once in a while to see how they do it over there. They don't throw it in the icebox. It's not supposed to be cold dough. The fresh dough bubbles when you put it in the oven, and the bubbles get a little burnt. You see the pizza, and it's got a lot of black spots, it's Italian pizza. If you see pizza that's straight brown, it's not Italian pizza.

We make the dough three or four times a day, because I believe in fresh dough. Besides, when you use fresh dough, the pizza comes out thin, not thick.

We start to close at 10 o'clock, but I never count the hours, because I'm a farmer. We go into the farm early in the morning, and we go home when the moon arrives. No problem.

I eat once a day, after I close. With wine. But I have one piece of pizza every day, to see if it comes out all right. Then, after I close, I sit down with my bottle of wine and I eat. When I eat, I like to sit down. There's no way I can sit down once I open the door in the morning.

I don't intend to retire. But I want my kids to take over the place. They've got to follow me. They've got to follow my idea. Like I said, I don't take the shortcuts.

Pizza has become considered a fast food. This one is slow food. Anything you do, when you do it too fast, it's no good. The way I make a pizza takes a lot of work. And I don't mind work.

Di Fara Pizza
1424 Avenue J, Brooklyn, NY, 718-258-1367.
RATING:

NICK ANGELIS

of Nick's Pizza

WHEN ASKED WHY, ARMED WITH A JOURNALISM DEGREE FROM New York's Hunter College, he ended up a pie man, albeit a great pie man, Nick Angelis shrugs his shoulders and says, "That's easy. It's what I always wanted to do." Nick's father Angelo's idea of a good time on the weekends was to pile everyone into his Ford Fairlane and head to Totonno's in Brooklyn. That's my kind of dad. Nick now belongs in the pantheon of great New York pie men that includes Patsy Lancieri, Patsy Grimaldi, the late Anthony and Jerry Pero of Totonno and the late John Sasso of the original John's. The crust Nick gets from his gas-fired brick ovens is nothing short of a miracle. It's crisp yet pliant, with just a hint of char and smokiness. Nick also has the good sense to use Corona Heights Pork Store coowner Frankie Cappezza's incomparable mozzarella and sausage on his pies in his Queens location. In his other stores he uses more local purveyors, for which he has earned respect. Nick makes the only cannoli I've ever truly loved—with a waffle iron, stuffed to order and topped with a sprinkling of pistachio nuts.

There are now three Nick's: one on Manhattan's Upper East Side, one in Rockville Centre on Long Island's South Shore and the original in Forest Hills, Queens. All three locations have become full-service Italian-American restaurants with salads and veal, shrimp, chicken and pasta dishes galore. The rest of the food is perfectly fine, but Nick's raîson d'être is still pizza. The cannoli is a bonus.

Nick says his mom still gives him a hard time for not becoming a lawyer or a doctor. Nick tells her, "What's the difference? One I'd wear a suit, and the one I chose I wear an apron." Angelis rarely questions the decision he made. "Most

days I have a great time." His idea of a great time isn't that much different from his dad's: "I love to go to Totonno's or some other great pizzeria with six or seven people and order a bunch of pizzas that come out of the oven every five minutes. That's my idea of heaven."

Nick's Pizza
108-26 Ascan Avenue (near Austin Street), Forest Hills, NY, 718-263-1126.
1814 Second Avenue (at 94th Street), New York, NY, 212-987-5700.
272 Sunrise Highway (between Morris and North Park Avenues), Rockville Centre, NY, 516-763-3278.
RATING: ✹ ✹ ✹ ✹

FLO CONSIGLIO

of Sally's Apizza

ACCORDING TO HIS WIDOW, FLO, WHO NOW RUNS THE SHOW AT Sally's Apizza, the late Sally (Salvatore) Consiglio was "gifted in many ways. If he could have afforded it there would have been many fields open to him." Pizza lovers are extremely thankful that Sal Consiglio utilized his considerable gifts in making perfect pies, with a slightly chewy, charred crust and just enough sauce and cheese for balance. Sally Consiglio perfected his pizza-making craft as a teenager in his uncle Frank Pepe's pizzeria (Sally's mother was Frank Pepe's sister Filamena). Flo, who met Sally when they were in grammar school, said that he was so small when he started making pizza that he had to stand on a box to knead the dough. Sally worked for Frank for four years until his father became ill, forcing Sally to become the principal breadwinner in his family. Needing to make more money, Sally opened his eponymous pizzeria in 1938, when he was eighteen. His mother, whose homemade pizza Sally adored, had to take the liquor license out in her name, because Sally was too young. Flo insists that even though her husband opened a couple of hundred yards from his uncle's pizzeria, there was never any bad blood between the two. Sally and Flo worked eighteen hours a day for many years turning out pizzas in their coal-fired brick oven for the Italian-American community that settled in New Haven to work in the local factories. Until he died, forty years after he opened the place, Sally Consiglio made every pie the Consiglio family sold, with mozzarella and sausage made locally, and fresh garlic and thyme on the tomato pies, made without mozzarella. Now Sally's two sons, Richard and Robert, are the pizzaioli, and their pies are every bit as good as their dad's. What's truly remarkable is that in the sixty-six years Sally's has been in business, only three people, Sally, Richard and Robert Consiglio, have ever made a pizza there. Talk about an owner-occupied pizzeria.

Sally's tomato pie, made with the aforementioned fresh herbs, California canned tomatoes and freshly grated pecorino Romano, is a revelation. It's a model of pizza flavor and texture balance. The absent mozzarella is not missed at all. And if you're lucky enough to be at Sally's in the summer, Flo and company make a great pizza with fresh local tomatoes, grated Romano, fresh basil and just enough mozzarella. The clam pie at Sally's, made with canned baby clams, is the only pie made there that doesn't belong in the great pizza pantheon. "It's just pizza," Flo Consiglio says, "and Sally knew that. But there was a lot of pride and passion that went into every pie Sally made, and I know we try to live up to his standards every day." 🍕

Sally's Apizza

237 Wooster Street (at Olive Street), New Haven, CT, 203-624-5271.
(Warning: This phone has been busy the last hundred times I have called.)
RATING: 🍊 🍊 🍊 🍊

> **NOTE:** One of the many pleasures of Sally's is that it's devoid of pretension or artifice. The wood paneling looks as if it's original, all the photos on the walls are slightly crooked, and there isn't a T-shirt, mug or cap for sale anywhere. Sally's feels like a club, which can be off-putting to nonmembers, but the only criteria for membership are a passion for the pizza and an adherence to the unstated rules. The best way to apply for membership is to tell Flo Consiglio how much you love the pizza at Sally's. And once you become a member, you'll be treated like family.

LAWRENCE CIMINIERI

of Totonno's Pizzeria Napolitano

IT'S BEEN EIGHTY YEARS SINCE ANTHONY (TOTONNO) PERO, THE immigrant son of a Neapolitan bread baker, left his pizza-maker's job at Lombardi's and opened his eponymous pizzeria in Coney Island. Remarkably, not much has changed. Pero's great grandson, Lawrence Ciminieri, is now making the pizza with the same care and fine ingredients: Brooklyn-made fresh mozzarella, Italian canned tomatoes, dough made fresh every day from flour, water, yeast and salt, a dusting of fresh Romano cheese and a splash of olive oil.

The legend of Totonno's has been fueled by two factors: the incredible pizza and the unique antisocial management style of the late Jerry Pero (Totonno's son). Lawrence Ciminieri still makes the remarkable pies the way Jerry did, moving them around the coal-fired oven like chess pieces to deal with the varying heat generated by the "hot spots" on the brick oven floor. A pile of burning coal sits on one side of the oven, imparting a smoky flavor to every pizza. The crust still comes out charred and blistered, with an outer layer of crispness that gives way to tender insides. A Totonno's pizza really does melt in your mouth.

Jerry Pero, who ran Totonno's with an iron pizza paddle from the early 1950s until 1991, was a screamer; he would scream at his siblings, his children and his customers. Lawrence says, "Jerry was eccentric and really cranky. Of course you'd be cranky too if you were standing before a 900°F oven all day. Anyways, Jerry would throw you out for the littlest things. If you asked if your pizza was ready, he would throw you out. If you asked for a slice, he would throw you out [Totonno's sells only whole pies]. At least once a year he'd be fighting with his brother and his sister so bad that he'd throw everybody out of the store. He would just turn off the lights and ask everybody, even the people who were in the middle of eating their pizza, to leave. The people who knew the drill wouldn't be fazed in the least by this. They'd just go around the corner and wait for a few

minutes. Then they'd go back in and finish their pizza. People are always coming in here and saying to me, 'Jerry threw me out once.' It was like a badge of honor."

Until 1978 Totonno's was open only Friday through Sunday, from noon until the fresh dough ran out. Of course no one but Jerry knew when the dough was running out, which made waiting in line an iffy proposition. A niece once told the *New York Daily News*, "He used to tell them to wait, even if he knew that he wasn't going to make any more pies. I told him: 'Jerry, you're gonna get killed doing that.' He didn't care. And the people kept coming back." They were invited to come back as long as they didn't ask too many questions. "How do you make pizza this good?" a Brooklyn College professor once asked Pero. He replied, "You stick to teaching, and I'll stick to pizza."

Pero didn't treat his immediate family any better. His niece Cookie (born Louise) stopped speaking to him in the early seventies. The precipitating incident? Lawrence Cimineri recalls, "My father asked me to get him a pie. I went into the store and told my [great] uncle Jerry that my father wanted a pizza. Jerry was really busy, so he said to me, 'I don't have time to make him a pizza. If your father is so hungry, tell him to go to Nathan's.' That was it. My mother and father were so mad at Jerry they didn't speak for fifteen years, even though they worked side by side in the shop."

Cookie and her husband, Joel, who spent seven years alongside Jerry learning the Totonno's secrets, took over Totonno's in 1991, when Jerry semiretired. By then the feuding family had had a rapprochement. Cookie remembers, "We were both visiting my aunt Julia in the hospital in 1986. As we're leaving her room Jerry turns to me and says, 'Hey, Louise, want to get something to eat?' And that was that. After all those years we started talking again." Jerry Pero died on May 31, 1994, having made peace with virtually everyone in his family, if not all of his customers.

By 1996 Totonno's was open five days a week (it's now open six), and Cookie and Joel always made sure they had enough dough on hand to feed everyone that came in the door. They took on new partners and opened a branch on Manhattan's Upper East Side in 1997. By then Lawrence had moved back to New York from Las Vegas, where he had been a food and beverage manager at Caesar's Palace. He recalls, "I had just been through a divorce, and I thought it was time to get back to doing the one thing in my life that I knew made people happy: making Totonno's pizza."

Lawrence and Cookie are now the principal keepers of the Totonno's flame. There are currently four Totonno's in the New York area, and I have had superb pizza at each of them in the past year. Lawrence trains every pizzaiolo in the original Coney Island shop, and they come back for a refresher course four times a year. "I have to make sure they don't develop bad habits when I'm not there," he says. Lawrence is proud of his multiethnic group of pie men. "Tashi in the 26th Street store makes a great pie, and he's from Tibet. So does Ozzie up on 81st Street, and he's from Mexico. I don't have any Italians making pizza for me. The Italians I talk to don't want to make pizza any more."

I asked Lawrence how he copes with the legend and the huge specter of Jerry. He told me Jerry himself supplied the answer to that question when he told him, "They're going to tell you your pizzas are not as good as mine. Don't be upset by it. They said the same thing to me." Lawrence says, "I just keep on making the pizza the Totonno's way, with passion and pride and good ingredients. If I do that, and we keep on building great ovens to make our pizza in, I figure we can't go too far wrong. And if we do get off track, and it gets back to Cookie, there will be hell to pay. You do not want my mother mad at you. It's not like Jerry, but take my word for it, she's plenty tough."

Totonno's Pizzeria Napolitano

1524 Neptune Avenue (between West 15th and West 16th Streets), Coney Island, NY, 718-372-8606, www.totonnos.com.
1544 Second Avenue (between 80th and 81st Streets), New York, NY, 212-327-2800.
462 Second Avenue (at 26th Street) New York, NY, 212-213-8800.
125 Tuckahoe Road, Yonkers, NY, 914-476-4446.

RATING: ✹ ✹ ✹ ✹

ACKNOWLEDGMENTS

IF YOU WRITE A BOOK ABOUT PIZZA, YOU HAVE TO SLICE UP THE work load. So now I must say grace and give thanks to all who aided and abetted me in this labor. First there is Vicky Bijur, wife, agent, first reader and editor, unflagging supporter and love of my life, who ate more pizza in the past twelve months than any rat in a pizza laboratory experiment ever would. And of course my son, Will, a good and funny and wise young soul who makes me the proudest father in the world. Will slyly smiled every time he asked, "Is there any pizza in the fridge that's off-limits to me and my friends?" All the other contributors, who inspire me with their graceful, casually elegant, and funny prose. The critics around the world, who toiled thanklessly so that all of us might enjoy a slice of heaven wherever we are. Jane Newman of Rizzoli, editor and pizza enthusiast, who came to me with the idea of writing a book on pizza. Barbara Anderson, who made a massive jumble of parts and words into a coherent whole without losing her cool. Joe Charap, my intern and editor- and writer-in-training, who helped immeasurably in putting this book across the finish line. Joe, I hope the book is punched up enough for you. My family, who were always there to encourage me: my brother Mike Levine and his wife, Carol, part-time New Haven residents and pizza enthusiasts; my brother Jesse Levine, his wife, Lynn, and their children, Samantha and Lauren, who showed up for a pizza in their town on a moment's notice; my cousin, Terry Sadin, whose spirit and passion for life and pizza is remarkable for anyone, much less an octogenarian; Bob and Meryl Meltzer, cousins, mensches and champions of Eddie's Pizza; Hilda Bijur, my patient and gracious mother-in-law, who sat through countless discussions about pizza; my brother-in-law, Arthur Bijur, his wife, Judy D'Mello, and their son, Ben, Hamptons pizza tasters and providers of warm and gracious hospitality; Sam Sifton, my former editor at the *New York Times* and my friend, who always added a touch of poetry to my passion; R. W.

Apple and his fantastic wife, Betsy, for all their support and use of their taste buds in Washington, D.C.; Kathleen McElroy and Nick Fox at the *Times*, who keep me keeping on at the paper of record; David Seitz and Peter Simmons at the *New York Times* permissions department; Joe Conason, my editor at the *New York Observer*, who gave license and birth to my being able to eat pizza (and other things) for a living; Maurizio DaRosa, Neapolitan pizza oracle, who accompanied me to Naples and Rome, and whose enthusiasm and love for pizza and the culture of pizza might exceed my own; Maurizio's mother, Rita, and brother Bruno, whose hospitality, warmth, and passion for food made my Italian journey a slice of heaven. All the pizza tasters around the country: Tony DiDio, Steve Schwartz and Mark Federman in New York; Andy Clurfeld, Maurizio DeRosa and Giancarlo Quaddalti in New Jersey; Ron Stanford in Philadelphia, Alan Schwartz in New Haven, Corby Kummer in Boston; John, Judy, Maya and DeDe Ayers and Don McLeese in Chicago; Stephen and Jane Usery in Minneapolis; Brad Thompson in Phoenix; and Larry Gonick and Dan Ruby in the Bay Area. Nancy Silverton, for her unflagging enthusiasm, hospitality and good taste; Betsy Amster and Barry Glassner, thanks for the war story exchange and your taste buds in Los Angeles; Bill Ayers, for his always provocative thinking; Vanessa Bortnick and Andrew Freeman of the Kimpton Group, for providing comfy beds in their wonderful hotels across the country at writerly rates; Richard Anderson and Carol Hollen of Northwest Airlines, who were the wind beneath my wings as I traveled across the country; Bob Rosen, Marcia Golub and their son, Zack, pizza lovers all; the McCoens, Joel, Fran and Pedro, food enthusiasts and generously spirited friends and neighbors; Eric Karpeles and Mike Sell, artists and sanitarium owners; Arietta Slade and Sam Felder, gracious country hosts, for the tip about Bar; Mitchell Charap and Karen Gilmore, thanks for the the use of your son and the car. And thanks most of all to the pizzaioli and pie men and women all over the world, who inspire and thrill me with their passion, dedication and skill.

A Slice of Heaven Glossary of Terms

Joe Charap

Cornicione: Italian term for the "lip" of the pizza, the outer edge of crust that puffs when cooked.

DOC (Denominazione di Origine Controllate): In 1955, Italy enacted DOC laws to safeguard the names, origins and characteristics of certain Italian cheeses. To date, only twenty-six of them are under the protection of the DOC, including *mozzarella di bufala*. From the *Cheese Primer*, by Steven Jenkins.

DOP (Denominazione di Origine Protetta): The mark is guaranteed by the European Union and was created to promote the authenticity and artisan characteristics of certain food and agricultural products.

Double-zero flour: In Italy, flour is classified either as I, 0, or 00, and refers to how finely ground the flour is and how much of the bran and germ have been removed. Double-zero flour is the most highly refined and is talcum-powder soft.

Fior di Latte: "Flower of the Milk," a soft, fresh mozzarella made of cow's milk. Italian law decrees that only cheese made from buffalo milk can be called mozzarella, yet *fior di latte* often receives the title of mozzarella regardless.

Grandma Pizza: Primarily found in Queens, New York, a sparsely topped, thin-crusted, crisp-bottomed rectangular pie cooked on a Sicilian pan.

Hole Structure: The pattern of air bubbles in bread dough, especially after it's baked. In France it's called *avéolage*.

Margherita: The classic Neapolitan pizza. Consists of tomato, mozzarella and basil.

Marinara: Also known as a Napoletana, this cheeseless pizza consists of tomato, olive oil, garlic and oregano.

Mozzarella di Bufala: A mozzarella made with water buffalo milk, which has a higher fat content than mozzarella made with cow's milk. Also known in America as buffalo mozzarella. *Mozzarella di bufala* has a tart and creamy taste and a slightly springy texture.

Pizza Bianca: Roman leavened flatbread less than an inch thick flavored with olive oil and salt and sold throughout the family-owned street bakeries of Rome.

Pizzaiolo: In Italy, a trained pizza maker is called a pizzaiolo. A pizzaiolo can make the pizzas and/or bake them. The feminine version of the word is pizzaiola, though according to Maurizio DeRosa, the only female pizza maker he's ever seen in Italy is Sophia Loren in the movies. The plural of the term is pizzaioli. In New York and New Haven the same person is called a "pie man."

San Marzano Tomato: Famed plum tomatoes from the town of San Marzano, Italy, often used to make pizza sauce because of low sugar content.

VPN (Vera Pizza Napoletana): The VPN is an international trade association, founded in 1984 in Naples, Italy, by Antonio Pace. Its purpose is to promote the culinary tradition of Neapolitan pizza and certification for those pizzeria/restaurants which produce Neapolitan pizza.

REPRINT PERMISSIONS

INDEX